PENGUIN HANDBOOKS

THE READ-ALOUD HANDBOOK

Jim Trelease is a frequent lecturer to parents, teachers, and professional groups on children, literature, and television. A graduate of the University of Massachusetts, he is an award-winning artist and writer for *The Springfield* (Mass.) *Daily News,* where his feature writing was awarded first prize in 1980 by the Associated Press and New England News Editors in their annual competition. His sports cartoons are included in the permanent collections of the baseball, basketball, and golf halls of fame. In addition, Mr. Trelease is a weekly visitor to classrooms throughout the Connecticut River Valley, sharing with children both his career as a journalist and his love of children's books. He lives in Springfield, Massachusetts, with his wife, Susan, and their two children.

The Read-Aloud Handbook

by
Jim Trelease

Photographs by Joanne Rathe

Penguin Books

Penguin Books Ltd, Harmondsworth,
Middlesex, England
Penguin Books, 625 Madison Avenue,
New York, New York 10022, U.S.A.
Penguin Books Australia Ltd, Ringwood,
Victoria, Australia
Penguin Books Canada Limited, 2801 John Street,
Markham, Ontario, Canada L3R 1B4
Penguin Books (N.Z.) Ltd, 182–190 Wairau Road,
Auckland 10, New Zealand

First published 1982
Reprinted 1982 (three times)

LIBRARY OF CONGRESS CATALOGING IN PUBLICATION DATA
Trelease, Jim.
The read-aloud handbook.
(Penguin handbooks)
Bibliography: p.
Includes index.
1. Oral reading. I. Title.
LB1573.5.T68   1982   372.6   82-9012
ISBN 0 14 046.534 0   AACR2

Printed in the United States of America by
Fairfield Graphics, Fairfield, Pennsylvania
Set in Fototronic Garamond

Portions of this work were originally published in pamphlet form.

Grateful acknowledgment is made to the following publishers for permission to re-
print excerpts from previously published material: Atheneum Publishers for *Pepper-
mints in the Parlor* by Barbara B. Wallace; copyright © Barbara B. Wallace, 1980.
Clarion Books/Ticknor & Fields for *Old Mother Witch* by Carol Carrick; copyright ©
Carol Carrick, 1975. Doubleday & Company, Inc., for *Early Del Rey* by Lester Del Rey.
Macmillan Publishing Co., Inc., for *The Lion, the Witch and the Wardrobe* by C. S.
Lewis; copyright 1950 by the Trustees of the Estate of C. S. Lewis; copyright ©
renewed Aretrum Owen Banfield, 1978.

To Elizabeth and Jamie—
the best audience a reader-aloud could hope to find.

And to Alvin R. Schmidt,
a ninth-grade English teacher who found the time twenty-seven years ago
to write to the parents of one of his students to tell
them that they had a talented child. The vote
of confidence has never been forgotten.

Contents

Acknowledgments

This book could not have been written without the support and cooperation of many friends, associates, neighbors, children, teachers and editors. I especially wish to acknowledge my everlasting gratitude to Mary A. Dryden, principal of New North Community School in Springfield, Massachusetts, for beginning it all by persuading me to visit her class fifteen years ago when she was teaching fifth grade.

I am deeply indebted to the editors of *The Springfield Daily News* for their long-standing support of staff involvement with the community's school children. It was this policy which provided the initial impetus for my experiences in the classroom. At the same time, I am particularly grateful to Associate Editor Jane Maroney of *The Springfield Morning Union,* whose guiding hand helped shape the initial concept of this book, Ruth Danckert, children's book editor of *The Springfield Sunday Republican,* and George R. Delisle of *The Springfield Daily News.*

For their assistance in preparing the photographs used in the book I am grateful to the following: Margo and Leigh Anderson; Dolores, Nathan, Shameka, and Nina Brice; Catherine Bryson; Karen Chartier and the children of Elias Brookings School; Ellie, Jonathan, Amy and Melissa Fernands; Jennifer Haley; Jack, Pat, John, Brian, Catie and Colleen Hoar; Nancy, Julie, Mark, Mary and Sheila Holland; Patricia Kelleher; Kathy, Ryan, Paul, Moira and Patrick Kelly; Mark Mamuszka; Linda and Meaghan McCormick; Debbie and Owen McLaughlin and the children of Holyoke Montessori Internationale; Mary, Danny, Darby and Jessica McLaughlin; Michael Nozzalillo; Scott Rogan; Andy and Jennifer Rostek; Todd Stewart; Jeff Sullivan and the children of New North Community School; Brian, Denis, Janet and Jeanne Trelease; and Susie, Christopher and Jennifer Wing.

In addition, I would like to thank my neighbor Shirley Uman, whose enthusiasm for my idea spilled over at a family reunion within hearing distance of a literary agent, Raphael Sagalyn, who carried it home for me to Penguin Books; Bernice E. Cullinan of New York University for her candid and painstaking advice; and my editor at Penguin, Kathryn Court, for her encouragement, thoroughness, understanding, and good humor.

Introduction

If we would get our parents to read to their preschool children 15 minutes a day, we could revolutionize the schools.
— Ruth Love,
Superintendent of Chicago Public Schools (1981)

Karen Chartier is a sixth-grade teacher in Springfield, Massachusetts, who begins school every year by reading aloud to her class. This particular year she began with a novel. Her wide-eyed new students listened attentively on that first day as she finished the first page and turned to the second.

At that moment, a student in the front row raised his hand. "Mrs. Chartier, you forgot to show us the picture on that first page," he said.

"Oh, I didn't forget," she explained. "It's just that this book doesn't have any pictures."

The student frowned for a second and then asked, "Then how are we supposed to know what the people look like in the story?"

That student has a problem, and so do millions of his peers in this nation of 42 million children where two out of every three children can't read, won't read, or hate to read. What that teacher was trying to do for that child and that class is what this book is all about: reading aloud to children to awaken their sleeping imaginations and improve their deteriorating language skills. Where this is done in school, it improves the atmosphere of the classroom. When it is done at home, it improves the quality of family life. But wherever it is done, the overwhelming result is that it improves children's attitudes toward books and reading.

These are facts that have been proven in hundreds of studies (many are referred to throughout this book) by educators and psychologists in thousands of classrooms and homes. The results are so decisive they are beyond debate. This handbook is an outgrowth of those findings, as well as a response to the only major decline in literacy skills since the founding of this nation. I have tried to bring to the writing a personal point of view—that of a parent, journalist, and frequent classroom instructor. In addition to my firsthand experiences with my own children and many school-children, I have included those of other parents and teachers.

I had been reading aloud to my daughter Elizabeth for several years when I was invited to speak to a sixth-grade class about my career as an artist with *The Springfield* (Mass.) *Daily News*. (I had been doing these talks on a weekly basis in the Connecticut River Valley for several years.)

After spending an hour with the class, talking about newspapers, illustrations, and cartoons, I gathered my materials and prepared to leave, when I noticed a book on the shelf near the door. It was *The Bears' House* by Marilyn Sachs and it caught my eye immediately because I'd just finished reading it to my daughter.

"Who's reading *The Bears' House?*" I asked the class. Several girls' hands went up.

"I just finished reading it," I said. Their eyes lit up. They couldn't believe it. This man, who had just told them stories about how he got started in newspapers, this man, whose drawings and stories they had been clipping out of the paper for the last month—this man was reading one of *their* books?

So I explained about my children, Elizabeth and Jamie, and how I read to each of them every night. I told them how, when my children were little, they were most interested in the pictures. That was fine with me because I was an artist and I was interested in the pictures, too. I told them how much I'd loved Maurice Sendak's *Where the Wild Things Are* because of how he drew the monsters. I loved to scan the Little Tim books to see how Edward Ardizzone drew the ocean and *Make Way for Ducklings* to see how Robert McCloskey drew the ducks.

"And did you know," I said, when I saw them perk up at the mention of the *Ducklings* classic, "that Mr. McCloskey had a dreadful time trying to draw those ducks? He finally brought six ducklings up to his apartment in order to get a closer look. In the end, because they kept moving around so much, do you know what he did? You may find this hard to believe, but I promise you it's true: In order to get them to hold still, he put them to sleep by getting them drunk on champagne!"

The class clapped and cheered their approval of McCloskey's unorthodox approach.

I went on to explain that as my children grew older, our read-aloud stories became longer and I began to realize that not only were the pictures beautiful in children's books but the stories were, too. "Now those books have become my hobby. We hated so much to return our favorites to the library, we decided to buy copies for ourselves. Today we have hundreds and hundreds." Again the eyes widened in wonder.

Then we talked about *The Bears' House:* what it was about (for those in the room who had not read it); what the students liked about it; and what else they had read by the same author. I asked the rest of the class what they had read lately. There was an avalanche of hands and a chorus of books. It was forty-five minutes before I could say good-bye. I stepped out into the corridor, where the teacher thanked me for coming. "But most of all," she said, "thank you for what you said about the books. You have no idea what it means for them to hear it from someone outside the classroom."

In the days following the visit I pondered what had happened in that classroom. The teacher subsequently wrote to say that the children had begged and begged to go to the library that afternoon in order to get some of the books I'd talked about. I wondered what it was that I had said that was so different. I had only talked about my family's favorite books.

All I was doing was giving book reports. As soon as I called it that I realized what was so special about it. It probably was the first time any of those children had ever heard an adult give not only a book report but an unsolicited book report—and that's the best kind. How many of them had ever hard a teacher say, "You'll have to bear with me today, class. I'm a little fuzzy-headed this morning. I stayed up until three o'clock this morning reading the most wonderful book. I just couldn't put it down. Would you like to hear what the book was about?" Of course they would!

I had talked animatedly about the characters, dramatically about the plots, warmly about the authors. I'd teased the children's interest by giving them a book report. But an even better description of it would be "a commercial." I'd started by selling them on newspapers and a career. And I'd concluded by selling them on books and reading.

From that day to this, I've never visited a class without asking before I left: "What have you read lately?" Speaking at nearly thirty schools a year over the last dozen years, I've exchanged book reports with thousands of children. Out of those numbers and years certain patterns have emerged that spurred me to write this book:

- Since the late 1960s there has been a dramatic decline in the number of books read by the children whose classrooms I've visited.
- The decline was so sharp that by 1979 when I asked, "What have you read lately?" the children were naming their classroom textbooks. That happened not once but numerous times.
- Lack of interest in reading was apparent in both public and private schools, in suburban as well as urban locales. In one private school, the entire sixth grade couldn't name more than five books they had read in the last three months. Either ignoring or ignorant of the reading problem at her school, the principal confided to me later that the school had begun to turn the corner—there was now a waiting list for enrollment. I shuddered and wondered if they really knew what they were waiting for.
- While the decline was general, it was not all-inclusive. Some classes overwhelmed me with their responses; they loved books and read voraciously. In each case that contagious enthusiasm was a direct result of a teacher's attitude. He or she loved books and shared that affection by reading aloud and talking to the class about books.
- In many cases, when teachers and parents witnessed the children's responses to my "commercials," they asked for a list of "good read-alouds." Some had tried reading aloud previously and had been stung by a dull book: the children were bored, the reader was bored, and the book was put away along with the whole idea of reading aloud.

When I realized there was no read-aloud listing available beyond the brief ones included in children's literature textbooks, I decided to do something about it. I would write a simple how-to guide for parents, teachers, and librarians on reading aloud to children, with a substantial list of recommended titles.

Very little of what is in this book is original. There are thousands of psychologists, librarians, and educators who know how remarkably effective reading aloud to children can be. What I have done is to collect evidence in support of its resurrection, to describe the various aids and techniques for reading aloud most effectively, and to provide an introductory booklist. I hope to persuade parents, teachers, and librarians to return to, or continue, an old practice and to help them make that practice a habit. This is not a book on teaching your child *how* to read. Instead, it is a book on teaching your child to *want* to read. All too often we mistakenly try to interest the child in reading *after* we've tried teaching him to read.

The first part of this book deals with the need to read aloud to children, when to do it and how to do it. I also discuss television, the largest single stumbling block to reading enjoyment and achievement in this country today, and how families can begin to cope with its pervasive influence. No discussion of children and books should take place without including television.

The second half of this book is a listing of 900 read-alouds, ranging in audience from toddlers to junior-high students. However, I do not recommend that a parent or teacher simply pick any book from the appropriate part of the list and begin reading to a child. As you will see in succeeding chapters, the key to success is matching the right book to the right child and coupling both with the right attitude by the reader.

Your 10-year-old may not want to hear the story of a Little League pitcher who is dying of leukemia *(Hang Tough, Paul Mather* by Alfred Slote). If the child is a nature lover, he probably would rather hear about the boy living with his ailing father on the edge of the Florida Everglades, searching daily for a legendary eight-foot rattlesnake *(Ironhead* by Mel Ellis).

I can promise that once you begin the daily experience of reading aloud to children, it will become one of the best parts of your day and the children's day, minutes and hours that will be treasured for years to come.

My children and I have sat in a one-room schoolhouse with Carol Ryrie Brink's *Caddie Woodlawn,* chased monsters with Maurice Sendak and Mercer Mayer, run away from home with Doris Burn's *Andrew Henry's Meadow,* and ridden the American plains with Louis L'Amour.

We have mourned the death of a father in *A Day No Pigs Would Die,* roamed the backwoods of the Ozarks with Wilson Rawls in *Where the Red Fern Grows,* groped down the dark subway passages of New York City with Felice Holman in *Slake's Limbo,* and swallowed magic potions with Judy Blume in *Freckle Juice.*

With *James and the Giant Peach* by Roald Dahl, we crossed the shark-infested waters of the North Atlantic; we battled a Caribbean hurricane in Theodore Taylor's *The Cay.* We have searched for wayward brothers and sisters, evaded wolves, lost friends, and learned how to make new ones. We have laughed, cried, shaken with fright, and shivered with delight. And, best of all, we did it together.

Along the way we discovered something about the universality of human experience—that we, too, have many of the hopes and fears of the people we read about.

The cost of such a wondrous experience is well within your means as a parent or teacher. It costs you time and interest. If you are willing to invest both, you can pick up a book, turn to a child, and begin today. I promise you, you will never want the experience to end.

A NOTE ON PRONOUNS

In the interests of smooth reading, I have generally avoided using "he or she" and instead I usually refer to the child as "he" and to the teacher as "she." This does reflect the numbers: a greater percentage of boys than girls have reading problems, and by far the larger proportion of elementary-school teachers is female. But of course this book is aimed at *all* adults—parents, teachers, loving neighbors—for the benefit of *all* children.

You may have tangible wealth untold:
Caskets of jewels and coffers of gold.
Richer than I you can never be—
I had a Mother who read to me.
        —"The Reading Mother" by Strickland Gillilan,
        from *Best Loved Poems of the American People*

The
Read-Aloud
Handbook

1
Why Read Aloud?

Perhaps it is only in childhood that books have any deep influence on our lives . . . in childhood all books are books of divination, telling us about the future, and like the fortune-teller who sees a long journey in the cards or death by water, they influence the future. I suppose that is why books excited us so much. What do we ever get nowadays from reading to equal the excitement and the revelation of those first fourteen years?

–Graham Greene,
The Lost Childhood and Other Essays

How and why does regular reading aloud strengthen children's reading, writing, and speaking?

One of the primary learning methods for children is imitation.[1] They imitate what they hear and what they see. It is this ability to imitate that allows the 15-month-old child to say his first words. By age 2, the average child expands his vocabulary to include nearly 300 words. That figure is tripled in the next year, reaches 1600 words by age 4 and 2100 by age 5. Considering that the average adult uses only 1800 different words in his daily vocabulary, the child's language development can only be considered monumental in scope.

Many parents are unaware of their role as a prime model in their child's language development. Much more obvious to them is the child's quickness to imitate television—especially the commercials. No matter how often children see a particular commercial, the same look of fascination returns to their eyes each time they watch it.

How great an effect does the commercial have on a child? At this imitative stage, the influence can be enormous. And, as I will point out in Chapter 7, it can be devastating in its long-range effects. I suspect that a few years ago you could find more 5-year-olds who could say McDonald's commercial for "two all-beef patties, special sauce, lettuce, cheese, pickles, onions, on a sesame-seed bun" than children who could recite their own telephone numbers and addresses.

This kind of commercial success does not happen by chance. It is carefully calculated by the agencies on Madison Avenue that are spending upwards of $50,000 a minute to ensure that your child is enraptured by the commercial.

That rapture is built upon a formula—admittedly an unofficial formula, but most certainly one that guides the advertising agencies. It was devised in the 1950s when they realized what a powerful tool they held in television.

When you break down the formula, you discover the following guidelines for selling to children:

1. Send your message to the child when he or she is still at a receptive age. Don't wait until he's 17 to try to sell him chocolate breakfast cereal. Get him when he's 5 or 6 years old.

2. Make sure the message has enough action and sparkle in it to catch and hold the child's attention. Avoid dull moments.

3. Make the message brief enough to whet the child's appetite, to make him want to see and hear it again and again. It should be finished before the child becomes bored.

We, as parents and teachers, would do well to learn something from Madison Avenue. We should take that three-part sales formula and use it to sell our product. And we most certainly have a product to sell. When the U.S. Department of Education is telling us that one out of every five American adults is functionally illiterate (which means that 20 percent of the adults in this country cannot read the directions on a can of soup), and that another 34 percent is only marginally literate (barely able to address an envelope), it is time for every educated adult to sell one product before all others in our homes and in our classrooms, and that product is READING.[2]

Despite some recent literacy gains among children, thanks to state policies of accountability along with Title I and Project Head Start (which frequently incorporate read-aloud practices within the daily curriculum), these remain difficult times in which to sell reading in America. Consider these statistics:

- Ninety-eight percent of the homes in America have a television set and nearly one out of every two families has more than one set.
- The average set is on for six and one-quarter hours a day.
- The television industry estimates that 2 million children *under* the age of 11 are still watching TV at midnight each night.
- The average kindergarten graduate has already seen more than 5,000 hours of television in his young lifetime.[3] That is more time than it takes to obtain a bachelor's degree.

Competing with that kind of monopoly is no small sales task. But it can be done. You, all by yourself, can instill a desire for books and reading in an entire family or class. If a plastic box in your living room can turn on your child to chocolate breakfast cereal, then you should be able to do ten times as much—because you are a sensitive, loving, and caring human being. (They have yet to invent the television set that can hug a child.) Using the television formula, here's the way to do it:

1. You read to children while they are still young enough to want to imitate what they are seeing and hearing.
2. You make sure the readings are interesting and exciting enough to hold their interest while you are building up their imaginations.
3. You keep the initial readings short enough to fit their attention spans and gradually lengthen both.

Few tasks present man with as monumental a challenge and few tasks are as far-reaching in their consequences as the challenge of learning to read. In describing his own childhood agonies with the printed word, Nobel Prize–winner John Steinbeck once wrote, "Some people there are who, being grown, forget the horrible task of learning to read. It is perhaps the greatest single effort that the human undertakes, and he must do it as a child. An adult is rarely successful in the undertaking. . . . For a thousand thousand years these humans have existed and they have only learned this trick—this magic—in the final ten thousand of the thousand thousand." [4] In pursuit of that magic and in an effort to ease the agony for young minds, the Federal government alone spends nearly $20 billion a year on teaching people how to read.

Nevertheless, for all the buying power and brain power expended in this war on ignorance, we continue to sustain heavy losses among our young:

- The Department of Education reports that 1 million teenagers between the ages of 12 and 17 cannot read at even a fourth-grade level.
- Eighty-one percent of U.S. colleges (including the prestigious Ivy League) have had to provide remedial composition courses for freshmen.[5]
- Our major city libraries are watching their circulation figures spiral downward.

If we are spending immense amounts of time and money in teaching children to read and they are *not* reading, we can only conclude that something is wrong. The problem is that we have concentrated exclusively on teaching the child *how* to read, and we have forgotten to teach him to *want* to read. To want to read. There is the key: desire. It is the prime mover, the magic ingredient. There is no success story written today—in the arts, business, education, athletics—in which desire does not play the leading role.

Contrary to popular opinion, desire is not something we are born with or that must come first from within. Winners aren't born, they're made; hundreds of coaches have taken teams with losing reputations, instilled desire in them, and directed them to championships. Readers aren't born, they're made; thousands of teachers instill desire each year in children who have been branded by parents and previous teachers as "losers," and by the end of the school year their desire to excel is a mainstay in their lives. Desire is planted—planted by parents and teachers who work at it.

How does one begin to instill in children the desire to read? That is something I believe we can learn from the man who has broken all records in the desire league, "Ronald McDonald." How did McDonald's instill that desire for their product and convince the American people that they "deserve a break today"? They did it by advertising over and over again, week after week, singing new praises, extolling new tastes, announcing new products.

Most parents do much the same thing with their children prior to their beginning school. They praise the virtues of school, the kindness of the teacher, the excitement of making new friends. In essence, they give the child a commercial for school. Unfortunately, it is only after the child has started school that most parents begin to think about motivating the child to be interested in books. The truth is that they should have begun motivating him years before. They should have started giving him book commercials in the first year of his life. They should have been reading to him and selling him early on the joys and discoveries waiting inside the covers of books.

Assuming this was not done, it is in school that the child begins to make his first noble efforts at reading—sound by sound, syllable by syllable, word by word. It is at this point that many parents and teachers make a mistake. They misread the child's early reading efforts as a sign that he loves to read and therefore doesn't need to be sold on it, or that continued reading by the adult to the child will rob the child of his initiative to read on his own. An indication of how widespread such reasoning is can be found in a national survey of teachers' read-aloud practices.[6] It was found that more than 60 percent of the third- and fourth-grade teachers did not read aloud regularly to their classes. By sixth grade, that percentage climbed to 74 percent. Interestingly, the grades that show the largest declines in read-aloud practices are the same grades that show the first signs of a national decline in grade-level reading performances by children—third and fourth grades.

At home, television combines with the parents' general disinterest in books to smother the beginning reader's desire to read the book he brought home from school or from the library. A Gallup Poll taken during the 1970s showed that 82 percent of the elementary-grade children polled had not read a book in the preceding month, although they each averaged more than one hundred hours of television during the same period.

In the classroom, too many of our children too quickly come to associate books and reading with ditto sheets, workbooks, tests, and homework. "Reading? That's work, not fun," they will tell you. Nearly 70 percent of the 233,000 sixth-graders polled by the California Department of Education in 1980 reported that they rarely read for pleasure. (In the same poll, an identical percentage of the students admitted to being heavy television watchers—four or more hours a day.)[7]

The "reading is work" mentality that children associate with books is supported in the findings of Richard Allington of the State University of New York.[8] Allington observed that remedial-reading classes spent a remarkably small amount of time reading in context without interruption. In fact, the average student read only forty-three consecutive words before being interrupted for questions or corrections. The poorest readers received the heaviest doses of skills instruction and consequently spent the least amount of time on the very objective—READING.

I am not suggesting that we abandon the teaching of reading skills.

They are, I am afraid, a necessary evil and most of today's children would never learn to read without them. However, I am suggesting that we balance the scales in our children's minds. It is imperative that we let our children know there is something more to reading than the practicing, the blendings, the vowel sounds, something more to it than the questions at the end of the chapter. And we must let them know this early, before they have permanently closed the door on reading for the rest of their lives.

The way to achieve this is to read to them every day, allowing them to finally sample the excitement and pleasures they've been practicing for but aren't quite ready or willing to accomplish on their own.

It can be done. Whether you are a teacher or a parent, don't tell me there isn't enough time—we find time for what we value. As a parent, I know first-hand how much time is wasted in a typical family day. And I know teachers who daily find the time to teach the skills *and* the love of reading—by reading to the class. If you care enough, you'll find the time.

Before a child can have an interest in reading, he must first have an awareness of it. The child who is unaware of the riches of literature certainly can have no desire for them.

Mrs. Ann Hallahan of Springfield, Massachusetts, offers an example of that axiom. Assigned at mid-year to teach a sixth-grade class of remedial students, Mrs. Hallahan shocked her new students by reading to them on her first day in class. The book was *Where the Red Fern Grows*.

A hardened, street-wise, proud group (mostly boys), they were insulted when she began reading to them. "How come you're reading to us? You think we're babies or something?" they wanted to know. After explaining that she didn't think anything of the kind but only wanted to share a favorite story with them, she continued reading *Where the Red Fern Grows*. Each day she opened the class with the next portion of the story and each day she was greeted with groans. "Not again today! How come nobody else ever made us listen like this?"

Mrs. Hallahan admitted to me later, "I almost lost heart." But she persevered, and after a few weeks (the book contained 212 pages), the tone of the class's morning remarks began to change. "You're going to read to us today, aren't you?" Or, "Don't forget the book, Mrs. Hallahan."

"I knew I had a winner," she confesses, "when on Friday, just when we were nearing the end of the book, one of the slowest boys in the class went home after school, got a library card, took out *Where the Red Fern Grows*, finished it himself, and came to school on Monday and told everyone how it ended.

"I didn't care about that. All I cared about was that I'd found the right key to open the lock on that boy's mind."

If the boy's parents had taken the time to introduce him to the book, the same task would have been accomplished. And if they had done it early enough, it's very probable he wouldn't have been in a remedial-reading class in the first place.

Amidst all the workbook pages and academic jargon, we daily overlook the very purpose of literature: to provide meaning in our lives. That, of course, is the purpose of all education. Child psychologist Bruno Bettelheim says that the finding of this meaning is the greatest need and most difficult achievement for any human being at any age. Who am I? Why am I here? What can I be? [9]

In his widely acclaimed work *The Uses of Enchantment,* Bettelheim writes that the two factors most responsible for giving the child this belief that he can make a significant contribution to life are: parents/teachers and literature.

Literature is considered such an important medium because—more than television, more than film, more than art or opaque projectors—literature brings us closest to the human heart. And of the two forms of literature (fiction and nonfiction), the one that brings us closest and presents the meaning of life most clearly to the child is fiction. That is the reason nearly all the recommendations for read-alouds at the back of this book are fiction.

What is it about fiction that brings it so close to the human heart? Three-time Pulitzer Prize–winning novelist and poet Robert Penn Warren declares that we read fiction because:

- We like it.
- There is conflict in it—and conflict is at the center of life.
- Its conflict wakes us up from the tedium of everyday life.
- It allows us to vent our emotions with tears, laughter, love, and hate.
- We hope its story will give us a clue to our own life story.
- It releases us from life's pressures by allowing us to escape into other people's lives.[10]

The child who has become accustomed to the tedium of the classroom cannot help but be awakened by the conflict in stories like *James and the Giant Peach* by Roald Dahl or *Mrs. Frisby and the Rats of NIMH* by Robert C. O'Brien. The awkward, freckle-faced 8-year-old discovers a ray of hope when she hears Hans Christian Andersen's *The Ugly Duckling.* It is through fiction's escapism—putting ourselves in the place of Snow White or Casey at the Bat or Mike Mulligan—that we stimulate the soul of creativity: the imagination. And it is this role-playing that leads us to an awareness of others and, most importantly, of ourselves.

Can we really believe that a child is going to develop a sense of "self" doing reading skills for forty minutes a day, five days a week, thirty weeks a year? Does an uninterrupted diet of skill and drill make a child want to escape *into* the world of books or *away* from it?

Reading aloud to children stimulates their interest, their emotional development, and their imagination. There is also a fourth area which is stimulated by reading aloud and it is a particularly vital area in today's world. It is the child's language. We have seen children's spongelike reaction to television commercials. They continue this imitative behavior with words until their language development peaks around age 13. They will speak the language primarily as they have heard it spoken.

Now, if the child hears the English language only as it is spoken by Archie Bunker, Laverne and Shirley, or Fonzie, then he has no alternative but to model his own speech on theirs. The danger with such modeling is that it is very different from the English language a student is asked to read, write, and speak in school or in the business world. A large portion of television's language is "street talk"—jargon and slang. It is poorly constructed and imprecise. It is hardly what a child needs as a model.

Children raised on a heavy diet of television and rock music are most readily recognized by a speech pattern that is punctuated every half-dozen words by "You know?" and "I mean, like . . ." The primal grunts and groans of a rock album may or may not have their merits as entertainment, but most decidedly they have neither the meaning nor the sensitivity children need to express their feelings clearly.

Literature's words, as opposed to those of the electronic media, offer a wealth of language for children to use. Because good literature is precise, intelligent, colorful, sensitive, and rich in meaning, it offers the child his best hope of expressing what he feels.

Hundreds of tests have been conducted to measure the effects of reading aloud upon language skills, and the results have been significantly positive.

In one study, twenty classes of Harlem 7-year-olds were read to for twenty minutes a day for one school year.[11] At the end of that time, the children were tested and compared with a control group that had not been read to. The experimental group showed significantly higher gains in vocabulary and reading comprehension.

In light of such statistics from one-year programs, imagine the results of a read-aloud program spread over several years. Imagine its effects upon both language and imagination.

For teachers and parents to ignore the warnings of widespread disinterest and illiteracy is to invite disaster for our children and our culture. Our goal is that all able-minded children read, write, and speak to their fullest capacities, and the road to it is clearly marked and defined. The first step in that direction is to pick up our books and begin reading to our children. A nation where 90 percent of the children can read and choose to read, instead of the present 50 percent, is not inconceivable.

2
When to Begin
Read-Aloud

Children who are not spoken to by live and responsive adults will not learn to speak properly. Children who are not answered will stop asking questions. They will become incurious. And children who are not told stories and who are not read to will have few reasons for wanting to learn to read.
                                        –Gail E. Haley,
                                        1971 Caldecott Medal acceptance speech

"How old must the child be before you start reading to him?" That is the question I am most often asked by parents. The next most often asked question is: "When is the child too old to be read to?"

In answer to the first question, begin as soon as possible. You may start the first day home from the hospital, and certainly you can begin by 6 months of age. But, you ask, how can the child understand what you are reading at that age? At this early stage of infancy we are not concerned with "understanding" as much as we are with "conditioning" the child to your voice and to books.

Dr. T. Berry Brazelton, chief of the child development unit of Boston Children's Hospital Medical Center, says that the new parent's most critical task during these early stages is learning how to calm the child, how to bring it under control, so he or she can begin to look around and listen when you pass on information.[1] Much the same task confronts the classroom teacher as she faces a new class each September.

The human voice is one of the most powerful tools a parent has for calming the child. At the earliest stages—there is even some evidence to suggest as early as the sixth or seventh month in the womb—a child is capable of discerning tone of voice: positive or negative, soothing or disturbing. He comes to associate certain tones with comfort and security. The baby is being conditioned—his first class in learning.

In exactly the same way that the child is conditioned by a soothing tone of voice to expect calmness and security, so, too, can the child be conditioned to the sound of the reading voice. Over a period of months the child will recognize it as an unthreatening sound, one that is associated with warmth, attention, and pretty pictures, and he will gravitate naturally to that sound.

Dorothy Butler demonstrates this thesis in *Cushla and Her Books,* where the parents began reading aloud to Cushla Yeoman at 4 months of age.[2] By 9 months the child was able to respond to the sight of certain books and convey to her parents that these were her favorites. By age 5 she had taught herself to read.

What makes Cushla's story so dramatic is the fact that she was born with chromosome damage which caused deformities of the spleen, kidney, and mouth cavity. It also produced muscle spasms—which prevented her from sleeping for more than two hours a night or holding anything in her hand until she was 3 years old—and hazy vision beyond her fingertips.

Until she was 3, the doctors diagnosed Cushla as "mentally and physically retarded" and recommended that she be institutionalized. Her parents, after seeing her early responses to books, refused; instead, they put her on a dose of fourteen read-aloud books a day. By age 5 the psychologists found her to be well above average in intelligence and a socially well-adjusted child.

If such attention and reading aloud could accomplish so much with Cushla, think how much can be achieved with children who have none or few of Cushla's handicaps.

Historical research offers the evidence of Puritan New England, where in 1765 John Adams noted that "a native American who cannot read or write is as rare an appearance as . . . a comet or an earthquake." Such verbal competence in our forefathers is attributed to the fact that the colonial child was exposed from infancy to the family's daily oral reading of the Bible.[3]

The crucial timing of such exposure has been discovered only in recent years, most powerfully by Professor Benjamin Bloom's famous study of 1,000 children's development profiles.[4] His findings demonstrated that 50 percent of the intelligence a child will have at maturity is already formed by age 4—at least a year before the child enters kindergarten.

The reason for such intense mental growth in so small a period of time is that children are at the height of their imitative powers during those years. Not only will they imitate the sounds of their home and family (and television set), but they will imitate also the actions of their parents, grandparents, and siblings. They are their first role models, their "super-heroes." If the child sees these heroes reading and involved with books, experience shows us that it is very likely that he will wish to do the same.

Martin Deutsch's study "The Disadvantaged Child and the Learning Process" demonstrates what happens when the role models do not stimulate the child.[5] In homes where conversation, questions, and reading are not encouraged, the child eventually enters school markedly short of the basic tools he will need to accomplish his tasks. He will ask fewer questions, use shorter sentences and have both a smaller vocabulary and a shorter attention span than his more advantaged classmates.

In studying methods to reverse such verbal shortcomings among children, Harvard psychologist Jerome Kagan found intensified one-to-one attention to be especially effective.[6] His studies indicated the advantages of reading to children and of listening attentively to their responses to the reading, but they also point to the desirability of reading to your children separately, if possible. I recognize this approach poses a problem for working mothers and fathers with more than one child. But somewhere in that seven-day week there must be time for your child to discover the specialness of you, one-on-one—even if it is only once or twice a week.

This is a good time to ask ourselves exactly why we are reading to children. Living as we do in a society that is so success oriented, it is a common mistake for parents to associate books only with skills. "If I read to my child," reasons the parent, "he will be smarter that much sooner and he'll be way ahead of the others in his class." On and on drones the achievement syndrome.

To be interested early in your child's intellectual growth is important and admirable. But you can expect negative consequences if this interest takes the form of an obsession with teaching your child to read, says Dr. Brazelton, who, along with his hospital work, research, and writing, has been a practicing pediatrician in Cambridge, Massachusetts, for twenty-six years.

"I've had children in my practice," Brazelton explained to National Public Radio's John Merrow, "who were reading from a dictionary at the age of 3½ or 4, and had learned to read and type successfully by the age of 4. But those kids went through a very tough time later on. They went through first grade successfully, but second grade they really bombed out on. And I have a feeling that they'd been pushed so hard from outside to learn to read early, that the cost of it didn't show up until later." [7]

Testimony to the importance of an *unforced* learning schedule in these formative years comes from all corners of the fields of psychology and education–including one that dates back nearly 3,000 years: "Avoid compulsion and let early education be a manner of amusement. Young children learn by games; compulsory education cannot remain in the soul," was the advice offered by Plato to parents.

None of these experts is saying that "early reading" is intrinsically bad; rather, they feel the early reader should arrive at that station naturally, on his own, without a structured time each day when the mother or father sits down with him and teaches him letters, sounds and syllables. That is the way Scout learned in Harper Lee's *To Kill a Mockingbird*–by sitting on the lap of a parent and listening, listening as the parent's finger moves over the pages, until gradually, in the child's own good time, a connection is made between the sound of a certain word and the appearance of certain letters on the page.

Prior to speaking to a group of children at a local library one day, I was stopped in the hallway by a grandmother. "Want to see something amazing?" she asked. When I expressed an interest, she sat on the floor, put her grandson on her lap, and handed him a book. The child, 3½ years old, began at once to read–easily, without stumbling, using marvelous expression and pointing to each word as he read. Anticipating my question, the grandmother whispered, "I began reading to him eight months ago. I'd put him on my lap and point to the words as I read. And then a month ago, it all fell into place for him."

"How does he like it?" I asked.

"He doesn't like it–he *loves* it," she said.

Much of that woman's achievement was accomplished by gradually conditioning her grandchild to look and listen when a book was being read. His senses of sight and hearing were pleased each time, along with the emotional pleasure of having Grandma's attention. By repeating this situation over and over again with a variety of books, the child developed a concept: Books are objects to be enjoyed; they bring pleasure.

By building this concept in the child's mind, the grandparent laid the foundation for the next accomplishment: the boy's attention span. Without a concept of what is happening and why, a child cannot and will not attend to something for any appreciable amount of time.

Here, for example, are two concepts entirely within the grasp of a 3-year-old: the telephone can be used to receive calls as well as make calls; books contain stories that give me pleasure if I listen and watch.

A nursery-school teacher told me recently of her experiences on the first day of school with these two concepts. All morning the 3-year-olds in her new class used the toy telephone to make pretend calls to their mothers for reassurances that they would be picked up and brought home. They dialed make-believe numbers, often talked for extended periods of time, and used telephone etiquette.

Understanding the concept of the telephone, these children were able to use and enjoy it for a considerable length of time. Their telephone attention span was excellent.

Let's compare that with story time in the same class. Thirty seconds after the story began, several of the children stood up and moved away from the circle, obviously bored. More children quickly joined them. Within two minutes, half the children had abandoned the story.

The difference between the attention spans for each of these two activities is based on the *concept* that each child brought to the activity. Where a child had little or no experience with books, it was impossible for him to have a concept of them and the pleasure they afford. No experience means no concept; no concept means no attention span.[8]

Parents and teachers are always fascinated with children who apparently "teach themselves" to read. However, as we have seen with Cushla and the grandchild at the local library, these children *do* have teachers—their role models. The majority of children who arrive in kindergarten already knowing how to read have never been formally taught to read, but they didn't pick it up out of thin air, either.

Over the past twenty-five years, studies done on "early readers," as well as those done on children who respond to initial classroom instruction without difficulty, indicate four factors which are present in the home environment of nearly every early reader:[9]

1. The child is read to on a regular basis. This is the most often cited factor among early readers. In Dolores Durkin's comprehensive 1966 study of early readers, every one of the seventy-nine children had been read to regularly. Additionally, the parents were avid readers and led by example. The reading aloud included not only books but package labels, street and truck signs, billboards, et cetera.

2. A wide variety of printed material—books, magazines, newspapers, comics—is available in the home.

3. Paper and pencil are readily available for the child. Durkin explained, "Almost without exception, the starting point of curiosity about

written language was an interest in scribbling and drawing. From this developed an interest in copying objects and letters of the alphabet."

4. The people in the child's home stimulate the child's interest in reading and writing by answering endless questions, praising the child's efforts at reading and writing, taking the child to the library frequently, buying books, writing stories that the child dictates, and displaying his paperwork in a prominent place in the home.

I want to emphasize that these four factors were present in the home of *every* child who was an early reader. None of these factors requires much more than interest on the part of the parent. There are no elaborate sound systems or learning machines involved, no bachelor or master's degrees; just a free public library card, some pencils and crayons, and cheap paper. (A small blackboard is another excellent aid if you want to go one step further.)

Beyond the materials, the program requires time: time to read to the child, time to post his drawings on the refrigerator door, time to answer questions, time to point out signs along the highway.

Time, a parent pointed out to me after a parent-teacher association meeting, is a rare commodity in her home. She works, her husband works, they don't have a lot of time to spare. I sympathized with her situation and gently pointed out that my wife and I have the same situation. "And just when I think there isn't enough time to spare for the night's reading," I told the parent, "I ask myself: 'Which is more precious—my time or my child? Which can I more easily afford to waste?'"

The woman nodded and slowly walked away. I wondered afterwards if she really understood, if she understood about the language bridges a parent builds with a child during those few minutes a day, bridges to adventure and imagination and, just as importantly, bridges between parent and child.

A year later, when a teacher in New Hampshire told me the story of Beth, I thought of that woman again. I wondered if she would have understood about Beth. "I've been a first-grade teacher for seventeen years," the teacher said, "and I have never had a child who didn't *want* to learn to read. That is, until this year.

"This year I had Beth as a student. The more I worked with her the more convinced I became that Beth didn't *want* to learn to read. Then I began to suspect that she already knew how to read but wouldn't admit it for some reason."

When the teacher talked to Beth's mother, she found the mother had similar suspicions. The following day the teacher took her student aside and said, "Beth, I think you've been fooling us. Do you know that? I think you already know how to read but for some reason you don't *want* to read. Is that true, Beth?"

Beth nodded.

"Will you tell me why?" asked the teacher.

"No," Beth replied.

At this point, the teacher asked a question that allowed Beth an escape route. "Do you think you could *ever* tell me why?"

The child thought for a moment and said, "Tomorrow."

The next morning Beth looked up at her teacher and whispered, "After lunch."

Sequestered in a room by themselves after lunch, Beth confided to the teacher that she was the oldest of four children. "The only time all day when I have my mother all to myself is when she reads to me at bedtime," she explained. She was afraid that if she admitted to being able to read by herself, then that was what she would be doing each night: reading alone. Beth felt her mother would go off to read to her sisters and brother and leave her without that intimate sharing time each night. As soon as the parent and teacher were able to convince Beth that her mother would continue their bedtime reading ritual, Beth became one of the best readers in the class.

"When do you start reading aloud to classroom children?" asks the teacher. On the very first day of school—whether you are teaching nursery school or kindergarten or seventh grade. And the way you hold that book, the warmth you extract from it, the laughter, the interest, and the emotion—all will tell your class something about you and how you feel about books, and the special place books and reading are going to hold in your class this year. The fifth-grade student who until now has associated books only with remedial classes or workbooks is going to experience a special treat on that first day. He's going to be introduced to a whole new concept of books and reading. He's going to be conditioned to the idea that books mean pleasure as well as work. You're going to show him the other side of the coin.

It's important for the teacher, just as it was for the parent, to establish in her own mind exactly why she is reading to the class.

The best answer is found in the definition of a teacher outlined by Nathan Pusey while president of Harvard.[10] "The close observer soon discovers that the teacher's task is not to implant facts but to place the subject to be learned in front of the learner and, through sympathy, emotion, imagination, and patience, to awaken in the learner the restless drive for answers and insights which enlarge the personal life and give it meaning." He could not have described the functions of reading aloud more accurately if he had been trying to. Children's literature arouses their imaginations, emotions, and sympathies. It awakens their desire to read, enlarges their lives, and provides a sense of purpose and identity for children.

Yes, you have to teach reading skills and math skills. They are necessary. But don't make the mistake of thinking they are the purpose of teaching or even the heart of the curriculum. Reading skills are facts; they have no life unto themselves. They cannot be loved, they cannot motivate.

On the other hand, *Charlotte's Web* by E. B. White can be loved by and will motivate a class. Most children and young adults have a strong need for books that curl up inside their lives, that take up residence in their dreams and ambitions.

Charlotte and her friends fill that need in young children; they reach out and beckon to their emotions and hopes and fears. There is no more important social experience in a child's life than friendship. And friendship is what *Charlotte's Web* is all about. It is the rare child who meets *Lassie Come Home* by Eric Knight or Jack London's *The Call of the Wild* and does not carry its story, its emotions, and its courage into the rest of his life.

I was unpacking a case of books before addressing a preschool parents group when a woman standing nearby gushed with pleasure when I put *Lassie Come Home* on the table.

"That book," she said, picking it up and caressing it, "and the teacher who read it to my sixth-grade class moved me more than any book or teacher I ever had in school. I can hardly wait for my daughter to be old enough for me to share this with her."

When you take time to read to your class you are not neglecting the curriculum. Reading *is* the curriculum. The principal ingredient of all learning and teaching is language. Not only is it the tool with which we communicate the lesson, it is also the product the student hands back to us—whether it is the language of math or science or history.

In that light, the classroom teacher who reads aloud helps the class to become better listeners and develop greater verbal skills. The more they hear other people's words, the greater becomes their desire to share their own through conversation and writing. Each read-aloud, then, is a language arts lesson, bolstering the four language arts: the art of reading, the art of listening, the art of writing, and the art of speaking.

Don't make the mistake of relegating read-aloud to the reading or language arts class exclusively. If you want your junior-high science class, history class, or civics class to be alive, then wrap the facts and figures, the dates and battles, in flesh and blood. Open your history class with five minutes from *A Bag of Marbles* by Joseph Joffo or Scott O'Dell's *Sarah Bishop*. Read *The Pond* by Robert Murphy to your science class each day.

Whether you are acting as a parent or as a teacher, when you read aloud to children you are fulfilling one of the noblest duties of cultured man. It is this sharing and enrichment that allows a culture to grow among people. Artists, writers, and musicians alone cannot keep a culture alive. They must be backed by the enthusiasm of a multitude of parents and teachers—people who treasure their heritage and will devote their energies to keeping its flame aglow. The mother who sits through music and dance recitals, the father who puts down the evening paper to help his son with a drawing of a tree, the teacher who reads to her class every day—they are the lifeblood of a culture. To them, more than to the artists, must fall the responsibility to "pass it on."

Almost like clockwork, after every speech I give on reading aloud, a worried parent approaches me and asks, "When is it too late? Is there a time when children are too old to be read to?" It is never too late, they are never too old—but it is never going to be as beneficial or as easy as it is when they are 2 years old or 6 years old.

Novelist and teacher Paula Fox, winner of the 1974 Newbery Medal for *The Slave Dancer,* read to her students at a branch of New York State University just as she had to her fifth-grade students years before. She found the older students loved the readings just as much as the younger ones had. "There was no tension of accomplishment or grades connected with the readings. It simply *was,* as literature should be," Fox explained.[11]

Because she has a captive audience, the classroom teacher holds a distinct advantage over the parent who suddenly wants to begin reading to a 13-year-old. Regardless of how well intentioned the parent may be, reading aloud to an adolescent at home can be difficult. During this period of social and emotional development, teenagers' out-of-school time is largely spent coping with body changes, sex drives, vocational anxieties, and the need to form an identity apart from that of their families. These kinds of concerns and their attendant schedules don't leave much time for Mom and Dad's reading aloud.

But the situation is not hopeless. When the child is in early adolescence, from 12 to 14, try sharing a small part of a book, a page or two, when you see he is at loose ends. This only has to be several times a week. Mention that you want to share something with him that you've read; downplay any motivational or educational aspects connected with the reading.

The older the child, the more difficult he is to corral. Here, as in early adolescence, you must pick your spots for reading aloud. Don't suggest that your daughter listen to a story when she's sitting down to watch her favorite television show or waiting for her boyfriend to call. Along with timing, consider the length of what you read. Keep it short—unless you see an interest for more.

Dorothy Mulligan, director of editorial services for the National School Volunteer Program in Alexandria, Virginia, confirms that there is no age limit to reading aloud. This is how she picked her spots for read-aloud:

"One summer our 22-year-old son had his four wisdom teeth pulled. A week later, after the stitches came out, one socket began to bleed. Late that night, the oral surgeon had to put in more stitches. Despite painkillers, Greg was miserable during the night. Nothing would calm him. And then I recalled what I had done for the kids whenever they were sick at night.

"First, I tried some of Greg's favorite authors—Mark Twain, Ray Bradbury, et cetera—but I couldn't find a section with enough action to still his moans. A lightbulb appeared in a balloon above my head; I reached for a *Reader's Digest.*

"Greg immediately quieted to listen to an article about how the music was selected to go into the space capsules. He is a violinist and one of the selections for the capsule was his favorite string quartet. Then I read about the kidnapping of a young girl, and then two more articles. By now he was lying quietly and told me he wanted to go to sleep."

Mrs. Mulligan says that her 17-year-old son, Mark, came down with a viral infection a few weeks later. The illness bothered him most at night.

"Several nights in a row he would vomit and complain of abdominal discomfort. This time I didn't wonder what to do—I got a *Reader's Digest.*

"I read about a 9-year-old who desperately needed to catch a fish for his family's dinner. Mark loves animals and never wants any living thing to be hurt, but he listened intently—until he fell asleep before the article ended."

Frequently, if the parent picks the right time and place, he or she can kill two birds with one stone—or story. Mrs. Mulligan recalls the week she and her family vacationed in a rustic cabin in Pennsylvania, minus television.

"That week I was reading *The Wheel on the School* [by Meindert DeJong], about children in a small Dutch school who put a wheel on the rooftop for a stork to use as a nest. I assumed that I was reading only for the younger three children, but learned differently when Greg, then 14, and my husband asked me not to read until they returned from playing tennis."

I found a similar situation when one of Elizabeth's girlfriends listened one evening to the chapter I was reading to Elizabeth from *Good Old Boy* by Willie Morris. She went home and insisted that her father get the book and read it to the entire family. The oldest son later used the book in a comparison study he did for eighth-grade English in which he compared *Good Old Boy* with *Tom Sawyer.*

The desire to read is not born in a child. It is planted—by parents and teachers.

Novelist and short-story writer Roald Dahl offers an example of this in an essay, "Lucky Break," from his book *The Wonderful Story of Henry Sugar.*

Tucked away in English boarding schools from age 8 to 18, Dahl's academic childhood was a disaster. "Those were days of horror," he writes, "of fierce discipline, of no talking in the dormitories, no running in the corridors, no untidiness of any sort, no this or that or the other, just rules, rules and still more rules that had to be obeyed. And the fear of the dreaded cane hung over us like the fear of death all the time." His teachers described him on his report cards as "incapable" and "of limited ideas." He hated school and school obviously hated him.

At last there came a ray of hope. One Saturday morning the boys were marched to the assembly hall. The masters departed for the local pubs and in walked Mrs. O'Connor, a neighborhood woman hired to "babysit" the boys for two and a half hours. Instead of babysitting, Mrs. O'Connor chose to read, talk about, and bring to life the whole of English literature. Her enthusiasm and love of books were so contagious and spellbinding that she became the highlight of the school week for Roald Dahl. As the weeks slipped by, she kindled his imagination and inspired a deep love of books. Within a year he'd become an insatiable reader, and Dahl credits Mrs. O'Connor with turning him into a reader, and thus a writer. Today, more than fifty years later, I know of no author who so captivates children, who so excites their imaginations, as Roald Dahl. His *James and the Giant Peach* is the finest read-aloud I have ever known.

How many minds and imaginations have remained unstirred because there was no Mrs. O'Connor? That child in your home or classroom—the one who never seems to be listening, who never completes his work on time, who appears to be forever looking out the window as though waiting for someone—is waiting for someone like Mrs. O'Connor. How long are you going to keep him waiting?

3
The Stages
of Read-Aloud

Few children learn to love books by themselves. Someone has to lure them into the wonderful world of the written word; someone has to show them the way.

—Orville Prescott,
A Father Reads to His Children

Staring at the thousands of books in the children's section of the local library, a parent is filled with the same panic that faces the beginning artist with an empty canvas: Where to begin?

I suggest that you first consider the child's age and maturity; then make your selections accordingly. Let's start with the infant level and work our way upward.

Until a child is 6 or 7 months old, I don't think it matters a great deal what you read, as long as you are reading. What is important at this stage is that the child becomes accustomed to the rhythmic sound of your reading voice and associates it with a peaceful, secure time of the day.

By 10 months of age, the child's sight and hearing are attuned enough for him to recognize familiar faces, objects, and voices. Therefore your selections should be books that stimulate those two senses—colorful pictures and exciting sounds upon which the child can focus easily. One of the reasons dear old Mother Goose has lasted so long is that she fills so well this rhythmic requirement:

> Hickory, dickory, dock,
> The mouse ran up the clock!

There is hardly a plot there, no great meaning, nothing other than rhyming sounds, fun sounds, sounds to stimulate a child who already takes delight in rocking back and forth in his crib repeating a single syllable over and over: "Ba, ba, ba, ba, ba, ba, ba . . ."

Since Mother Goose so wisely populated her rhymes with people as well as animals, the child's visual world is also expanded—particularly with many of the exciting recent editions. My favorite Mother Goose is the one edited by Watty Piper and illustrated by the Hildebrandt brothers. The pictures, large and brightly painted, are perfect for young children. Grade-school children also can enjoy Mother Goose, especially in Wallace Tripp's collection, *Granfa' Grig Had a Pig,* which contains hundreds of minutely detailed drawings that add not only a sense of humor to the rhymes but an element of sense as well. Your neighborhood library or bookstore has these and others. Each year sees another artist's version of Mother Goose in print and I hope the list grows longer and longer.

Have you ever noticed how many of the Mother Goose rhymes can be applied to a child's everyday activities? "Hush-a-Bye Baby" (sleeping and waking); "Deedle, Deedle, Dumpling" (going to bed); "One, Two, Buckle My Shoe" (getting dressed); "Pat-a-Cake" (eating); "Little Jack Horner" (eating); "London Bridge" (falling down); "Jack and Jill" (falling down); "Little Bo Peep" (losing toys); "Humpty Dumpty" (falling down); "What Can the Matter Be?" (crying); "Rub-a-Dub-Dub" (bathing).

Many parents find that singing or reciting these rhymes during the appropriate activity further reinforces both rhyme and activity in the child's mind. Long-playing records of these rhymes are available at your library and local record store.

Mother Goose is your child's first language lesson. Author and editor Clifton Fadiman, writing in *Empty Pages* as the chairman of the Council for Basic Education's Commission on Writing, notes: "If you read the most famous of all rhymes, 'Jack and Jill,' your child will, after listening to the third line, have learned the excellent word *fetch*. This word has a useful, precise meaning, a little different from *get.* It should not be allowed to disappear. Mother Goose will see to that." [1]

Recent research has proven that speech and music are stored in separate parts of the brain.[2] Therefore, when you sing a nursery rhyme to your child you are expanding even wider your child's early learning. Later, when your child becomes interested in the alphabet, pick up Joan Walsh Anglund's *In a Pumpkin Shell,* a Mother Goose alphabet book.

One factor that is often overlooked by parents is the inability of children under 18 months of age to easily understand complicated illustrations that adults recognize instantly. Book illustrations consisting of many little figures running here and there may be charming to adults but they are incomprehensible to young children. An adult can recognize instantly a three-dimensional rabbit when it is reduced to one dimension on a page, but a 14-month-old child is just beginning this complicated process. To help the child in this task, the picture books you choose in the early stages should be simple. Some of the very best for this purpose are those by Dutch author-artist Dick Bruna.

Internationally recognized, the Bruna books are masterpieces of simplicity: simple black outlines, solid colors of red, yellow, blue, and green against plain backgrounds. His subjects are simple enough to border on caricature. Bruna packs language, story, emotion, and color into 12 pages. After *Mother Goose,* among your first books should be one of the more than thirty little Dick Bruna books (see Index to Treasury).

During the toddler stage, an important parental role is serving as a kind of welcoming committee for the child, welcoming him to your world. Just think of yourself as the host of a huge party. Your child is the guest of honor. Naturally, you want to introduce him to all the invited guests in order to make him feel at home.

You do this by helping him learn the names of all the objects that surround him, the things that move, things that make noises, the things that shine. Picture books are perfect teaching vehicles at this stage. Point to the various items illustrated in the book, call them by name, ask the child to say the name with you, praise him enthusiastically for his efforts.

Dr. Fitzhugh Dodson, psychologist and author of *How to Parent* and *How to Father,* recommends that you include your department store mail-order catalogues in this "label-the-environment" activity. With your help and reinforcement, your 11-month-old can be pointing correctly to household items as you say them.

Must reading at this stage is Dorothy Kunhardt's *Pat the Bunny,* a little book that enables the toddler to use all his senses—to smell the flowers, feel the beard, lift the cloth, pat the fur, and see his reflection. *Pat the Bunny* is never thrown out by a family; it is worn out.

Since familiarity with pictures and words is essential at this "labeling" stage, it's a good idea to purchase several simple picture books to keep in the home along with those you borrow from the library. Not only does this give you a start in building your children's personal library (see Chapter 6), but you also will avoid the embarrassment of returning torn books to the library. Many publishers are marketing their toddler books with reinforced, durable covers and laminated pages. Keep a book in the crib and playpen at all times.

Frequently the 2-year-old who has been read to regularly can be seen toddling along with his favorite book, looking for someone to read to him. When I say "favorite" I mean just that. He has already developed literary tastes. Between now and when he is 6, he'll probably have several favorites, books he asks for often, maybe even nightly, for months on end. All too frequently this favoritism irritates parents who tire of reading the same book. Dr. Bruno Bettelheim believes that such a book fills a personal need of the child. Some fear or concern is being allayed by the book. He finds nightly courage or comfort in its characters or setting. Once we realize this, we should be able to tolerate reading the same words night after night. And Bettelheim offers this hope to weary parents: When a child has gotten all he can from the book or when the problems that directed him to the book have been outgrown, he'll be ready to move on to something else.[3]

A wonderful example of how firmly attached a child can become to a certain book is provided by *Mike's House* by Julia Sauer. She tells the story of a boy who only wants to hear the story *Mike Mulligan and His Steam Shovel* by Virginia Lee Burton. It's the only book he'll take out of the library. He comes to associate the library and the book so closely that he thinks of the library as Mike's House. Children who have heard and enjoyed *Mike Mulligan and His Steam Shovel* will find a new favorite in Mrs. Sauer's book.

Mike Mulligan and His Steam Shovel offers a perfect example of how long-lasting the love of books can be when we plant it at the right time in a child's mind. "I had no idea how deep those roots went," a nursery-school teacher told me one day after a workshop, "until last year when I was hiking the Appalachian Trail with my husband, my 19-year-old college freshman son, and a group of friends. We'd been climbing for about three hours and had just taken a rest by the side of the trail when I heard my son begin to recite some familiar words.

"I couldn't believe it," she told me. "Sitting there on a log, he regaled the group with a verbatim recitation of the entire story of Mike Mulligan—at age 19."

How deep do the roots go? Very deep and very strong when you take the time to plant the seeds correctly.

During these early years and even later, your read-aloud effort should be balanced by the outside experiences you bring to the child. It simply is not enough to just read to the child—except in extreme cases like Cushla Yeoman's.

"Reading begins with that first recorded experience," says Phyllis Halloran, first-grade teacher and a national reading consultant for the Learning Institute. "It is that experience, together with all the others to follow, that allows the child to react and respond to ideas in a book."

To the child who has never seen a flower, a plane, or a puppy, pictures of a flower, a plane, and a puppy hold little attraction. They are, instead, obstacles to overcome on the page. But having played and romped with a puppy, having picked and smelled a flower, "the child now has an experience bank from which he can draw interpretations and appreciations," Mrs. Halloran explains.

I saw firsthand the importance of experience when I was reading *Slake's Limbo* to Elizabeth when she was 11. The novel tells of a young boy chased by a gang into the New York City subway system. In his desperation, he stumbles on an old construction mistake in the tunneling and for the next 120 days lives in the subterranean cave surrounded by the grime, noise, and danger of the speeding trains.

A child in Idaho who has never stood clutching her parent's hand on a subway platform will enjoy this story but most certainly she cannot bring to it the same personal interpretation that Elizabeth could. She was introduced to subways when she was 7 years old and found them frightening almost beyond reassurance. No one knew better than Elizabeth how much courage it took for Aremis Slake to walk those rails each day. Experience, says the axiom, is the best teacher, and no one knows that better than reading teachers.

No parent of young children needs to be told how incredibly active they are or how short are their attention spans. Bearing this in mind, we cannot expect young children to be interested in reading a book whenever *we* happen to be. After all, there's a whole new world out there waiting to be explored by them; that book can wait. And it will. Let it wait until the child is calm and unwound.

Most of us who have read to children for a long time have found it helpful to establish a flexible routine for reading—a time when the child has few other distractions, a time toward which the child can look forward, from which he can gather security, a time as dependable as lunch time, nap time or bath time.

The time of day my family usually chose was bedtime—both in the afternoon before naps and in the evening. These are the times when the child looks for security, appreciates the physical closeness, and is tired enough to stay in one place. This is also an appropriate time to introduce children to the various "bedtime" books—stories like *Bedtime for Frances* by Russell Hoban, *Goodnight Moon* by Margaret Wise Brown, *Goodnight, Goodnight* by Eve Rice, *Wake Up and Goodnight* by Charlotte Zolotow, and *A Bedtime Story* by Joan Levine. These books all deal sensitively and lightly with the bedtime customs of animals as well as people.

As you increase the number of picture books you read to the child, keep in mind that between the ages of 1 and 3 children will continue to respond best to illustrations that are easily viewed, like those in the Harry the Dirty Dog series by Gene Zion.

As the child grows, if you stay tuned to his moods and needs, you'll know when he needs his books. When Jamie reached nursery-school age he wanted to be read to before leaving for school each day. Obviously he found some support in the reading which he carried with him into the day. This practice continued until he was in third grade, and it was in addition to our nightly bedtime sessions.

The physical growth of the child also means that his interests and needs are growing. He'll be asking millions of questions over the next few years, and his capacity for language from age 2 until age 5 has been described by Kornei Chukovsky, the Russian poet and literary historian, as "near-genius." [4] As the principal architect of this building stage, your reading material should keep pace with the child's growth.

Because of this high-level curiosity, many children will enjoy nonfiction books as much as fiction at this point. Peter Spier has produced a series of books that are excellent for this stage: *Crash! Bang! Boom!* (a book of noises), *Gobble, Growl, Grunt* (a book of animal sounds), *Fast-Slow, High-Low* (a book of opposites). You also must not miss Ruth Krauss's *A Hole Is to Dig*.

Stop and think for a moment, think of all the things that fascinate children: holes, cars, snow, Daddies, birds, stars, trucks, dogs, rain, cows, Mommies, planes, cats, storms, babies. At this stage in their lives, children are interested in everything. Fortunately, for nearly every subject of interest to a child there is a corresponding book. For example, when I last looked there were eighteen different books—fiction and nonfiction—published on the subject of snow. You haven't seen what books can do for children's imaginations until you've read Virginia Lee Burton's *Katy and the Big Snow* to a child or class as the winter's first snowflakes fall outside your window. What excitement!

When you see that your child or class has developed a fascination for a particular subject, check your neighborhood library for a book on it. The subject listing in the card catalogue will show what the library has on its shelves, and a handy reference guide in all libraries, *Subject Guide to Children's Books in Print,* will show what is available outside the library as well. This volume can be especially helpful with sixth-, seventh- and eighth-grade students who frequently develop strong appetites for one particular subject and are willing to devour any book about it.

Frequently, if your library doesn't have a particular book, the staff can obtain a copy for you through a regional library lending service to which they may belong. Or, thanks to your interest, they may order a copy from the publisher for the library's own collection. In looking for an out-of-print children's book, many used-book stores will advertise nationally in their trade papers and magazines to help you locate the book. There is usually a nominal fee for such services, and except in the case of rare books, the search is often successful.

During the period between 2 and 5 years of age, your child's desire to imitate his parent will extend to reading books. In some cases, by the time the child is 4 he can recite a book verbatim, page by page. Notice I said "recite" and not "read," because in the majority of cases the child has merely memorized what you've been reading to him. He'll boast that he is reading—and that's fine. Reward and praise his effort. Let him know how much you admire someone who can read. If he keeps it up, his approximations gradually will come closer to the text and eventually he will be reading naturally.

One excellent means of building the confidence, imagination and vocabulary of prereaders is through the use of "wordless" books—picture books consisting of simple plots but no words. The pictures tell the story. This has become an increasingly sophisticated and popular medium in recent years; there are more than a hundred wordless books currently available (see Wordless Books). To start, you'll want to obtain the wordless books of Mercer Mayer and John Goodall. And don't miss Shirley Hughes's *Up and Up* and Lynd Ward's classic *The Silver Pony.*

All these books offer children the chance to "read" by privately interpreting the sequence of pictures and developing the story through their own experiences and in their own words. Such actions will be essential later when they really begin to read, but for now they build a healthy sense of self-esteem and accomplishment.

As your child becomes more and more at home in the world, his confidence will grow and, in direct proportion, so will his sense of humor and adventure. I doubt there has ever been an author who stimulated these senses in young children as well as Dr. Seuss. And what Mother Goose does for toddlers' sense of sound, Dr. Seuss does for preschoolers and up. Seuss refers to his writings as "logical nonsense": children find the sights and sounds logical while adults find them nonsensical. What matters here, of course, is the child, and the fact that he is drawn into the book by Seuss's verbal gymnastics and humor.

Although Seuss has written a staggering number of books, I feel his most appropriate stories for read-aloud are those with a story line *(If I Ran the Zoo)* and definitely *not* his "controlled vocabulary" books *(Cat in the Hat)*. The latter are intended to be read *by* the child, not *to* him. Bear in mind that while the average first-grade student reads from a primer with only 350 vocabulary words in it, his *listening* vocabulary approaches 10,000 words, according to the Council for Basic Education. Frequent reading aloud of "controlled vocabulary" books is an insult to the listening vocabulary of your child. (See Index to Treasury for recommended Dr. Seuss read-alouds).

Even before the child is ready for kindergarten, he can pride himself on having a sense of humor—especially if it has been cultivated with some simple joke and riddle books. Start with something simple like *Bennett Cerf's Books of Animal Riddles* or *Bennett Cerf's Book of Laughs.* The child will love memorizing jokes from these books and trying them out on family and friends. Nothing builds self-confidence like a well-told and well-received joke.[5]

The joke book can be an effective tool for all ages. Reading consultant Bill Halloran of the Learning Institute suggests that every teacher begin the day with a joke. "All over the country teachers are starting out the day with, 'Take out your books.' Why can't they ease into the day with an elephant joke? Start the day with some knock-knock jokes and the kids will be with you for the rest of the day. Go to the library and get the joke and riddle books, leave them around your classroom. Before you know it, even the kids who hate to read will be reading them. And that's the beginning. Reading because they *want* to."

Bernard Waber is an author and illustrator who has his finger on every child's laugh pulse. In his four Lyle books, beginning with *The House on East 88th Street,* children are introduced to a lovable alligator who will touch their hearts as well as their funnybones. The most popular of all the Waber books is *Ira Sleeps Over,* the story of a child's first sleep-over and the trauma of deciding whether or not to bring his teddy bear along to his friend's house.

Ira's adventure brings us to the need for adventure stories that support the growing child who is ready, in his own mind at least, to go out and challenge the world. Nothing has served to fill this need in the last 2,000 years as well as the fairy tale.

I know what you may be thinking. "Fairy tales? Is he kidding? Why, those things are positively frightening. Nobody tells those to children any more. Children see enough violence on television—they don't need kids pushing witches into ovens, and evil spells and poisoned apples."

Stop for a minute and remind yourself how long the fairy tale has been with us—through all those years, in every nation, in every civilization, in every time. Surely there must be something important here, an insight so important as to transcend time and mountains and cultures to arrive in the twentieth century still intact. There are, for example, nearly 400 different versions of *Cinderella* from hundreds of cultures. Nevertheless, they all tell the same story—a truly universal story.

What characterizes the fairy tale—sets it apart from the rest of children's literature—is the fact that it speaks to the very heart and soul of the child. It admits to the child what so many parents and teachers spend hours trying to cover up or avoid. The fairy tale confirms what the child has been thinking all along—that it is a cold, cruel world out there and it's waiting to eat him alive.

Now, if that were all the fairy tale said, it would have died out long ago. But it goes one step further. It addresses itself to the child's sense of courage and adventure. The tale advises the child: Take your courage in hand and go out to meet that world head on. According to Bruno Bettelheim, the fairy tale offers this promise: If you have courage and if you persist, you can overcome any obstacle, conquer any foe. And best of all, you can achieve your heart's desire.

By recognizing the child's daily fears, by addressing his courage and confidence, and by offering him hope, the fairy tale presents the child with a means by which he can understand his world and himself.[6]

The true fairy tale boasts both a hero and a happy ending. Today more than ever, our children need to hear such stories and know that heroes are blessed with happy lives. We must offer that hope to our children as often and as early as possible. A few years ago, a Talent Preservation Project in New York City considered the problem of "underachievers"—very bright children who were wasting away at the bottom of their high-school classes. Included among the observations of that investigation was this one made by the staff psychologist: When these 300 teenagers were asked to name their heroes, to indicate those whom they most admired in life, 298 were unable to think of anyone.[7]

We have every reason to believe there is a direct connection between a child's heroes and heroines—his role models and motivators—and that child's self-image and achievements.

If there is one flaw in the fairy tale, it is that the most popular traditional tales are top-heavy with heroes and short on heroines. Readers-aloud will want to try *The Maid of the North* by Ethel Johnston Phelps, a collection of twenty-one traditional tales about nontraditional, courageous, resourceful, and witty heroines from a variety of ethnic cultures. They are fast-moving and dramatic enough to please all children.

When you read fairy tales to young children it is a good idea to choose books that deal with a single tale. Large volumes containing dozens of stories frequently are too heavy (and sometimes too complicated) for the child to handle comfortably. Up until second grade, children are intimidated by heavy books. They prefer books that are light and easy to hold. Later you can move up to the larger books.

I suggest you start with the simple tales as interpreted by artist Paul Galdone: *The Three Bears, Little Red Riding Hood, The Three Billy Goats Gruff, The Three Little Pigs,* and *The Gingerbread Boy* (see Index to Treasury for a list of Paul Galdone books).

From here you can progress gradually in length and complexity as the child's maturity and imagination demand. Two of today's best illustrators, Nancy Ekholm Burkert and Trina Schart Hyman, have done glorious versions of *Snow White* that are not to be missed. Hyman's *Sleeping Beauty* is my personal favorite among the volumes of single fairy tales.

Some may quarrel with the fact that many of these simpler retellings depart from the language of the original Grimm versions. I can only assume that if these two men were writing today they would use the language and idiom of our time and not of a time departed. I am less concerned with the language of the tales than I am with the meanings, particularly when the child is 5 years and older. Too often the modern adaptations emasculate the tale, leaving children with nothing but charming pap. While I don't recommend *Hansel and Gretel* for 3- and 4-year-olds, I most heartily urge it upon children of 5 and older who wonder to themselves: How long could I survive alone out there if nobody loved me? To dramatically alter *Hansel and Gretel* is to rob your child of its essential meaning.

Once your child or class is ready for the longer and more complicated tales, try the collections of Grimm and Andersen—collections where only the language has been modernized; the meanings remain untouched. Certainly one of the best anthologies available today is *The Fairy Tale Treasury,* edited by Virginia Haviland of the Library of Congress and illustrated by Raymond Briggs. This volume includes, among others, the most popular tales by Jacobs, Andersen, Perrault, and the Brothers Grimm, and runs from the simple *Henny Penny* to the more complex *The Ugly Duckling.*

The strong flavor of adventure in fairy tales and their obvious success have been extended and developed by many of today's best writers and illustrators. Edward Ardizzone's series of Little Tim books features children who save floundering ships, subdue runaway locomotives, and rescue drowning friends from the thundering surf. Each calls for children with courage to face enormous odds.

Maurice Sendak's *Where the Wild Things Are,* one of the best-selling children's books of all time, deals with a child's rage at his parent and his subsequent triumphs in the land of monsters. Ludwig Bemelmans allows his heroine Madeline to enter numerous horrendous predicaments, always to emerge devilishly triumphant. In William Steig's *Sylvester and the Magic Pebble* the hero is turned into a stone (talk about predicaments and a cruel world!), but finally emerges triumphant through his own persistence and the unfailing love of his parents.

Even when you go beyond the picture book, some of the best writers for children often follow the lead of the fairy tale. Natalie Babbitt confronts a 10-year-old girl in *Tuck Everlasting* with a kidnapping, a jailbreak, a murder, and a life-or-death decision. No life-leeched pap here! And no adult or child can read this book without coming to terms with some of life's basic issues.

It is this internal struggle to find out how we feel or who we are that is so central to the idea of reading. More than helping them to read better, more than exposing them to good writing, more than developing their imagination, when we read aloud to children we are helping them to find themselves and to discover some meaning in the scheme of things. When Robert Penn Warren wrote, "We turn to fiction for some slight hint about the story in the life we live," he meant children as much as adults. All the best qualities of great adult fiction can be found in great children's literature, but particularly in the fairy tale. When Professor Richard Abrahamson of the University of Houston studied the "Children's Choices for 1979," a list of favorite books chosen by children across the United States, he found most children preferred books with "episodic plots involving confrontation with a problem and characters who have opposing points of view . . ." [8]

Teachers and parents often ask me, "When do you stop the picture books and start with the 'big' books—the novels?" Although I understand their impatience to get on with the business of growing up, I wince whenever I hear them phrase it that way.

First of all, there is no such time as "a time to stop the picture books." I know nursery-school teachers who read Judith Viorst's *Alexander and the Terrible, Horrible, No Good, Very Bad Day* to their classes and I know a high-school English teacher who reads it to his sophomores twice a year— once in September and, by popular demand, again in June.

Shouldn't those 15-year-olds have outgrown a picture book like *Alexander and the Terrible, Horrible, No Good, Very Bad Day?* Not by my standards. I read a picture book *(Ira Sleeps Over)* to every adult group I address and no one ever objects; in fact, it may be the best part of my entire presentation. A good story is a good story. Beautiful and stirring pictures can move 15-year-olds as well as 5-year-olds. The picture book should be on the reading list of every class in every grade through twelve years of school.

You say your eighth-grade class wouldn't sit still for a picture book? They'd be insulted? Not if you picked the right book and matched it with the right moment and the right attitude on the part of the reader. Try reading *The Shrinking of Treehorn* by Florence Parry Heide to teenagers. I can almost guarantee there will be someone at your desk at the end of the class asking, "What was the name of that book again?"

Writing in *The Reading Journal,* William Coughlin, Jr., director of English education at the University of Lowell (Massachusetts), explained the difficulties he encountered in trying to teach literary form (plot, setting, character) to secondary-school students.[9] The complexity and subtlety of the text he was using, Herman Melville's *Moby Dick,* appeared to overwhelm the class. Coughlin began to wonder if the mistake was in trying to teach a simple idea with a complex book. Why not introduce the concepts of plot and point of view through a simple book and then apply them to a complex work?

Coughlin chose to work with Leo Lionni's *Frederick,* a picture book he describes as "a story of less than 600 words, but the beautifully structured craftsmanship with which its elements of form interrelated exhibited perfectly what I wanted my students to see when they read." The response by his class was immediate and the results positive. In the same article, co-author Brendan Desilets explained how picture books are used in a similar manner at Bedford (Massachusetts) High School. Both authors agree that "to ignore children's literature in the high school classroom is to overlook a valuable resource for teaching advanced reading skills."

Since many elementary-school teachers only have the opportunity to read to a mixture of slow, medium, and fast students, your initial read-aloud plan should call for material that is within the range of *all* the children in the room. In succeeding readings you can increase the caliber of the books and challenge the group's abilities. Of course, if you are teaching a gifted or top-level class you can begin at a much higher level.

One of the first criteria for lengthening the read-aloud session beyond picture books is the attention span of the child or class. It is no secret among teachers that children's attention spans appear to be growing shorter each year. It is in this battle to expand their attention spans that reading aloud can be particularly effective. A good story, peopled by well-developed characters moving in a suspenseful plot, cannot help but hold children's attention. The more this happens—as with an athlete in training—the stronger becomes the child's listening endurance.

The analogy to athletes is appropriate because of the conditioning factor in both. As the runner must accustom himself to self-discipline, so the child must be conditioned to listen for set periods of time if he is to understand and appreciate the story. And just as the runner doesn't achieve endurance overnight, neither do listeners. You must start slowly and build. Let the mental, social, and emotional level of your class or child guide you in your selections.

If the class has had experience in being read to, you can move quickly to longer books or longer reading sessions. If it is a new experience, keep your readings short. This gradual conditioning process applies to almost all grades and ages.

If I had a second-grade class with a short attention span at the start of the school year, I'd start with picture books like Bernard Waber's *Ira Sleeps Over, The Aminal* by Lorna Balian, *The Biggest Bear* by Lynd Ward, Steven Kellogg's *The Island of the Skog,* and *Sleeping Beauty* by the Brothers Grimm. Then we'd move to picture books with more words—perhaps the Bill Peet books (see Index to Treasury). And then one day I'd read a picture book and tie in a poem from Shel Silverstein's *Where the Sidewalk Ends.* In another week or so, I would add two poems to the end of the picture book, or perhaps a poem in the morning and a poem in the afternoon when we came back from lunch.

As I felt their interest and enthusiasm grow, I'd move to a series of interconnected read-aloud books, such as Bernard Waber's Lyle series. I would also introduce the children to the series by Carol and Donald Carrick about a young boy named Christopher—six beautiful stories which I'd spread through an entire week. In this series, the class will follow Christopher through his first sleep-out alone with his dog Bodger *(Sleep Out);* they can empathize with Christopher as he worries about Bodger being caught in an electrical storm *(Lost in the Storm);* they can grieve with Christopher when he must come to terms with his loss after Bodger is killed *(The Accident);* they can grow with him as he finds the replacement for Bodger—a dog abandoned on the wharf *(The Foundling);* they can rejoice with him and his new dog, Ben, in their adventure on the river after a flash flood *(The Washout);* and they can plot with him to control a neighborhood nuisance *(Ben and the Porcupine).* Six books, six days, all linked by the common thread of one family and their concern for each other and their pets. From these single-sitting books I'd move to a book like Roald Dahl's *The Magic Finger,* which can be spread over several days.

My own judgment and the attention of my child or class would indicate my next move. If the attention span was still short, I'd stay with the shorter stories for a while longer. Don't rush it. Soon, though, the class or child will be ready for the short novel—something between 60 and 100 pages long. I'd start with one like *My Father's Dragon* by Ruth Stiles Gannett or *Lafcadio, the Lion Who Shot Back* by Shel Silverstein. The former is the first book in a fantasy adventure series *(Elmer and the Dragon; The Dragons of Blueland)* with a gentle blend of drama and humor. *Lafcadio, the Lion Who Shot Back* has all the storytelling charm and humor of Silverstein's poetry and can be read to an experienced kindergarten class as well as to a sixth-grade class.

I remember a sixth-grade teacher who told me her class appeared annoyed when she announced that she was going to read *Lafcadio, the Lion Who Shot Back.* They already had been read four lengthy novels and now looked down their noses at what they called a "little kid's book." Of course, she knew they'd love it and also that they needed a change of pace from the serious novel they'd just finished *(Incident at Hawk's Hill* by Allan W. Eckert). When she finished the first chapter, they pleaded for another. It turned out to be one of the class favorites that year.

Having been read a few short novels, your class or child may be ready for the full-length novel. Perhaps the biggest difference between reading aloud the short novel and the full-length novel is the amount of description in the latter. The shorter book keeps its description to a minimum, whereas the longer book allows for greater development of character, plot, and setting.

These descriptive passages require the imagination—the right side of the brain—to build a picture of what's being read. However, if the imagination has been shriveling in front of the television for years, then it is going to be weak and unable to do any heavy lifting or building. Like any muscle in the body, the imagination cannot be built in a day or a week. It stands to reason that the child or class that has been read to regularly will have less trouble in using its imagination with these descriptive passages than will beginners.

In our home we began reading to Jamie a year earlier than we did to

Elizabeth (largely because he was the second child and we were that much smarter the second time around). As a result, Jamie was ready for his first full-length novel by the time he was in kindergarten. Elizabeth wasn't ready until first grade. The reading and listening experience of the child or class should not be your only guide. Since each child has his or her own development timetable, we cannot expect all children to arrive at the novel stage at the same time, even if they are read to regularly.

How will you know if they are ready for a full-length novel? Does the child ask you each night to keep reading? What kinds of questions does he ask about the stories you read? Are the descriptions or characters confusing for him?

The first novel I read to Jamie would be my first choice a thousand times over, for almost any child or class—*James and the Giant Peach*. I know a kindergarten teacher who ends her year with this book and I know a sixth-grade teacher who has started her September class with it for seventeen years. Any book that can hold the attention and lift the imaginations of 6-year-olds as well as 11-year-olds has to have magic in it. And *James and the Giant Peach* has that.

Once a child or class has reached the novel stage, it is increasingly important for the adult to preview the book before reading it aloud. The length of such books allows them to treat subject matter that can be very sensitive, far more so than a picture book could. As the reader, you should first familiarize yourself with the subject and the author's approach. Ask yourself as you read it through, "Can my child or class handle not only the vocabulary and the complexity of this story, but its emotions as well? Is there anything here that will do more harm than good to my child or class? Anything that might embarrass someone?"

Along with enabling you to avoid this kind of damaging situation, reading it ahead of time will enable you to read it the second time to the class or child with more confidence, accenting important passages, leaving out dull ones (I mark these lightly in pencil in the margins), and providing sound effects to dramatize the story line (I'm always ready to knock on a table or wall where the story calls for a "knock at the door").

Let me offer two personal experiences concerning story selection and reading ahead.

When Jamie was in first grade, I picked out a book by Elliott Arnold called *Brave Jimmy Stone*. It is a dramatic and touching story that describes a boy and his father on a hunting trip. They are two days away from civilization when the father falls and breaks a leg and the boy has to travel through a blizzard to get help. It was a short novel, just the right pace for Jamie, and the vocabulary was well within his grasp.

Mistakenly I considered only the intellectual level of the story and ignored the emotional level. It wasn't until Jamie woke up crying for the second straight night that I realized that I had forgotten about the emotional side of the story. Jamie had thought that because this was happening to Jimmy Stone and his father, it probably would happen to Jamie Trelease and his father, also. He was too young to deal with the realistic emotional drama of the scenes and became blind to the difference between fact and fiction. *Brave Jimmy Stone* is worth reading. It is a beautiful book. The mistake was mine in reading it too soon. I should have waited until Jamie was in third grade.

The embarrassing moment avoided by my wife when she was reading *Lafcadio, the Lion Who Shot Back* to her fifth-grade class points out the need for previewing read-alouds and the importance of staying flexible in our readings. Susan had not read the entire book ahead of time but was staying three chapters ahead of the class in her preparation each night. Suddenly one night she stood in front of me exclaiming, "What am I going to do? I just got to the part where Lafcadio goes to Chicago and has a suit made for himself out of marshmallows. What am I going to do?"

When I expressed bewilderment, Susan explained that there was an overweight child in her class whom the children cruelly had nicknamed "Marshmallow." To make matters worse, she said, the word appeared throughout the next chapter, also. "I know that as soon as I read the word 'marshmallow,' every head in the room is going to turn toward that child. He's going to hate this book and he's going to hate me for reading it. I just can't do that to him. But I've already started the book with the class and they love it."

We solved the problem with a little flexibility: Taking a pencil, we crossed out every "marshmallow" in the text and replaced it with "M & M's." She finished the book and the children never knew the difference, though she didn't leave the book around the room for the kids to examine as she normally would have done.

Sooner or later the question of censorship arises, perhaps not over the word "marshmallow" but over others. My own creed is that I censor everything—what I read to myself and what I read aloud. I do it all the time. If I don't like something I'm reading, I usually skip over it, as most people do. If there is something in the text that will detract from the book's impact or disturb your class or child, skip it or change it. You're running the program, not the person who wrote the book, who has no idea what the problems are in your classroom or home.

If you edit calmly you can save many books that ordinarily might have to be scrapped for classroom consumption. A teacher in South Hadley, Massachusetts, confirmed this approach in reading Lois Duncan's *Killing*

Mr. Griffin to her eighth-grade remedial-reading class. Her students were 13-year-olds reading on a third-grade level. The story of four teenagers who decide to kidnap and frighten their overstrict English teacher is controversial enough, but the occasional four-letter words if read aloud could put the teacher in hot water. Nevertheless, she knew the story was worth saving. In reading it to her class she skipped or changed the swear words and read on. The resulting class attention and enthusiasm were sky-high. By the middle of the book, half the class had tried in vain to find a copy in the school library in order to read it for themselves.

"I choose to read one chapter a day, no more. That way," the teacher explains, "if a child is absent, he doesn't miss too much of the story. I also do the reading at the beginning of the class. As a result, I never have to call for order. They are 'shush-ing' each other as they walk in the door. There is perfect order at the sound of the bell and seldom is there a late arrival."

But more importantly, they became involved in the story. They immediately recognized the peer pressures that fertilized the kidnapping scheme. They took sides and began to form judgments about the characters, putting themselves in their places. These eighth-grade remedial students had become emotionally, intellectually, and socially involved in the story.

"For me," the teacher enthuses, "that is a dream come true."

Several questions often are raised about a book like *Killing Mr. Griffin*. First, what kind of subject matter is that for kids? In reply I refer you to Robert C. O'Brien's speech in accepting his 1972 Newbery Medal for *Mrs. Frisby and the Rats of NIMH*. O'Brien saw the mind as a seed. As the seed grows, it puts down roots, opens its leaves, and looks around. "It learns about love," O'Brien noted, "about hate, fear, sadness, courage, kindness. But all of them come to life in books in a way that is peculiarly suitable for examination, for contemplation, and evaluation . . .

"Did I mention bad guys?" O'Brien asked. "Did I say Long John Silver? Long John Silver is a liar; he is unctious, greedy, tricky; he is a thief. Then why do we like him better than anybody else in the book?

"Here is where examination and evaluation come into play," O'Brien explained. "The mind learns that it is not easy to separate good from bad; they become deviously intertwined. From books it learns that not all doors are simply open and shut . . ." [10]

The second question arising from a book like *Killing Mr. Griffin* is: Won't remedial students reading on a third-grade level miss much of the meaning of the story?

Fader and McNeil answer this question in their book, *Hooked on Books*. Dr. Daniel Fader writes of his experiences in turning reluctant readers into willing readers, particularly at the W. J. Maxey Boys' Training School in Michigan. Many of the delinquent boys at the school were semiliterate, but that didn't stop them from reading books that interested them. Fader points to the boy who wanted to read Nathaniel Hawthorne's *The Scarlet Letter*. When the boy was cautioned that the book might be too difficult, he replied, "Ain't this the one about a whore?" When he was told that, indeed, that description came fairly close to the mark, he proceeded to read it. "If it was a book about a whore, it was a book for him," Fader wrote.

The author convincingly points out that his experiences at Maxey show that children definitely can read and understand without knowing every word in the book. [11]

Semi-literate readers do not need semi-literate books. The simplistic language of much of the life-leeched literature inflicted upon the average schoolchild is not justifiable from any standpoint. Bright, average, dull—however one classifies the child—he is immeasurably better off with books that are too difficult for him than books that are too simple. . . . Reading is a peculiarly personal interaction between a reader and a book . . . but *in no case* does this interaction demand an understanding of every word by the reader. The threshold . . . even in many complex books, can be pleasurably crossed by many simple readers.

By citing Dr. Fader's argument here I am not suggesting that every book you read aloud be over the head of your audience. A child hears a story on at least three different levels: intellectual, emotional, and social. In the Maxey and South Hadley incidents, while the students were on a third-grade intellectual level, their emotional and social levels were often those of their own age or older.

While on the subject of junior- and senior-high school students who are reluctant readers, I think it is important to note that they, too, should be conditioned gradually to the reading-aloud process. In working with these slower students you must first consider the kind of class you have and work from there. I remember the remedial-reading teacher who told me about her frustrations in trying to find the right book for the worst class she'd ever had. This happened to be a sixth-grade class but the lesson applies to all grade levels. First she tried *Charlotte's Web;* they thought it was corny. Then she tried *Charlie and the Chocolate Factory* by Roald Dahl; half the class liked it, half didn't. At last she struck upon *J.T.* by Jane Wagner, the story of a black boy straddling the edge of delinquency. The class loved it so much that half of them found extra copies and finished it ahead of her.

The teacher admitted that her mistake was in not tailoring her first selections to the kind of class she had—a group of restless, nonreading, street-wise, inner-city kids. Make your *initial* choices for a group like that something they can relate to, win their interest, catch their hearts and ears. A few selections of this kind and you'll have won their confidence, after which you can broaden the scope of your reading and introduce them to other times and other places than their own.

Humor or light verse or suspense are perfect introductions to read-aloud for older reluctant readers. Try beginning each day with a poem from *Where the Sidewalk Ends* or a short piece from one of *Reader's Digest*'s outstanding anthologies. Two of the most popular features in *Reader's Digest* have recently been collected in paperback form: *Unforgettable Characters* and *Drama in Real Life*. Following the magazine's formula, all the stories are short, attention-grabbing, and true.

In a similar vein is *Paul Harvey's The Rest of the Story,* two volumes containing nearly 200 tales drawn from history and contemporary life. Originally used for Harvey's popular radio program of the same name, the stories are only four minutes in length and each is highlighted by an O. Henry ending. A few weeks of these short selections is all you'll need before launching your class into a novel.

You might also keep in mind that all your reading selections do not have to be complete works. If, in your leisure reading, you find a magazine article, newspaper column, or a book chapter that you think the class or child would enjoy, read it aloud to them. It might whet their appetites enough to read the book themselves or become a regular reader of that newspaper columnist. You'll know you've scored when a student stops you in the hall between classes and asks, "Did you read Mike Royko this morning? Wasn't it great?" Remember: Awareness must come before desire.

The youngster being conditioned to reading aloud is much like a runner in training. One of the problems that faces a runner after he has acquired some proficiency is the boredom associated with repetitive training. Long-distance runners combat this boredom by varying the length and routes of their training runs. Readers-aloud face a similar predicament in conditioning children in listening. To solve this problem, readers should imitate the runner—vary your reading routes. Read a three-sitting story after a week of one-sittings. Or do a series of short stories from *Free to Be You and Me*.

Just as you should remember to challenge the mental level of your audience, it also is important to realize that you don't have to challenge them *all* the time. Do *you* choose for your personal reading only those books that challenge you? Do you read only the editorial page of the newspaper or do you read the comics and Ann Landers too?

If we are to give our children an overview of the literary spectrum available to them, then we should vary the scenery: animal stories like *Lassie Come Home* and George Selden's *Cricket in Times Square;* family stories like *Roll of Thunder, Hear My Cry* by Mildred Taylor and Franklyn Mayer's *Me and Caleb;* historical stories like Carol Ryrie Brink's *Caddie Woodlawn* and *My Brother, the Wind* by G. Clifton Wisler; funny stories like *Freckle Juice* and Barbara Robinson's *The Best Christmas Pageant Ever;* sad stories like *Bridge to Terabithia* by Katherine Paterson and *A Day No Pigs Would Die;* scary stories like William Sleator's *Among the Dolls* and *Old Mother Witch* by Carol Carrick; sports stories like *It's a Mile From Here to Glory* by Robert C. Lee and *Hang Tough, Paul Mather.*

A parent may choose to challenge a child's mind with each read-aloud and take care of the child's emotional needs in other ways. But classroom teachers are limited in the ways they reach and touch children. Each day millions of children arrive in American classrooms in search of more than reading and math skills. They are looking for a light in the darkness of their lives, a Good Samaritan who will stop and bandage a bruised heart or ego.

Books can do much to ease those hurts. Katherine Paterson spoke eloquently about the healing salve of books when she accepted the 1979 National Book Award for *The Great Gilly Hopkins,* a book that offers hope and affection to those thousands of children who have found themselves rated "disposable"—foster children.

Mrs. Paterson told her Carnegie Hall audience, "A teacher had read aloud *The Great Gilly Hopkins* to her class and Eddie, another foster child, hearing in the story of Gilly his own story, did something that apparently flabbergasted everyone who knew him. He fell in love with a book. Can you imagine how that made me feel? Here was a 12-year-old who knew far better than I what my story was about, and he did me the honor of claiming it for himself. It seemed to me that anyone who liked a book as much as Eddie did should have a copy of his own, so I sent him one. On Saturday I got this letter:

Dear Mrs. Paterson:
   Thank you for the book, *The Great Gilly Hopkins.* I love the book. I'm on page 16.

Your friend always,
Eddie Young[12]

When considering material to read aloud to children, two areas often overlooked are poetry and comic books.

"Children never hear poetry any more," laments Professor Leland Jacobs of Columbia University. "They come to nursery school and they know the jingles from television but they don't know Mother Goose."

The problem is that most parents and teachers assume that children hate poetry. They are right in such assumptions if they are talking about obscure or long descriptive poetry filled with obsolete figures of speech to which children are introduced by having to memorize or analyze it.

On the other hand, when children are introduced to the right poems in the right manner, they love poetry. This love is easily recognized in children's universal love of song—which is just poetry set to music. A child cannot help but begin life with a love of poetry if you consider that the first sound he hears is a poem: the rhythmic beat of his mother's heart. The love of such rhythm stays until it is driven from the child by unthinking and insensitive teachers in his home or classroom.

In making your poetry selections, it would be helpful to bear in mind what Bernice Cullinan, New York University professor of early childhood and elementary education, says in her book *Literature and the Child:* "Children's poetry choices remain stable and consistent over the years. Many children today, like those of 50 years ago, prefer humorous poems. Most children do not like sentimental and serious poetry, or poems difficult to understand. Poetry with clear-cut rhyme and rhythm is well liked; poetry that depends heavily upon imagery is not." [13]

The rules for retaining or developing a love of poetry within children are: read it aloud; read it often; keep it simple; keep it joyous or spooky or exciting. Remember, poetry appreciation is like a ball. "It is more caught than taught," explains Jacobs. For this purpose, keep an anthology of poetry handy at the bedside or on the teacher's desk. Mother Goose and Shel Silverstein's *Where the Sidewalk Ends,* both mentioned earlier in this chapter, are outstanding examples of Anthologies and are included in the Treasury.

Frequently you can link an appropriate poem with a book you are reading aloud, either before or after the story, later in the day, or on days when your schedule doesn't leave enough time for the day's chapter.

Samples of the many story-poem combinations you might choose are listed on page 62. (The volume in which the poem can be found is listed above each group.)

The Best Loved Poems
of the American People

Call of the Wild	"The Spell of the Yukon"
The Little House	"The House With Nobody in It"
A Taste of Blackberries	"The Child's First Grief"
Old Mother Witch	"Somebody's Mother"
Catch a Killer	"The Bank Thief"
Sing Down the Moon	"The Indian Hunter"
Old Arthur	"Bum"
The Elves and the Shoemaker	"Be the Best of Whatever You Are"
Matt's Mitt	"Casey at the Bat"
Mike Mulligan and His	
Steam Shovel	"It Couldn't Be Done"

Now We Are Six

The Leatherman	"The Charcoal-Burner"
How I Hunted the Little	
Fellows	"Binker"

Piper, Pipe That Song Again

The Snowy Day	"Snow in the City"
Snow-Bound	"Stopping by Woods on a Snowy Evening"
Storm Boy	"The Reason for the Pelican"
Grasshopper and the Unwise	
Owl	"Little Talk"

The Golden Treasury of Poetry

The Man in the Box	"The Battle of Blenheim"
The Indian in the Cupboard	"George Who Played with a Dangerous Toy and Suffered a Catastrophe"
The Reluctant Dragon	"The Tale of Custard the Dragon"
Chocolate Fever	"Griselda"
The Maggie B.	"Pirate Story"

Where the Sidewalk Ends

Search for Delicious	"Peanut-Butter Sandwich"
The Book of Giant Stories	"Me and My Giant"
No Fighting, No Biting!	"The Crocodile's Toothache"

By familiarizing yourself with the Poetry books listed in the Treasury, you will be able to come up with many more combinations of your own.

Along with accomplishing many of the aims of all good literature, poetry has one aspect that sets it apart from the rest. It is an excellent medium for training the disciplines of listening and reading that are such integral parts of your read-aloud program.

"Poetry," explained Donald Barr while headmaster of the Dalton School, "cannot be skimmed. It must be read word for word." Because it is bound by meter and rhythm, every word and every syllable counts. Children quickly come to sense this and discipline their attention in order to stay tuned. There is no room for the skimming that is so prevalent in prose. Barr adds that such unfortunate habits often rob literature of its subtle meanings. "But poetry will not bear it. It is a great discipline." [14]

The other area commonly overlooked for read-aloud is the comic book. But no ordinary comic. No boy or girl should be allowed to escape childhood without being introduced to the comic *Tintin*.

If you looked closely at Dustin Hoffman while he was reading a bedtime story to his son in *Kramer vs. Kramer,* you would have noticed he was reading *Tintin.* Or if you looked closely at the list of favorite read-alouds offered by historian Arthur Schlesinger, Jr., in *The New York Times Book Review,* you would have found Hergé's *Tintin* between *Huckleberry Finn* and the Greek myths.[15]

Begun as a comic strip in Belgium in 1929, *Tintin* now reaches, in comic-book form, thirty countries in twenty-two languages and is sold only in quality bookstores. The subject of this success is a 17-year-old reporter (Tintin) who, along with his dog and a cast of colorful and zany characters, travels around the globe in pursuit of mad scientists, spies, and saboteurs.

Two years are spent researching and drawing the 700 illustrations in each issue. These pictures vary in size, shape, and perspective, and run as many as fifteen panels to a page. Their sequence, with its minute detail and on-running dialogue, inhibits the child from understanding the book by merely looking at the pictures, as he can with most comics. To be understood, *Tintin* must be read—and that is the key for parents and teachers who care about reading. Each issue contains 8,000 words. The beautiful part of it is that children are unaware they are reading 8,000 words. They are reading for the fun of it—the important first step toward all other kinds of reading.

Introduce your child to *Tintin* and the comics page of your daily newspaper by first reading them aloud. Young children must be shown how a comic "works": the sequence of the panels, how to tell when a character is thinking and when he is speaking. A comic can be viewed as nothing more than a sequential diagram of conversation—a language blue-print. Once the blueprint is understood, the child will be ready and willing to follow it on his own without your reading it aloud.

Parents and teachers who provide a wide variety of reading materials for the child need not fear that the child or class will develop a "comic-book mentality." A recent study showed that more top students (nearly 100 percent), in all grades, read comics or comic books than did lower students.[16]

4
The Do's and Don'ts of Read-Aloud

Writing begins long before the marriage of pencils and paper. It begins with sounds, that is to say with words and simple clusters of words that are taken in by small children until they find themselves living in a world of vocables. If that world is rich and exciting, the transition to handling it in a new medium—writing—is made smoother. The first and conceivably the most important instructor in composition is the teacher, parent, or older sibling who reads aloud to the small child.
> —Clifton Fadiman,
> *Empty Pages: A Search for Writing Competence in School and Society*

Do's

• Begin reading to children as soon as possible. The younger you start them, the better.

• Use Mother Goose rhymes and songs to stimulate the infant's language. Simple but boldly drawn picture books will help arouse the child's senses of sight and curiosity.

• Read as often as you and the child (or class) have time for.

• Try to set aside at least one traditional time each day for a story. In my home, favorite story times are before going to bed and before leaving for school.

• Remember that the art of listening is an acquired one. It must be taught and cultivated gradually—it doesn't happen overnight.

• Picture books can be read easily to a family of children widely separated in age. Novels, however, pose a problem. If there are more than two years between the children, each child would benefit greatly if you read to him or her individually. This requires more effort on the part of the parents but it will reap rewards in direct proportion to the effort expended. You will reinforce the specialness of each child.

• Start with picture books and build to storybooks and novels.

• Vary the length and subject matter of your readings.

• Follow through with your reading. If you start a book, it is your responsibility to continue it—unless it turns out to be bad book. Don't leave the child or class hanging for three or four days between chapters and expect their interest to be sustained.

• Occasionally read above the children's intellectual level and challenge their minds.

• Avoid long descriptive passages until the child's imagination and attention span are capable of handling them. There is nothing wrong with shortening or eliminating them. Prereading helps to locate such passages and they can then be marked with a pencil in the margin.

• If your chapters are long or if you don't have enough time each day to finish an entire chapter, find a suspenseful spot at which to stop. Leave the audience hanging; they'll be counting the minutes until the next reading.

• Allow your listeners a few minutes to settle down and adjust their feet and minds to the story. If it's a novel, you might begin by asking if anyone remembers what happened when you left off yesterday. Mood is an important factor in listening. An authoritarian "Now stop that and settle down! Sit up straight. Pay attention" is not conducive to a receptive audience.

• If you are reading a picture book, make sure the children can see the pictures easily. In class, with the children in a semicircle around you, seat yourself just slightly above them so that the children in the back row can see the pictures above the heads of the others.

• In reading a novel, position yourself where both you and the children are comfortable. In the classroom, whether you are sitting on the edge of your desk or standing, your head should be above the heads of your listeners for your voice to carry to the far side of the room. Do not sit at your desk and read or stand in front of brightly lit windows, which strain the eyes of your audience.

• Remember that even sixth-grade students love a good picture book now and then.

• Allow time for class and home discussion after reading a story. Thoughts, hopes, fears, and discoveries are aroused by a book. Allow them to surface and help the child to deal with them through verbal, written, or artistic expression if the child is so inclined. Do not turn discussions into quizzes or insist upon prying story interpretations from the child.

• Remember that reading aloud comes naturally to very few people. To do it successfully and with ease you must practice.

• Use plenty of expression when reading. If possible, change your tone of voice to fit the dialogue.

• Adjust your pace to fit the story. During a suspenseful part, slow down, draw your words out, bring your listeners to the edge of their chairs.

• The most common mistake in reading aloud—whether the reader is a 7-year-old or a 40-year-old—is reading too fast. Read slowly enough for the child to build mental pictures of what he just heard you read. Slow down enough for the children to see the pictures in the book without feeling hurried. Reading quickly allows no time for the reader to use vocal expression.

• Preview the book by reading it to yourself ahead of time. Such advance reading allows you to spot material you may wish to shorten, eliminate, or elaborate on.

• Bring the author to life, as well as his book. Pick up Lee Bennett Hopkins's paperbacks of interviews with children's authors, *Books Are by People* and *More Books by More People.* Consult *Something About the Author* at the library. Read the information about the author on your book's dust jacket. Either before or during the reading, tell your audience something about the author. Let them know that books are written by people, not by machines.

• Add a third dimension to the book whenever possible. For example: have a bowl of blueberries ready to be eaten during or after the reading of Robert McCloskey's *Blueberries for Sal;* bring a harmonica and a lemon to class before reading McCloskey's *Lentil;* visit the owls at the zoo in conjunction with Farley Mowat's *Owls in the Family.*

• Reluctant readers or unusually active children frequently find it difficult to just sit and listen. Paper, crayons, and pencils allow them to keep their hands busy while listening.

• Bring a book with you whenever you travel with a child. That traffic jam on the way to the beach or the long wait at the dentist's office is a perfect time for a chapter or two.

• Fathers should make an extra effort to read to their children. Because 90 percent of primary-school teachers are women, young boys often associate reading with women and schoolwork. And just as unfortunately, too many fathers prefer to be seen playing catch in the driveway with their sons than taking them to the library. It is not by chance that most of the students in remedial-reading classes are boys. A father's early involvement with books and reading can do much to elevate books to at least the same status as baseball gloves and hockey sticks in a boy's estimation.

• Regulate the amount of time your children spend in front of the television. Excessive television viewing is habit-forming and damaging to a child's development.

• Arrange for time each day—in the classroom or in the home—for the child to read by himself (even if "read" only means turning pages and looking at the pictures). All your read-aloud motivation goes for naught if the time is not available to put it into practice.

• Lead by example. Make sure your children see you reading for pleasure other than at read-aloud time. Share with them your enthusiasm for whatever you are reading.

Don'ts

• Don't read stories that you don't enjoy yourself. Your dislike will show in the reading, and that defeats your purpose.

• Don't continue reading a book once it is obvious that it was a poor choice. Admit the mistake and choose another. (You can avoid this by prereading the book yourself.)

• If you are a teacher, don't feel you have to tie every book to classwork. Don't confine the broad spectrum of literature to the narrow limits of the curriculum.

• Consider the intellectual, social, and emotional level of your audience in making a read-aloud selection. Challenge them, but don't overwhelm them.

• Don't read above a child's emotional level.

• Don't select a book that many of the children already have heard or seen on television. Once a novel's plot is known, much of their interest is lost. You can, however, read a book ahead of its appearance on television or at the movies. Afterwards, encourage the children to see the movie. It's a good way for them to see how much more can be portrayed in print than on the screen.

• Don't be fooled by awards. Just because a book won an award doesn't guarantee that it will make a good read-aloud. In most cases, a book award is given for the quality of the writing, not for its read-aloud qualities.

• Don't start a reading if you are not going to have enough time to do it justice. Having to stop after one or two pages only serves to frustrate, rather than stimulate, the child's interest in reading.

• Don't be unnerved by questions during the reading, particularly from very young children. Answer their questions patiently. Don't put them off. Don't rush your answers. There is no time limit for reading a book but there is a time limit on a child's inquisitiveness. Foster that curiosity with patient answers—then resume your reading.

• Don't use the book as a threat—"If you don't pick up your room, no story tonight!" As soon as the child or class sees that you've turned the book into a weapon, they'll change their attitude about books from positive to negative.

• Don't try to compete with television. If you say, "Which do you want, a story or TV?" they will usually choose the latter. That is like saying to a 9-year-old, "Which do you want, vegetables or a donut?" Since *you* are the adult, *you* choose. "The television goes off at eight-thirty in this house. If you want a story before bed, that's fine. If not, that's fine, too. But no television after eight-thirty." But don't let books appear to be responsible for depriving the children of viewing time.

5
What Makes a
Good Read-Aloud?

The prime function, therefore, of the children's book writer is to write a book that is so absorbing, exciting, funny, fast and beautiful that the child will fall in love with it. And that first love affair between the young child and the young book will hopefully lead to other loves for other books and when that happens the battle is probably won. The child will have found a crock of gold. He will also have gained something that will help to carry him most marvelously through the tangles of his later years.

> –Roald Dahl,
> from a Knopf publicity release

Perhaps the most common mistake of parents and teachers when examining children's books is the assumption that children have a separate set of literary standards from adults. It is this theory that frequently turns many children away from books. As an adult you would not tolerate the life-leeched literature we frequently insist on feeding our children. C. S. Lewis, the author of the Narnia Chronicles, suggests this rule of thumb when considering the worth of a children's book: "A book which is enjoyed only by children is a bad children's story. The good ones last. A waltz which you can like only when you are waltzing is a bad waltz." [1] In much the same way, a book which is not worth reading at age 50 is not worth reading at age 10, either.

Before we ask ourselves if a book is a good read-aloud, we should first consider: Is it a good book? What makes a good book for you as an adult? Most importantly, the book must hold your interest. Children make the same demand. They have no more appetite for boredom than you do, and perhaps they have less.

Books and readers are very much like fishing rods and fish. Since the object of every good book is to catch readers, it should come equipped with a hook—a piece of the story's framework that grabs the reader and holds him through all 24 pages or all 224 pages. There must be just the right amount of tension in the story line: it must be loose enough to kindle the reader's imagination, yet tight enough to keep the reader's constant attention.

The hook in picture books, by necessity, must be right up front. There is seldom enough room to hide it because the reader must be captured early in so few pages. To make sure that the reader doesn't escape, a good picture book comes with two hooks: the story and the illustrations, the latter being the more important. If the story is sharp but the pictures dull, or vice versa, the audience will lose interest. To be most effective they must work together, pleasing the child's eye and ear, teasing his curiosity, and holding his attention. The perfect example of this is *Where the Wild Things Are.* The story hook is: Will Max ever return home? The picture hook: Are those ferocious monsters going to eat him up?

The problem for most teachers and parents is finding good fiction for older children—short novels and novels. Sometimes the hook is right there, waiting for you in the first sentence, as in the opening line from Jay Williams's *The Hero from Otherwhere:*

It was a case of hate at first sight.

Another fine example is the first three sentences of *Charlotte's Web:*

"Where's Papa going with that ax?" said Fern to her mother as they were setting the table for breakfast.

"Out to the hoghouse," replied Mrs. Arable. "Some pigs were born last night."

Or, as in the case of *James and the Giant Peach,* the first page enthralls you:

Here is James Henry Trotter when he was about four years old.

Up until this time, he had had a happy life, living peacefully with his mother and father in a beautiful house beside the sea. There were always plenty of other children for him to play with, and there was the sandy beach for him to run about on, and the ocean to paddle in. It was the perfect life for a small boy.

Then, one day, James' mother and father went to London to do some shopping, and a terrible thing happened. Both of them suddenly got eaten up (in full daylight, mind you, and on a crowded street) by an enormous angry rhinoceros which had escaped from the London zoo.

Other books, like *Roll of Thunder, Hear My Cry* or *The Pond,* don't set the hook for ten or twenty pages into the book. If you have to wait longer than that to be pulled in, the book probably won't make a good read-aloud.

Just as adult books sometimes start off by holding our interest but end up dying in our laps halfway through, so can children's novels. You cannot judge a book by its first few chapters any more than you can by its cover. The only way to judge a book is to read it all the way through. If it holds your interest and if you think it would also appeal to children, ask yourself these questions, posed by Professor Edward Rosenheim, Jr., of the University of Chicago:

- Will the book call into play the child's imagination?
- Will it invite the exercise of compassion or humor?
- Will it exploit the capacity for being curious?
- Will its language challenge the child's awareness of rhythms and structures?
- Will its characters and events call for—and even strengthen—an understanding of human motives and circumstances?
- Will it provide the joy that comes with achievement, understanding, and new encounters? [2]

If you can answer yes to most of those questions, you are holding a good book, perhaps even a great book. But is it a good read-aloud?

To answer that question, you must apply a further set of standards. In the same way that every poem cannot be set to music and made into a song, so, too, every story is not meant to be read aloud. Three factors primarily determine the success of any good book that is to be read aloud: the writing, the reader, and the audience. If even one factor is negative, the book will fail as a read-aloud.

To begin with, let's consider the writing. Assuming that the book already possesses the criteria called for by Rosenheim, what else is needed?

First, it is important to keep in mind that nearly all parents and teachers are pressed for time. Few adults have the time to read for an hour at a time and few children have the time to listen that long—unless it is to avoid a math test. In addition, reading aloud can be physically tiring for the reader after ten or fifteen minutes.

In my experience the most successful read-aloud approach is one that whets the child's appetite in small doses of ten to twenty minutes. Of course, if the child clamors for more and you have the energy and time, by all means continue for as long as the interest or your voice holds. If, on the other hand, you can only read for short bursts of time, the length of your books should allow you to finish them in a reasonable amount of time. In spending months on one book, no matter how good it is, you are testing the child's or class's interest and patience. You also are limiting them to one book. I feel you do more for a child by reading two books in one month than one book in two months.

Therefore, considering the short amount of time usually available, a good read-aloud book should:

1. *Be fast-paced in its plot, allowing children's interest to be hooked as soon as possible.* For the older child, pace is less important and more description can be included in the story.

Great read-aloud authors use not only an opening story hook but also hasten the pace with chapter hooks. Theodore Taylor does this in nearly every chapter of *The Cay,* the story of a blind boy and an old man (Timothy) marooned on a tiny Caribbean island. Consider these opening lines from chapters in *The Cay:*

Like silent, hungry sharks that swim in the darkness of the sea, the German submarines arrived in the middle of the night.

We were torpedoed at about three-o'clock in the morning of April 6, 1942, two days after leaving Panama.

One morning in the middle of May, I awakened to hear Timothy taking great breaths. It sounded as though he were fighting for air.

There is also the cliffhanger hook at the end of a chapter and this, too, distinguishes the great read-aloud. Louis L'Amour, the best-selling western writer of all time, uses the cliffhanger with great skill. Although *Down the Long Hills* was not written with the juvenile market in mind, it is a wise parent, teacher, or librarian who adds it to his or her library. Read aloud these chapter endings and imagine children's reactions. They will beg for the next chapter. They will remind you throughout the next day not to forget the day's chapter:

> He knew he had to get away from there. They must leave right away. For that big Indian, he felt sure, was going to come back.
>
> Old Three-Paws thrust his huge head from the bush and stared at the horse. The stallion blew shrilly, then reared on his hind legs, his front legs pawing, and then Old Three-Paws charged.
>
> Cal eased back the hammer on the pistol, and the click was loud in the silence.

2. *Contain clear, rounded characters.* Children should see character unfold and grow with the story. For character development, few writers can compare with C. S. Lewis, whose 1950 novel, *The Lion, the Witch and the Wardrobe,* is a modern classic of fantasy. Lewis brings the main characters to life in just one paragraph (the first) and without a word of dialogue:

> Once there were four children whose names were Peter, Susan, Edmund and Lucy. This story is about something that happened to them when they were sent away from London during the war because of the air-raids. They were sent to the house of an old Professor who lived in the heart of the country, ten miles from the nearest railway station and two miles from the nearest post office. He had no wife and he lived in a very large house with a housekeeper called Mrs. Macready and three servants. (Their names were Ivy, Margaret, and Betty, but they do not come into the story much.) He himself was a very old man with shaggy white hair, which grew over most of his face as well on his head, and they liked him almost at once; but on the first evening when he came out to meet them at the front door he was so odd-looking that Lucy (who was the youngest) was a little afraid of him, and Edmund (who was the next youngest) wanted to laugh and had to keep on pretending he was blowing his nose to hide it.

3. *Include crisp, easy-to-read dialogue.* Good dialogue definitely increases a book's readability. However, *too* much dialogue can present problems. Story dialogue is read best by altering the pitch of your voice between characters. The more characters involved in the conversation, the more shifting must be done by the reader, as well as by the listener who is taking his cue from the reader as to who is speaking in the story. Too many switches eventually trip the reader and listener.

Remember to pace yourself when reading dialogue aloud. Give yourself enough time between different characters' "voices." This slight pause also indicates to your audience that someone else is about to speak.

4. *Keep long descriptive passages to a minimum, at least at the start.* This frequently means eliminating certain classics from your read-aloud library. Writing in *The New York Times* on the joys of reading aloud to his children, historian Arthur Schlesinger, Jr. (a staunch advocate of reading *only* the classics), recalled his disappointment in re-experiencing the classic *Swiss Family Robinson* by J. R. Wyss as a read-aloud: "I had forgotten the inordinate amount of time the Robinson family spends a) praying and b) massacring great numbers of inoffensive animals."

This is not to suggest there is no room for description in read-aloud. Consider these two paragraphs of fast-moving description, rich in simile and metaphor, from Barbara Brooks Wallace's *Peppermints in the Parlor.* In this scene from the first chapter, the newly orphaned Emily arrives at the mansion home of her aunt and uncle, fully expecting a warm welcome, but finds her relatives replaced by two strangers:

Both were women, one plump as a pudding in a lavender, full-skirted dress. All Emily could see of her head, however, was a tiny lace doily set on a crown of greying hair. She kept her face bent over a pair of long knitting needles and was busy plying them as if she had no interest whatsoever in the new arrival. But it was the figure beside her that made Emily's blood suddenly freeze.

Click! Click! Click! To the curiously grim tune of the knitting needles, her eyes rose slowly up, up, up past the waist of a deadly black skirt, past a gold medallion with a glittering ruby eye in its center, past a high black collar coiled around a white, serpent-thin neck, past a chin sharp as an ice pick, past thin bloodless lips under a pale nose so pinched it seemed air could never pass through it, and arriving finally at the meanest, wickedest, evilest pair of eyes Emily had ever seen in her whole life!

Few language devices are as enriching and important as simile and metaphor. They clarify and expand the subject under discussion and provide opportunity for the intellectual exercise known as comparison: "plump as a pudding"; "a crown of greying hair"; "grim tune of the knitting needles"; "glittering ruby eye"; "serpent-thin neck." Such figurative language sharpens not only the eye with which a child views the world but the mind's eye as well. It is worth noting the excellent economy in Wallace's description—no words are wasted and two adjectives are never used where one would suffice. This keeps the narrative pace moving, a prime consideration for reading aloud to children.

Along with the quality of writing, a book's read-aloud success is determined also by the reader. Even the best read-aloud will fail if the person reading it stumbles over words, loses his place, or reads unenthusiastically. It is imperative that *you* like the story, that *you* are interested in its characters and outcome. If you know ahead of time that you cannot bring your heart to a certain book, don't read it. There are too many available that you do like to waste your time on one you dislike.

Along with your interest, you must also consider the individual reading style we each bring to a story. The teacher who reads in a monotone will not do as much justice to a book as one who can give an expressive rendering. The good reader senses when to drop his or her voice almost to a whisper in the picture book *Old Mother Witch*. Coaxed by fellow trick-or-treaters, young David creeps onto the porch of cranky old Mrs. Oliver, whom neighborhood children have named "Old Mother Witch." On his way across the darkened porch, David trips over an overturned garbage can. At this point, the reader's voice should drop to a worried whisper.

"Oh boy," muttered David. "Now I'm really in for it. She must have heard that." [Reader is now slightly bent over.]
As he scrambled to his feet his hand reached out. What he tripped over [pause] was [pause again] something soft. He screamed and heard the others scream and run down the block. He had touched [long pause] skin and a [pause] pair of eyeglasses. It was a body. It was [pause, voice whispers in horror] Mrs. Oliver.

This story's sensitive message, its impact and drama, can be tripled in strength by reading it aloud in the right manner. The tone of the reader has an effect upon the listener in much the same manner that background music does in a movie or radio program.

The last factor in determining the read-aloud's success is the listener. If the material is too far over the head of your audience, no matter how good the story is or how well it is read, it will fail. It is important to carefully match a book with its appropriate audience. Don't read what you think the child or class *ought* to hear. Good children's books were not written to be used as textbooks. They were written to be enjoyed. Ask yourself, "If I were sitting out there listening, is this what I would want to hear?"

There is, however, no grade in education—from kindergarten through college—that cannot relate in some way to the picture book *Alexander and the Terrible, Horrible, No Good, Very Bad Day*. Every level discovers something in the book that others may have missed. Yet I know teachers and parents (and a few school librarians) who tell sixth graders, for instance, to put that book back on the library shelf and pick something more on their own level. In so doing, they show their ignorance of both children and their books.

"What happened to the classics?" you may ask. "Don't you believe in reading great literature to children?"

Nothing happened to the classics—but something happened to children: their imaginations went to sleep in front of the television set twenty-five years ago. Reading a classic to a child whose imagination is in a state of retarded development will not foster a love of literature in that child. Instead, it may result in boredom and frustration. I believe you should start with good, simple stories and build to the classics.

What precisely is a classic? There are two schools of thought regarding classics. There are those who define a classic as any book which ought to be read by (or to) children because: their teacher/principal/superintendent or parent/grandparent read it as a child; the author has been dead for more than fifty years; and the right people will be impressed by seeing it in the curriculum or on the bookshelf.

The more enlightened school prefers Webster's definition: "a work of the highest class and of acknowledged excellence." Within this framework I find two categories: early classics like the fairy tales of Andersen and Grimm and Perrault, *Pinocchio* by Carlo Collodi, and *Otto of the Silver Hand* by Howard Pyle; and modern classics like *Charlotte's Web, The Lion, the Witch and the Wardrobe,* and *James and the Giant Peach*.

Among the early classics I have listed in the Treasury are: Jack London's *The Call of the Wild; Dick Whittington and His Cat; Heart of Ice* by Benjamin Appel; *Mother Goose;* Kenneth Grahame's *The Reluctant Dragon; Robin Hood;* Frances Hodgson Burnett's *The Secret Garden;* Beatrix Potter's *The Tale of Peter Rabbit; A Wonder Book* by Nathaniel Hawthorne; and L. Frank Baum's *The Wonderful Wizard of Oz*. Some obvious choices like Mark Twain's *Tom Sawyer* and Robert Louis Stevenson's *Treasure Island* have been omitted here because they already are required reading for literature classes in many school systems.

6
Home and Public Libraries

The library is not a shrine for the worship of books. It is not a temple where literary incense must be burned. . . . A library, to modify the famous metaphor of Socrates, should be the delivery room for the birth of ideas.
—Norman Cousins,
ALA *Bulletin* (October 1954)

Long before children are introduced to their neighborhood public library, books should be a part of their lives. Begin a home library as soon as the child is born. If you can provide shelving in the child's room for such books, all the better. The sooner children become accustomed to the sight of the covers, bindings, and pages of books, the sooner they will begin to develop the concept that books are a part of daily life.

Admittedly, we were late in starting our home library for Elizabeth, our first child. Public library books were heavily relied upon until she was about 4 years old—the time when her younger brother, Jamie, was born. Since we had begun to see the positive effects of reading aloud to Elizabeth, my wife and I decided at that point to begin the children's home library. We had no idea, of course, that this library would eventually serve not only the children but their parents as well. Within a few years of Jamie's birth, Susan took a teaching degree in elementary education and now uses the books every day in her classes. It was the reaction of my own children and of those in my wife's classes to these books that first inspired me to write this handbook.

I'd like to make a few suggestions that may prove helpful to those beginning a home library, particularly if you have children under the age of 4.

Divide your books into two categories: expensive and inexpensive. The higher priced or fragile books should be placed up on shelves out of the reach of sticky fingers, dribbles, and errant crayons. While out of reach, they should still be within sight—as a kind of goal. On lower shelves and within easy reach should be the less expensive and, if possible, more durable books. If the replacement price is low enough, you'll have fewer qualms about the child "playing" with the books. This "playing" is an important factor in a child's attachment to books. He must have ample opportunity to feel them, taste them, and see them.

At the same time, parents act as role models in the way they treat books (carefully and affectionately) and the way they speak of books ("And here's our old friend Little Toot. We haven't seen him in a long time.") Children should be encouraged to become as affectionate with a book as they are with a teddy bear. Young children should be encouraged to bring books into every corner of their lives, from playpen and crib to the potty and car.

Where space permits, have many of the home library's books positioned on the shelf with the cover facing out. These covers serve as stimulants to the child's imagination, causing him to wonder what is happening both in the picture and inside the book. This inspires one of the foundation stones for all learning—a sense of curiosity.

This sense of curiosity will become even more acute as the child grows older. When Jamie was around 9 or 10 years old, I remember finding him lying in bed one morning, staring at the top shelf of his bookcase. Because of space limitations, all but a few of the books were shelved with bindings facing outward, thus obscuring the covers.

"See that book up there, Dad? The one named *Trigger John's Son?* What's it about?" he asked.

"I haven't read it myself," I said, "but I think it's about an orphan boy who constantly gets himself into mischief. A little like *Homer Price,* I think. Why do you ask?"

"Oh, I was just thinking about it," Jamie explained. "Sometimes when I wake up, I just look up at the titles and, if it's a book I haven't seen or read, I try to figure what it's about from the title."

This incident also shows one of the advantages of having a home library as well as a public library. These periods of idleness and daydreaming most often strike children at times when they are far removed from distractions—in their own room or home. The buzz of activity in many public libraries is not especially conducive to daydreaming, and school libraries (many of which are now bastardized into "media centers") are often the least conducive of all. The important thing to remember is that it is during these intervals of unoccupied leisure that the child's imagination does its window shopping. How much it eventually buys is determined by how much you have on display.

I know of no greater tribute to the warmth and inspiration offered by a home library than that given by Lester Del Rey, author of more than forty books and one of the most respected authors of science fiction.[1]

I am a compulsive reader, however, and always have been. That began during my first year of schooling when a marvelous teacher taught me to read well before I could even pronounce many of the words correctly. There were no extensive magazine stands or good libraries in the little farming community of southeastern Minnesota where I grew up. But I was lucky. My father had an excellent home library. I ploughed my way happily through the complete works of Darwin, Gibbons's *Decline and Fall,* and the marvelous works of Jules Verne and H. G. Wells. I learned to enjoy Shakespeare without really knowing the difference between a play and a novel. And I spent about equal time going through the Bible several times and reading the collected works of Robert Ingersoll.

By all the standard criteria, I should have had a miserable childhood. We often moved from one poor farm to another—acting as northern sharecroppers, if you like—and there were plenty of times when we didn't have much to eat. I was expected to do most of a man's hard manual labor in the woods and fields from the age of nine. But truth is that I look back on it all as a very happy period. And reading had a lot to do with that, along with a deep sense of emotional security given by my father. Also, there were many times when the dollar-a-day wage I earned when working with my father was supplemented by the kind loan of some popular work of fiction from the farmer for whom we worked. I read a lot of books after I should have been sleeping, with no light other than the full moonlight! People also saved their used magazines and gave them to me.

In 1927, when I was barely twelve, my father moved to a small town where I could have a chance to attend high school, and my horizons were suddenly broadened by the availability of books and magazines from quite a good local library. It was there I discovered the works of Edgar Rice Burroughs, as well as quite a few early works that could be called science fiction . . ."

That quotation from his introduction to *Early Del Rey,* an anthology of his earliest writings, also illustrates that money is no obstacle in compiling a home library. Obviously, the Del Reys were poor—but not poor in spirit or dedication. The Del Rey home library also served as a "greenhouse" until Lester was introduced to the limitless wonders of the public library.

Before discussing further the role of the public library, I would like to offer several ideas I have used in building a good home library for children. The principal problems are cost, where to buy the books, and which books to buy. (The solutions I offer should also be of help to patrons who cannot locate a particular book in their local library or are puzzled by which of the "new arrivals" in children's fiction are worth reading.)

While inflation has more than doubled the cost of children's books in the last five years, it is not an insurmountable obstacle to a good home library if you combine the following information with a little ingenuity.

On the bright side of the financial ledger is the cheering fact that more and more children's publishers are issuing their own books in paperback, usually within a year of hardcover publication. Some are published simultaneously in paperback. The hardcover is aimed at schools and libraries while the softcover is aimed at parents and school book clubs. The paperback editions are at least half the price of the hardcover.

Over the years I've made it a habit never to visit a new city or town without checking the Yellow Pages for a secondhand bookstore. These shops frequently are gold mines for book-shopping parents or teachers. I'm in the secondhand department of Johnson's Bookstore (in Springfield, Massachusetts) so often that many of the customers, and even some of the employees, think I work there. Your local Salvation Army thrift shop is another good source for children's book bargains. It also pays to check in advance with your local public library, as well as those in surrounding communities, for the date of its annual "discard" sale.

I fully recognize the qualities of a brand-new book—its bright, crisp pages, its clean smell. But in an age of daily inflation, such books are a luxury that is often unaffordable to parents. If that is the case, remember that the words and story and pictures are the same in a used book as they are in a new book. Barring damage, one reads as well as the other.

Most schools today subscribe to one of several young people's paperback book clubs. These clubs offer nearly forty monthly selections at half price. The paperback your child pays $1.00 for in class will cost $1.95 in the bookstore and $7.95 in hardcover. Not only are many excellent books available through these clubs, but they are being offered in paperback sometimes within a year of their hardback publication, as well. Encourage your child's school to belong to one of these clubs and look over the selection sheets each month. By adding your choices for the family library to the child's selections, you'll be saving a considerable expense as well as showing the child your interest in books.

The question of durability frequently arises in discussing paperbacks. If the book is to be used only as a read-aloud by a teacher or parent, then this is not a problem. But if it is going to be handled by a family of children or circulated through a classroom, its durability becomes important. My own solution, and one which has had considerable testing, is to protect the paperback with clear plastic self-sticking shelf paper, which can be bought in your local supermarket or discount department store.

Because our books are used not only by the immediate family but also by neighborhood children and by my wife's students, they must stand up to constant wear. This laminating system gives paperbacks a strength that even some hardcovers don't possess.

I first open the book fully so that both its front and back covers are spread out on the plastic sheet. This enables me to gauge the amount I'll need to cut from the roll. Allowing for an inch overlap all around the book, I cut the plastic. This piece is then peeled and rolled gently onto the book's cover, wrapping the overlapping inch around the edges. I also cut strips (or use scraps) to cover the area inside the book where the cover and pages meet at the spine, front and back.

This procedure prevents attractive covers from picking up kitchen-table stains or becoming torn, and greatly reduces the most frequent damage to children's paperbacks—separation at the spine.

Nearly every city in America now has a bookstore that specializes in paperbacks, and a juvenile section usually is included. Make a habit of visiting this section at least every two weeks to review new arrivals. If your bookseller does not carry a particular line or book, badger him until he does. "Why don't you have any Bill Peet books? You certainly are missing out on a great author and illustrator. When are you going to order some?" In addition, most major publishing houses in the juvenile market will send you their catalogues of titles upon request. These can then be ordered through your bookstore or directly from the publisher.

Another often-neglected source of savings for the teacher is the book wholesaler (or jobber) who supplies your school library. A handsome discount is given for nearly every purchase your school makes from that jobber. When you want to order a book for yourself, ask your school librarian to add it to her regular order and pay her accordingly. Although jobbers most often deal in hardcover, some handle paperbacks as well. Take advantage of the discounts available to you, which can run from 25 percent to as much as 45 percent. If the book is for your classroom, you are entitled to a sales tax exemption, and if you are paying for it out of your own pocket you can write off the entire cost on your personal income tax as a business (teaching) expense.

If you are searching for a particular book that is unavailable at your local bookstore, I recommend that you write to the publisher. There will be no discount but at least you will avoid the handling costs that retail stores frequently charge.

Parents who are looking for the best literary bargain available should consider a subscription to *Cricket: The Magazine for Children*. Geared for children between ages 3 and 12, *Cricket*'s monthly offering includes more than twenty stories and features from many of today's finest artists and writers, a potpourri of literature: poetry, fiction, nonfiction, humor, fables, mystery, and sports. The price of each issue represents a substantial savings for a family when you consider that many of its features have previously appeared in book form at five times the price of the magazine. If you haven't seen a copy, check the children's department of your local library.

How should you decide which books to buy? This handbook, with its list of read-alouds, should solve at least part of that problem. You'll also find that neighbors, friends, librarians, and teachers who read aloud are eager to share the names of their favorites.

If your child's teacher reads aloud, she probably has a long list of choices she can't possibly get to in the course of the year. At your next parent-teacher conference, ask her for some recommendations. She may even have one she thinks is particularly pertinent to your child.

Dr. Charles Reasoner, a New York University elementary-education professor who serves as a consultant to Dell Publishing Company on its juvenile and young adult paperbacks, has published four Dell paperbacks which describe and suggest related activities for the most popular Yearling books. The four books are *Releasing Children to Literature, Where the Readers Are, When Children Read,* and *Bringing Children and Books Together*. These volumes are an invaluable asset to anyone involved with children and literature, as is *Literature and the Child* by Bernice E. Cullinan, a comprehensive textbook of specific teaching ideas and activities centered on hundreds of children's books.

Your neighborhood library subscribes to several journals that regularly review new children's books, including *The Horn Book, Kirkus Reviews, Publishers Weekly, School Library Journal,* and *Booklist.* These will give you an excellent sense of what is new, good, bad, or indifferent in children's literature. Unfortunately, many people are unaware of these periodicals, but librarians will be happy to share them with you.

One of the most effective publications on children's books—which pays special attention to read-alouds—is a monthly newsletter published by Jan Lieberman of the University of Santa Clara. Entitled *"T'N'T" (Tips and Titles of Books for Grades K-6),* the newsletter is geared for busy parents and teachers. Each issue offers a selection of approximately nine books with their synopses. A cross section of literature is covered, old and new, fiction, nonfiction, and poetry, sometimes tied together under a common theme (for example, an October Halloween issue). As a former elementary-schoolteacher, Jan Lieberman knows children, what they like, what they read, and how they learn. Her book synopses often contain creative tips on related activities. One of the best things about Lieberman's newsletter is that it is *free.* Those interested need only send five SASE to: Jan Lieberman, Department of Education, University of Santa Clara, Santa Clara, Calif., 95053.

Many libraries have areas for "new arrivals" in the children's books section, which parents should check regularly. If no such section exists in your library, ask your children's librarian to start one. They save parents, teachers, and children much time in keeping abreast of what's new in children's books.

Many large metropolitan newspapers publish reviews of new juvenile books. *The New York Times,* for example, publishes special supplements each spring and fall to its Sunday Book Review, reviewing the best in recent children's publications.

Under the title "Children's Books [year]", the Library of Congress publishes an excellent list and review of the year's outstanding books for preschool through junior high. It is available for $1.00 from the Superintendent of Documents, U.S. Government Printing Office, Washington, D.C., 20402 (Library of Congress Card Number 65-60015).

A smaller annual list is offered by the American Library Association (50 E. Huron St., Chicago, Ill., 60611) and also is available from your public library. A compact retrospective listing entitled "Children's Books of International Interest" also is published by the ALA. It lists titles and offers synopses of many of the modern classics, most of which make excellent read-alouds.

In your search for which books to buy for your home or classroom library and which books to read aloud to children, look to guidebooks, friends, teachers, librarians, and reviews. But always reserve the final decision for yourself. Only *you* know the level and interests of your children. Only you can appreciate their special needs and capacities.

Occasionally you will make a mistake. The book will be boring or too far above or below the child. The best thing to do in that case is to admit the mistake quickly and go on to another book. But such mistakes will occur less frequently when you take the time to seek the advice of experts in the field.

As important and convenient as a home library is, it cannot replace a public library. The home library should act as an appetizer, stimulating the child's taste for the vast richness offered by the free public library. It is a town's or city's most important cultural and intellectual asset, and dollar-for-dollar is the greatest bargain known to civilized man. Nevertheless, in this age of declining literacy and skyrocketing inflation, libraries face increasingly difficult times.

"What can be done to turn things around for library circulations?" the chairman asked the library director at a recent trustees' meeting I attended.

"Well," the director hedged for a moment, "a good Depression might help . . ."

There were chuckles around the table (although the banker and two business owners laughed least), but the truth of the statement was lost on none of us. It is only in hard times that we appreciate the community services we receive for free. America's free public library systems received unprecedented use during the Depression years when other forms of entertainment or enlightenment were too costly.

The modern family's addiction to television and shopping malls, along with rising municipal costs, has led to curtailed library services in many major cities. If Norman Cousins was correct, and I believe he was, in calling the library "the delivery room for the birth of ideas," then the closing of library branches or the curtailment of their hours amounts to the abortion of ideas, a crippling of the American mind.

Some libraries, attempting to survive the cultural and economic crises, have begun to shed old habits in favor of new vigor. They are calling attention to themselves and offering a fighting resistance to television. Sadly, not all libraries are able to do so; there are still some that don't have either the money, the community support, or the staff leadership to initiate such changes.

If, as a parent or teacher, you feel your local library is not adjusting to the times, protect your rights as a taxpayer and become involved. Join with your friends to form a "Friends of the Library" group which can, among other things, lobby local government or the library administration for positive change. In the majority of cases, however, it is not the staff but the community that needs prodding. In such cases libraries cannot afford to stand by and wring their hands over the decline in reading habits. If they are to survive they must:

1. Shed the image of "Marian the Librarian" who governs the stacks with a rule of silence in favor of an image that shouts to the community, "Hey! Come on in—look what we've got for free!"
2. Sell the healthful advantages of its services to the community in much the same way we sell the United Way, Catholic Charities, United Jewish Appeal, and the March of Dimes.
3. Become competitive with television.

Such goals are not unrealistic. Already they are being accomplished in cities and towns where the library:

- Begins at the beginning—by distributing library material to expectant new parents through prenatal clinics and maternity wards.
- Provides registration tables at nursery and elementary schools in the first week of school to distribute library information and register parents and children for cards.
- Maintains a constant campaign to stress reading aloud to children, in the home and in the classroom. The campaign is instructive, inspirational, and year-round. Parents and teachers are a library's "sales representatives"; the product line's success depends largely on how well they are motivated and trained.
- Fights fire with fire. If 70 percent of the community's parents are watching television each evening, they are a captive audience for this fifteen-second commercial: "The Springfield Public Library wants to know—Did you read to your child tonight?" (The voice-over image on the screen is a reading parent nestled with his children.) The state of Idaho now offers spot announcements for radio and television which feature the governor asking, "Have you read to your child today?"
- Instructs parents and teachers on read-aloud by offering demonstrations and "talking book" tapes as models. Many of today's adults were raised on television; they need to see or hear an example of how

to read to children—the expression, the pace, how to tie the pictures into the story, and how to discuss a book when it is finished.

- Sponsors "foster grandparent" programs which connect senior citizens with children and allow the "grandparent" an opportunity to read to, talk to, and listen to the child.
- Uses the local newspaper to print the list of new books acquired each month. The large metropolitan newspapers are usually unwilling, but the smaller dailies and local weeklies are happy to receive such notices. Semiannual listings of new acquisitions are printed on recycled paper and left in beauty parlors, barber shops, shopping malls, pediatricians' offices, nursery schools, and supermarkets.
- Knows that children are motivated in much the same way as adults—most of them initially pick their books by the appearance of the cover. (Paperback publishers realized this human inclination thirty years ago.) The library staff clears enough shelf space to display 150 to 200 children's books with the covers face out. By the end of the day all are usually in circulation, and they are replaced on the shelf by fresh ones the next day. This library staff—like its bookstore counterpart—realizes it is burying a major selling factor every time a book is shelved with only the spine showing.
- Creates a climate that welcomes children with open arms. Its walls festooned with colorful posters, the library brings books alive with tanks of fish and cages of gerbils, hamsters, and rabbits. It offers an outlet for the imagination that books inspire by having pencils, crayons, and paper readily available for children who want to come in and draw.
- Schedules its service hours for the convenience of the patrons and not the convenience of the staff or labor union. In this day and age, the idea of a library being closed on Sundays makes about as much sense as scheduling a picnic in January. Twice as many people in the community are free to use the library on Sunday as on Monday. Nevertheless, the vast majority of American libraries are closed on Sundays. In the last two decades, such tradition-bound institutions as the Roman Catholic Church and the YMCA have adjusted their long-standing service schedules to fit the changing American weekend lifestyle. And they have accomplished these changes while facing many of the manpower and financial shortages that confront today's libraries.
- Enlists the aid of the private sector to advertise library programs. The library—with its "Friends" committee—convinces paper companies and printers to donate paper and printing costs for fliers and pamphlets. It persuades sign companies, mass-transit authorities, and the

news media to donate advertising space for a yearly campaign that portrays the free public library as the best and most important bargain in town.

School libraries, while facing the same cultural challenges, possess none of the autonomy exercised by their free public counterparts. They all too frequently are bound by school budgets which place them at the bottom of the priority list.

School librarians continue to struggle against school policies which allow teachers and administrators to use the library as a "Siberia" to which they banish children who are disrupting classes. What could be more damaging to a library's image than to have it portrayed as a punishment? What a difference appears in those schools where the library is a port in the storm, a place that invites you to curl up with a book, a spawning ground for a lifelong love of libraries—instead of a lifelong dread.

More school administrators must recognize the enormously positive effect a good librarian can have upon a school. I have seen them successfully used by principals as prime motivators for a hitherto lethargic faculty. These cases are the direct opposite of those in which a library staff position is filled by a teacher who has simply grown weary of either the classroom or, worse, children; a person who is generally ignorant of children's books. One bad school librarian can undo the work of a dozen good reading teachers.

Exciting things can happen when a public library joins hands with parents, teachers, and the private sector. Consider this example. Many librarians have grown discouraged, seeing their patrons continually lured away by television shows that are based on the library's offerings—books. Many classics and best-sellers have been filmed or shown on television— and even advertised in such a way as to suggest that television discovered the book in the first place. Look at just a partial listing of the many children's books adapted for TV: *The Headless Horseman; The Gift of the Magi; Charlotte's Web; How the Grinch Stole Christmas; Little Women; Tom Sawyer; The Snow Goose; The Lion, the Witch and the Wardrobe; The Adventures of Pinocchio; Where the Lilies Bloom; Little House on the Prairie; Cricket in Times Square;* and *A Christmas Carol.*

The staff at one library decided finally to claim what was rightfully theirs. With the cooperation of their local daily newspaper, the staff obtained nearly 200 photographs that had been mailed out by the networks to television editors to publicize their shows. All of these photographs dealt with productions—for adults and children—that were book adaptations. The pictures were labeled with the book's title and then mounted and displayed throughout the system's eight branches with headlines: "If you missed the movie, there's no need to miss the book. We've got it!"; "If you liked the movie, you'll *love* the book!"; or "TV only gave you half the story. We've got the *rest of the story.*" The presentation was arranged for easy display in the library foyers as well as in schools, banks, and store windows during National Library Week and Children's Book Week and served as an eye-catching, aggressive advertisement for the public library.

Unlimited possibilities exist for such private-public cooperation. The major paperback publishers have reaped huge success from thirty-second book commercials on radio. Libraries can utilize the same "teaser" techniques by convincing the local telephone company to donate whatever is necessary for "dial-a-story" commercials aimed at children. Since nobody claims to be more interested in words than AT&T, why not ask them to prove it by helping?

Watching my children eat breakfast one morning several years ago, it occurred to me that if we want to send book messages to the largest number of children in one place at one time, all we have to do is put them on the back of a cereal box. Judging from my classroom discussions with thousands of school children, I strongly suspect that more children voluntarily read the back of cereal boxes each day than any other form of print. And what is on these boxes? Advertisements for ballpoint pens, T-shirts, and model trains. That is not very exciting stuff, but at a time when more American children are eating breakfast alone than at any other time in the last hundred years, anything to read is better than staring at what is in the bowl.

What would happen, I wonder, if the back of the cereal box contained an advertisement for libraries? To my way of thinking, the best kind of library advertisement would be a chapter from a children's book; a chapter so funny, so intriguing, or so exciting that it would bring those young breakfast readers to the library door first thing after school. Imagine how the publishers would compete to have their book chosen; imagine how authors would love it. Moms would go out of their way to buy that particular brand—not because it had less sugar, not because it was cheaper, but because it sent their children to the library.

But what about the pens and the T-shirts? Alternate them every month with book chapters, if need be. But I don't think you'd have to. The largest cereal manufacturer in America, controlling 45 percent of the U.S. cereal market, netted $185 million in 1980. I don't believe they need those T-shirts and pens but I *do* think they would love to be known as the cereal company that lured one million kids into libraries so they could finish *Freckle Juice* by Judy Blume.

Impossible? Not if you make literacy—the ability to read, write, and communicate clearly—the business of *all* America and not just that of teachers and librarians. If all sectors of the community work together to bring the excitement of books into our homes early enough and to develop libraries that are truly "delivery rooms for ideas," then we need not fear an electronic Pied Piper stealing our children's minds and imaginations.

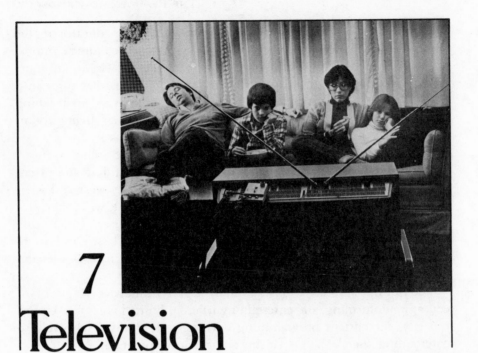

7
Television

I believe television is going to be the test of the modern world, and that in this new opportunity to see beyond the range of our vision we shall discover either a new and unbearable disturbance of the general peace or a saving radiance in the sky. We shall stand or fall by television—of that I am quite sure.

—E. B. White
from "Removal from Town,"
Harper's Magazine (October 1938)

In its short lifetime, television has become the major stumbling block to literacy in America. For all its technological achievement, television's negative impact on children's reading habits—and therefore their thinking—is enormous. In this chapter I suggest a method of dealing with television. As this approach is used in my own home and as I have seen it used in countless other homes, it is a reasonable and workable solution to the problem. However, in order to make it work, parents must believe in it, must understand fully why they are using it and what the consequences are to family and child if it is not used.

This understanding is just as important for teachers as it is for parents. True, the classroom teacher, principal, and guidance counselor have no immediate control over the television sets in pupils' homes. But they *are* in the education business, and television is the prime educator in the world today. It is the school's primary competitor for children's minds.

Educators spend millions of dollars and thousands of classroom hours teaching children how to cope with the hard-core drugs that come into their lives. But they spend no time or money, relatively, in teaching children how to cope with the soft-core drug in their living room: television.

TV has been described by author Marie Winn as the "plug-in drug," and not without reason. Its control of children is demanding and extensive. It will largely determine how they talk, what they wear and what they won't wear, what they eat and what they won't eat, what they play and what they won't play, what they will read and what they will not read. Our children must be taught in the home and in the classroom how to cope with television. They must be taught to control *it* instead of letting it control *them.*

I do not think of television as a totally negative influence. As a tool for educating, informing, and entertaining it has unlimited potential. Unfortunately, the current programming devotes itself almost exclusively to entertaining, thereby falling far short of its natural potential. As entertainment it should be treated as dessert and not be allowed to become the principal meal in our children's lives.

The first serious alarm was sounded by a small cluster of educators in 1964 when the scores were computed for that year's college admission tests. That year's high-school seniors, born in the late 1940s, were the first generation to be raised on a steady television diet. Their Scholastic Aptitude Test scores showed a decline from previous years, a decline which has continued for seventeen of the past nineteen years.

Naturally there are those in the television industry who claim that these lowered standards have nothing to do with their medium. Social scientists, educators, and psychologists respond loudly that there is every connection between the two. Television, they declare, interrupts the largest and most instructive class in childhood: life experience.

Paul Copperman, president of the Institute of Reading Development and author of *The Literacy Hoax,* sees the interruption in these terms: "Consider what a child misses during the 15,000 hours [from birth to age 17] he spends in front of the TV screen. He is not working in the garage with his father, or in the garden with his mother. He is not doing homework, or reading, or collecting stamps. He is not cleaning his room, washing the supper dishes, or cutting the lawn. He is not listening to a discussion about community politics among his parents and their friends. He is not playing baseball or going fishing, or painting pictures. Exactly what does television offer that is so valuable that it can replace all of these activities?"[1]

The most recent alarm was sounded by the state of California's Department of Education with the announcement of its findings from a scholastic achievement test in reading, writing, and mathematics that was administered to sixth- and twelfth-grade students in 1980. (One of the factors which lends great significance and credibility to this test is the number of students involved: half a million children.) Buried in the test was a question that appeared to have nothing to do with the students' classwork but in actuality had very much to do with it. The question was: How much time do you spend watching TV each day? It was the one question that more students (99 percent) chose to answer than any other in the exam.

When the educators finished compiling the scores on the 500,000 exams, they began to correlate each child's grade with the number of hours the student spent watching television. Their findings showed conclusively that the more time the student spent watching TV, the lower the achievement score; the less time, the higher the score. Interestingly, these statistics proved true regardless of the child's IQ, social background, or study practices (all of which were queried in the exam process).[2]

Today's television programming is a serious impediment to children's personal growth because of both what it offers and what it does *not* offer:

1. *Television is the direct opposite of reading.* In breaking its program into eight-minute commercial segments (shorter for shows like *Sesame Street*), it requires and fosters a short attention span. Reading, on the other hand, requires and encourages longer attention spans in children. Good children's books are written to hold children's attention, not interrupt it. Because of the need to hold viewers until the next commercial message, the content of television shows is almost constant action. Reading also offers action but not nearly as much, and reading fills the considerable space between action scenes with subtle character development. Television is relentless; no time is allowed to ponder characters' thoughts or to recall their words because the dialogue and film move too quickly. The need to scrutinize is a critical need among young children and it is constantly ignored by television. Books, however, encourage a critical reaction; the reader moves at his own pace as opposed to that of the director or sponsor. The reader can stop to ponder the character's next move, the feathers in his hat, or the meaning of a sentence. Having done so, he can resume where he left off without having missed any part of the story.

2. *For young children television is an antisocial experience, while reading is a social experience.* The 3-year-old sits passively in front of the screen, oblivious to what is going on around him. Conversation during the program is seldom if ever encouraged by the child or by the parents. On the other hand, the 3-year-old with a book must be read to by another person—parent, sibling, or grandparent. The child is a participant as well as a receiver when he engages in discussion during and after the story. This process continues to an even greater degree when the child attends school and compares his own reactions to a story with those of his classmates. The poet T. S. Eliot pointed to the antisocial nature of television when he described it as "a medium of entertainment which permits millions of people to listen to the same joke at the same time and yet remain lonely."

3. *Television deprives the child of his most important learning tool: his questions.* Children learn the most by questioning. For the thirty-three hours a week that the average 5-year-old spends in front of the set, he can neither ask a question nor receive an answer.

4. *Television interrupts the most important language lesson in a child's life: family conversation.* Studies show that the average kindergarten graduate has already seen 5,000 hours of television in his young lifetime. Those are 5,000 hours during which he engaged in little or no conversation.

5. *Television provides a language tool that is the direct opposite of what children find in the classroom.* The child who writes and speaks the language of Vinnie Barbarino from *Welcome Back, Kotter* or Robert Blake on *Baretta* is verbally crippling himself for the classroom, where the books are written in standard English, not street language.

6. *Television presents material in a manner that is the direct opposite of the classroom's.* Television's messages are based almost entirely on pictures and our emotions in response to those pictures. Conversely, the classroom relies heavily on reading, the spoken word, and a critical response to those words, not just raw emotion. School also requires large amounts of time to be spent on a task. These minutes spent doing things like multiplication tables and spelling can often be boring and repetitious when compared with watching *The Dukes of Hazzard,* but they are critical for learning.

7. *Television is unable to portray the most intelligent act known to man: thinking.* In 1980 Squire Rushnell, vice-president in charge of ABC's children's programming, said that certain fine children's books cannot be

adapted for television. Much of the character development in these books, Rushnell noted, takes place inside the character's head. He said, "You simply can't put thinking on the screen." As a result, a child almost never sees a TV performer thinking through a problem.[3]

8. *Television encourages deceptive thinking.* In *Teaching as a Conserving Activity,* educator Neil Postman points out that it is implicit in every one of television's commercials that there is no problem which cannot be solved by simple artificial means.[4] Whether the problem is anxiety or common diarrhea, nervous tension or the common cold, a simple tablet or spray solves the problem. Seldom is mention ever made of headaches being a sign of more serious illness, nor is the suggestion ever made that elbow grease and hard work are viable alternatives to stains and boredom. Instead of thinking through our problems, television promotes the "easy way." The cumulative effect of such thinking is enormous when you consider that between ages 1 and 17 the average child is exposed to 350,000 commercials.

9. *Television, by vying for children's time and attention with a constant diet of unchallenging simplistic entertainment, stimulates antischool and antireading feeling among children.* A 1977 study showed that the majority of the preschool and primary-school students examined felt that school and books were a waste of time.[5] Offered the same story on television and in book form, 69 percent of the second-grade students chose television. That figure increased to 86 percent among the third-grade pupils—the grade where national reading skills begin to decline.

10. *Television has a negative effect on children's vital knowledge after age 10, according to the Schramm study of 6,000 school children.*[6] It does help, the report goes on to say, in building vocabulary for younger children, but this stops by age 10. This finding is supported by the fact that today's kindergarteners have the highest reading-readiness scores ever achieved at that level and yet these same students tail off dismally by fourth and fifth grades.

11. *Television stifles the imagination.* Consider for a moment this single paragraph from Eric Knight's classic, *Lassie Come Home:*

Yet, if it were almost a miracle, in his heart Joe Carraclough tried to believe in that miracle—that somehow, wonderfully, inexplicably, his dog would be there some day; there, waiting by the school gate. Each day as he came out of school, his eyes would turn to the spot where

Lassie had always waited. And each day there was nothing there, and Joe Carraclough would walk home slowly, silently, stolidly as did the people of his country.

If a dozen people were to read or hear those words, they would have a dozen different images of the scene, what the boy looked like, the school, the gate, the lonely road home. As soon as the story is placed on film there is no longer any room for imagination. The director does all your imagining for you.

12. *Television overpowers and desensitizes a child's sense of sympathy for suffering, while books heighten the reader's sense of sympathy.* Extensive research in the past ten years clearly shows that television's bombardment of the child with continual acts of violence (18,000 acts viewed between the ages of 3 and 17) makes the child insensitive to violence and its victims—most of whom he is conditioned to believe die cleanly or crawl inconsequently offstage.[7]

Though literature could never be labeled a nonviolent medium, it cannot begin to approach television's extreme. Frank Mankiewicz and Joel Swerdlow noted in *Remote Control: Television and the Manipulation of American Life* that you would have to see all thirty-seven of Shakespeare's plays in order to see the same number of acts of human violence (fifty-four) that you would see in just three evenings of prime-time television.

13. *Television is a passive activity and discourages creative play.* The virtual disappearance of neighborhood games like I spy, kick the can, spud, hopscotch, Johnny-jump-the-pony, stickball, red light, Simon says, flies up, giant steps, and statue attests to that.

Compared to reading, television is still the more passive of the two activities. In reading, educators point out, a child must actively use a variety of skills involving sounds, spelling rules, blendings, as well as constructing mental images of the scene described in the book. Television requires no such mental activity.

When children do leave the set in order to play, it is often to imitate performers they have seen. In many cases, the imitations are of violent shows. During a week of camping at a lake in Maine, I found the campground's 5- and 6-year-olds gathering each morning in the tent-roofed assembly area to peddle their Big Wheels. They were not interested in the lakefront, the sand, the fish, or the chipmunks on the forest trails. Instead they gathered, rain or shine, to stage their daily imitation of *The Dukes of Hazzard,* complete with yodeling the show's theme song as they careened into one other.

14. *Television is psychologically addictive.* In schools and homes where students voluntarily have removed themselves from TV viewing, their subsequent class discussions and journals report the addictive nature of their attachment to television: it draws upon their idle time and there is an urgency to watch it in order to fulfill peer and family pressure.

15. *Television has been described by former First Lady Betty Ford as "the greatest babysitter of all time," but it also is reported to be the nation's second largest obstacle to family harmony.* In a 1980 survey by the Roper Organization, 4,000 men and women listed money as the most frequent subject of fights between husband and wife. Television and children tied for second, and produced three times as many arguments as did sex.

16. *Television's conception of childhood, rather than being progressive, is regressive—a throwback, in fact, to the Middle Ages.* In *Teaching as a Conserving Activity,* Postman points to Philippe Ariès's research, which shows that until the 1600s children over the age of 5 were treated and governed as though they were adults.[8] After the seventeenth century, society developed a concept of childhood which insulated children from the shock of instant adulthood until they were mature enough to meet it. "Television," Postman declares, "all by itself, may bring an end to childhood." Present-day TV programming offers its nightly messages on incest, murder, abortion, rape, moral and political corruption, and general physical mayhem to 85 million people—including 5.6 million children between the ages of 2 and 11 who are still watching at 10:30 p.m.[9] The afternoon soap operas offer a similar message to still another young audience. Of the twenty-one children (ages 7 to 9) in my wife's second-grade class one year, all but four of them were *daily* soap opera viewers.

Bob Keeshan, most often heard in the role of his TV character Captain Kangaroo, places the prime responsibility for television's negative influence upon the parent. In a 1979 interview with John Merrow on National Public Radio's *Options in Education,* Keeshan said, "Television is the great national babysitter. It's not the disease in itself, but a symptom of a greater disease that exists between parent and child and the parent-child relationship. A parent today simply doesn't have time for the child, and the child is a very low priority item, and there's this magic box that flickers pictures all day long, and it's a convenient babysitter. I'm busy, go watch television . . . The most direct answer to all our problems with television and children is the parent, because if the parent is an effective parent, we're not going to have it." [10]

Keeshan represents one of the few bright spots in television's thirty-year association with children. He's been actively engaged over the past twenty-five years in stretching children's imaginations and attention spans with shows that always include the reading of at least one complete children's book each morning. Next to the book's author, Virginia Lee Burton, Captain Kangaroo is probably the most responsible for making *Mike Mulligan and His Steam Shovel* the most widely loved book among American children today. I have found in my lecture travels that no book and no person so universally evoke such warm and affectionate recognition from both teachers and parents as do *Mike Mulligan and His Steam Shovel* and Captain Kangaroo.

In recent years Keeshan has incorporated in his shows suggestions for parents on learning activities in which they can and should engage their children. He represents what can be accomplished when television is used correctly, both as a teacher and as an entertainer. The network's response to Keeshan's pioneering creative involvement with the nation's children since December 1955 was revealed in October 1981 when CBS cut in half the show's sixty-minute format and rescheduled it for an hour earlier (7 a.m.), in a move that one syndicated columnist-critic, Jerry Krupnick of the Newhouse News Service, portrayed as "mugging Captain Kangaroo and shoving him down the stairs." Three months later the network shoved him almost out of sight by dropping him to the 6:30 a.m. slot. Considering television's traditional disregard for children's education, the wonder is that they've allowed the Captain to last as long as they have. *The Mickey Mouse Club,* which debuted on a rival network the same week as *Captain Kangaroo,* lasted only two years.

Keeshan's call for parental control of the television set is more easily said than done, as any parent can tell you who has ever tried it. I know firsthand.

My family's restricted viewing began in 1974, at about the time I'd begun to notice a growing television addiction in my fourth-grade daughter and kindergarten son. There had even begun a deterioration of our long-standing read-aloud time each night because, in their words, it "took too much time away from the TV."

One evening while visiting Marty and Joan Wood of Longmeadow, Massachusetts, I noticed that their four teenage children went right to their homework after excusing themselves from the dinner table.

I asked the parents, "Your television broken?"

"No," replied Marty. "Why?"

"Well, it's only six forty-five and the kids are already doing homework."

Joan explained, "Oh, we don't allow television on school nights."

"That's a noble philosophy—but how in the world do you enforce it?" I asked.

"It is a house *law*," stated Marty. And for the next hour and a half, husband and wife detailed for me the positive changes that had occurred in their family and home since they put that "law" into effect.

That evening was a turning point for my family. After hearing the details of the plan, my wife Susan agreed wholeheartedly to back it. "On one condition," she added.

"What's that?" I asked.

"*You* be the one to tell them," she said.

After supper the next night we brought the children into our bedroom, surrounded them with pillows and quilts, and I calmly began, "Jamie . . . Elizabeth . . . Mom and I have decided that there will be no more television on school nights in this house—forever."

Their reaction was predictable: they started to cry. What came as a shock to us was that they cried for four solid months. Every night, despite explanations on our part, they cried. We tried to impress upon them that the rule was not meant as a punishment; we listed all the positive reasons for such a rule. They cried louder.

The peer group pressure was enormous, particularly for Elizabeth. "There's nothing to talk about in school anymore," she sobbed. "All the kids were talking about *Starsky and Hutch* at lunch today and I didn't even see it."

There was even peer pressure from other parents directed at Susan and me. "But, Jim," they would ask, "not even for an hour after supper?" in a tone that suggested our plan was a new form of child abuse. "And what about all the National Geographic specials? Aren't you going to let the kids watch *those?*" they'd ask.

It should be pointed out that a great many parents use National Geographic specials, Jacques Cousteau specials, and *Sesame Street* as the salve on their consciences. I can count on one hand the number of children I know who actually like those specials. Given the choice, as the vast majority are, they'll choose *Happy Days* or *Kojak* every time.

As difficult as it was at first, we persevered and resisted both kinds of peer pressure. We lived with the tears, the pleadings, the conniving. "Dad, my teacher says there is a special show on tonight that I have to watch. She said don't come to school tomorrow if you haven't seen the show," Elizabeth would say after supper.

After three months my wife and I began to see the things happen that the Woods had predicted. Suddenly we had the time each night as a family to read aloud, to read to ourselves, to do homework at an unhurried pace, to learn how to play chess and checkers and Scrabble, to make the plastic models that had been collecting dust in the closet for two years, to bake cakes and cookies, to write thank-you notes to aunts and uncles, to do household chores and take baths and showers without World War III breaking out, to play on all the parish sports teams, to draw and paint and color, and—best of all—to talk with each other, ask questions and answer questions.

Our children's imaginations were coming back to life again.

For the first year, the decision was a heavy one for all of us. With time it grew lighter. Jamie, being younger, had never developed the acute taste for television that Elizabeth had, and he lost the habit fairly easily. It took Elizabeth longer to adjust, largely because she'd been allowed such a steady dose for so long.

Over the years the plan was modified until it worked like this:

1. The television is turned off at supper time and not turned on again until the children are in bed, Monday through Thursday.

2. Each child is allowed to watch one school night show a week (subject to parents' approval). Homework, chores, et cetera must be finished beforehand.

3. Weekend television is limited to any two of the three nights. The remaining night is reserved for homework and other activities. The children make their selections separately.

The suggestion to modify the original diet and allow one school night show a week came from my wife during the third year of the plan and it met with my immediate resistance. Only reluctantly did I agree to give it a try.

As it turned out, it was an excellent addition. By limiting the choice to one show a week, we forced the child to be discriminating in his or her selections, to distinguish worth from trash. They became very choosy, refusing to waste the privilege, and began using a critical eye in evaluating shows.

The habit of watching, however, continued to decrease while other interests expanded. By the time Elizabeth was a ninth-grade student, she didn't bother to use her school-night option more than three or four times in the course of the entire year. More than half the time Jamie forgot until the week was over. "Hey!" he'd say on Saturday. "I never watched my show this week. Why didn't somebody remind me?"

We structured the diet to allow the family to control the television and not the other way around. Perhaps this particular diet won't work for your family, but a similar one would—if you have the courage and determination to make it work.

If you are going to require your children to curtail their TV viewing, if you are going to create a three-hour void in their daily lives, then *you* must make a commitment to fill that void. *You* have to produce the crayons and paper, *you* have to teach them how to play checkers, *you* have to help with the cookie mix. And most importantly, *you* must pick up those books—books to be read to the child, books to be read by the child, books to be read to yourself—even when you have a headache, even when you're tired, even when you're worried about your checkbook. You'll be surprised. Just as that book will take your child's mind off television, it also will take your mind off the headache or checkbook.

A short time after the release of the fifty-two American hostages by the Iranian government in January 1981, I had the opportunity to address the children's librarians of the Massachusetts Library Association. As the fourth member of a panel on "Children's Television: Friend or Foe?" I was preceded by three speakers who went to great lengths to praise the medium and its efforts in stimulating children's minds, both in the classroom and at home.

In my opening remarks I reminded the audience of the recent events in Iran and the unprecedented worldwide daily coverage by the media throughout the 444 days.

Isn't it interesting that with all the marvelous computerized and transistorized accomplishments of TV—including those you've heard espoused by the previous speakers today—we've yet to hear any of the hostages say, "Thank God we had TV! It got us through our darkest hours. We could never have survived without it."

We have, however, heard hostage after hostage pay tribute to the one element that appears to be the savior of the hostages' sanity: their imaginations. Upon their release they . . . detailed for State Department doctors the intricate "daydreaming" which allowed them to escape their tormentors many times a day. One captive fantasized a train trip from India to England, including a mental script for seating arrangements, passenger descriptions—even a dining car menu. Another remodeled his parents' home—inch by inch, making mental notes of what he would use for wallpaper, paneling and flooring.[11]

And nearly all the hostages [I reminded the librarians] made daily fantasy trips home to their families—walking through their children's rooms, mowing lawns, hosting backyard barbecues. Psychologists have been studying such "daydreaming" since the Korean War and they have found it serves two immediate purposes: it allows the prisoner momentary escape and it serves as a constant reminder of who they are and why they are there.

My point in mentioning this is to remind you that a great many of our children face a future in which they will someday be hostages: hostages to bad marriages, hostages to unhappy jobs and careers, hostages to illnesses or neighborhoods. How well they survive their captivity—however long it may be—may well be determined by their imaginations, their ability to dream and hold fast to those dreams.[12]

From this capacity to dream springs the very progress of the human race. Without the willingness to wonder, notes the great Russian children's poet Kornei Chukovsky, there would be no new hypotheses, inventions, or experiments.[13] Science and technology would be at a standstill. Albert Einstein reaffirmed this when he stated: "The gift of fantasy has meant more to me than my talent for absorbing positive knowledge."

Einstein was speaking not only for himself but for mankind. From the very beginning, man appears to have recognized the need to feed and preserve his imagination. Beginning with the caveman who stood before his brothers at the evening fire and detailed the drama of his journey across the mountains, through the bards and strolling minstrels, evangelists and itinerant players, to the writers of modern prose and poetry, mankind has been inspired, instructed, warned, soothed, and regaled by stories. A Greek poet sharing with his neighbors the travels of Homer, a Jewish mother detailing for her daughter the story of Ruth, a German forester spinning for his children the tale of Hansel and Gretel, a French schoolteacher reading Perrault's *Cinderella* to the class, a black woman in Tennessee sharing the story of her African ancestor with her grandchild, Alex Haley.

It is this sense of family, this sense of history, this sense of culture, that is being robbed by the flickering blue light of television. Its overwhelming presence encourages our society to speak less, feel less, and imagine less.

Several years ago Sylvia Ashton-Warner, an internationally recognized authority on teaching and learning, spent a year teaching and observing in an American community. Afterwards, in *Spearpoint: "Teacher" in America,* she wrote of her concern about what television was doing to the human condition here. In stripping them of a third dimension, she noted, television leaves us with children who are daily less capable of dreaming. "You don't get far without a dream to lure. A dream keeps you looking forward. . . . Man does not live by bread alone but by dreams also. . . . Man does not die from breadlessness but from dreamlessness also." [14]

The substitute for dreams is boredom—bored children, bored parents, an entire culture held hostage by boredom. If such a condition seems farfetched or inconceivable, consider the fact that in 1978 there were 200,000 teenagers and adults in Atlanta, Georgia, who couldn't read—couldn't read books, newspapers, phone books, or menus. As their imaginations die a little each day from undernourishment, think of the hopelessness and boredom that must envelop their lives. Now multiply that boredom by as many other major American cities you can name.

You don't have to throw out the television. All you have to do is control it. When it is used correctly, it can inform, entertain and, occasionally, even inspire. Used incorrectly, television will control your family. It will limit its language, its dreams, its achievements. The choice is yours.

Many of today's educators have become increasingly concerned over the condition of children's listening skills. "It is *the* most important communications skill and very little is done with it at any educational level," states educator Rhoderick J. Elen in *Elementary English*.[15] Since reading comprehension feeds directly from listening comprehension, it stands to reason that many of our current reading problems can be attributed to a breakdown in children's listening skills.

There is little argument that reading aloud is one of the best stimulants for listening skills, but there are several others which deserve the attention of parents, teachers, and librarians: records, radio drama, and tape recorders. While these devices lack the immediacy of a live person (who can answer a child's questions), they do fill the gap when an adult is unavailable.

Records of children's songs, rhymes, and stories should be among the family's first purchases after books. They offer rhythms and distinct vocalizing, both of which fill important needs in young children. Neighborhood libraries and record shops have extensive children's record collections from which to choose.

Included among the library's recordings you will find copies of old radio dramas like *Superman, The Green Hornet, The Lone Ranger, Sergeant Preston of the Yukon, Fibber McGee and Molly,* and *Inner Sanctum.* These are excellent stimulants to listening and imagining for older children.

In *Remote Control: Television and the Manipulation of American Life,* Mankiewicz and Swerdlow describe how much more mental exercise is demanded by the reader or radio listener than by the television viewer: "[The reader or listener] must give all the characters faces and features, they must be tall or short, pretty or plain. He must provide clothes, mannerisms and modes of expression. . . . He must be an architect and an interior decorator."

Though television all but eliminated radio drama during the 1950s, its sole survivor, *CBS Radio Mystery Theater,* is alive and well five nights a week and is heard on more than 200 stations. Its "mystery" label covers a variety of offerings—occult, macabre, detective, suspense, and humor. Recognizing the large number of young people in his nightly audience of 3.6 million, director Himan Brown (who handled the same chores for *Inner Sanctum* during radio's golden era) has incorporated numerous literary classics into the series and has earned commendations from the National Education Association and the American Library Association. Among the adaptations were: *Hamlet, Macbeth, The Phantom of the Opera, Jane Eyre,* and *Tom Sawyer, Detective.*

"Radio drama—storytelling—is as close an activity to reading as you can find," Brown declares. "In fact, listening leads to reading." He turns to a letter from a grateful listener. "Thank you for giving my child back the world of fantasy," he quotes. "Today's children have lost the world of fantasy, they've lost the beauty of the spoken word. If you were a camp counselor you remember those ghost stories around the camp fire each night. Children love to listen—if you give them the chance. The best stories are right up here in your head."

Since *Mystery Theater* was broadcast in our area at an hour that was too late for my children when they were younger (9 or 10 is about the right age to start on *Mystery Theater),* I attached a timer to the radio and tape recorder. In this way we were able to hear the shows at a more convenient hour and built up an extensive tape library for use on long car trips.

Unfortunately, the vast majority of youngsters are unaware of radio drama. Introduce them to it through recordings and *Mystery Theater;* then watch the curtain lift on their imaginations and listening skills. After you have explained how the various sound effects were achieved for the shows, their ambitions will grow. They'll be asking, "Can we try one? Could we put on our own radio show with the tape recorder?"

That is when the learning swings into high gear—with script writers, directors, performers, sound technicians, and musicians. You'll see first-hand how listening skills lead to better speaking, writing, and reading.

Most public libraries now boast a large collection of long-playing records and cassettes featuring great literature read aloud. The readers include not only featured names of the theater like Alexander Scourby, Orson Welles, and James Earl Jones but a host of literary figures reading their own work: Eudora Welty, John Cheever, John Updike, Shirley Jackson,

William Saroyan, and Howard Fast. As one listens to James Earl Jones read Richard Wright's description of fear from *Native Son,* one cannot help but want to read or reread the book. Since most library collections of the spoken word are strong in the field of adult literature, these records can be especially pertinent to the curriculum of the junior and senior high school teachers.[16]

The cassette tape recorder could be the handiest listening device known to man, barring, of course, the human ear. Its low cost and simple operation make it a must item for every classroom and home, as a source of both instruction and entertainment. One of its obvious but often overlooked uses is for "talking books," similar to those used by the blind. In recent years, classroom teachers have begun to incorporate the recorder into their learning centers, but parents still haven't realized its enormous potential. Dr. Marie Carbo, a learning-disabilities specialist and resource teacher, has been taping stories and books for her students and has achieved "phenomenal" results. Her students all have severe learning handicaps, they are disabled, educable retarded, emotionally disturbed, and severely speech-impaired children.[17]

By listening to the tape and following the story in his book, each child is free to move at his own pace and has a constant language model as a companion—the tape. There also is the additional reinforcement from repeated playings of the tape. Dr. Carbo keeps the pace of her taped story slow enough for the child to follow and indicates when the page should be turned. As the individual child's reading ability improves, she increases the pace of the story and the size of the word groupings.

Describing a particular case, Dr. Carbo says, "The greatest gain in word recognition (fifteen months) was made by Tommy, a sixth-grade boy reading on a 2.2 level. Prior to working with the tapes he had faltered and stumbled over second-grade words while his body actually shook with fear and discomfort. Understandably, he hated to read. Because a beloved teacher had once read *Charlotte's Web* to him, he asked me to record his favorite chapter from this book. I recorded one paragraph on each cassette side so that Tommy could choose to read either one or two paragraphs daily. The first time that he listened to a recording (five times) and then read the passage silently to himself (twice), he was able to read the passage to me perfectly with excellent expression and without fear. After this momentous event, Tommy worked hard. At last he knew he was capable of learning to read and was willing to give it all he could. The result was a fifteen-month gain in word recognition at the end of only three months. Every learning-disabled child in the program experienced immediate success with her or his individually recorded books," explains Dr. Carbo.

If such phenomenal results are possible with learning-disabled children, think of what can be done with children who have fewer hurdles to hold them back.

Although many commercial recordings are available, the sound of a parent's or teacher's voice reading at an unhurried pace (some recordings move too quickly) will carry far more meaning than will a stranger's. Tape-record those Mother Goose rhymes and have them playing during the day when you are busy. When lectures take me away from home in the evening, I usually tape that night's chapter from the book I am reading to the children. With the lights out and the tape whispering beside them, an extra air of mystery is added to story time. (One of the advantages of old-time radio theater was that it could be listened to in bed with the lights out, thus providing the imagination with a blank piece of paper on which to draw.)

It is important to remember, however, that the cassette recorder is not an unqualified replacement for the personal touch of a live parent or teacher. Nothing is as good as the living, responsive voice and the person behind it.

Although all read-alouds foster listening skills, some books deal specifically with this subject. Peter Spier's *Crash! Bang! Boom!* and Ann McGovern's *Too Much Noise* both treat sounds in a picture book format. *Don't Forget the Bacon* by Pat Hutchins, *Nobody Listens to Andrew* by Elizabeth Guilfoile, *That Noodle-head Epaminondas* by Eve Merriam, and *The Cat Who Wore a Pot on Her Head* by Jan Slepian and Ann Seidler are picture books which deal with the problems of *not* listening.

For older children, the gift of language is demonstrated dramatically in these stories of mute children: *Burnish Me Bright* and its sequels *Far in the Day* and *The Silent Voice* by Julia Cunningham; *Child of the Silent Night,* the nonfiction story of Laura Bridgman, by Edith Fisher Hunter; *The Half-A-Moon Inn* by Paul Fleischman; *Our John Willie* by Catherine Cookson; and *A Certain Small Shepherd* by Rebecca Caudill. Children in sixth grade and up are quick to catch the irony of *The Shrinking of Treehorn* and *Treehorn's Treasure,* both by Florence Parry Heide, which wittily portray adults' penchants for holding one-way conversations with children.

8
Sustained
Silent Reading:
Reading-Aloud's Natural Partner

With the tests, with the "methods," with the class structures, with the teacher's determination to teach . . . no one had ever had much time in school to just read the damn books. They were always practicing up to read, and the practice itself was so unnecessary, or so difficult, or so boring you were likely to figure that the task you were practicing for must combine those qualities and so reject it or be afraid of it.
                                                    —James Herndon,
                                                    How to Survive in Your Native Land

After finishing my forty-five-minute career talk to the fourth-grade students at Brunton School in Springfield, Massachusetts, I debated whether to ask my usual question: What have you read lately? A week before, I'd asked the question of a fifth-grade class in the same school system and came away depressed by the lack of response. Only four children in the room had been able to think of anything they had read lately. I was embarrassed for the class, the teacher, the system, and the city. Reluctantly, I now asked the question again, dreading another disappointing response.

But those wonderful fourth-grade pupils surprised me. For forty-five minutes they spouted the names of the books they had been reading. I could barely get a word in edgewise as their enthusiasm and excitement flooded the room.

Later, as I was leaving, I asked the teacher, Terri Cullinane, "What have you done to those kids? I haven't seen a class this excited by books in years."

"Two things," she answered. "We—the other teachers and I—read aloud to them every day, and SSR." (SSR is an acronym for Sustained Silent Reading.) "Every day when we go to lunch, each child leaves his library book on his desk. It is ready and waiting for him when he returns after lunch. We read quietly for ten minutes, close our books, and go on with classwork."

Terri explained that the SSR program had been in effect only a few months but already the faculty had seen a dramatic change in reading habits and attitude among the children.

"Ten minutes a day may not seem like much time but think of it this way: ten minutes a day for five days. That's almost a solid hour of reading and it puts the child well into the book, much further, by the way, than most of them would be if they were left to read it on their own time."

SSR is one of those common-sense ideas that is so obvious and uncomplicated that it is easily overlooked in today's complex educational scheme. Sadly, 99 percent of our school systems (and nearly 100 percent of our homes) either haven't heard about it or can't spare the time to try it.

Its basic principle is simple. Reading is, among other things, a skill, and like all skills, the more you use it the better you become at it. Conversely, the less reading you do, the more difficult it is. It is no secret among educators that today's students are assigned 50 percent less reading than their counterparts in the early 1960s. In *The Literacy Hoax,* Copperman points out that the average Soviet high-school student is required to read more English literature than the average American student. He also reports that the decline in reading skills has required twenty of the largest textbook publishers to downgrade the reading level of their books to two full grades below the grade in which they are to be used.

Since literature serves as the prime model for writing, any decline in reading time will affect writing skills. Nearly 80 percent of the incoming journalism majors at West Virginia University in 1979 failed the grammar test. Far from being an isolated case, West Virginia's experience is typical of many colleges throughout the nation.

As reading and writing skills continue to decline, the nation's schools increase the hours of skills instruction, search for new instruction methods, change publishers, and wring their hands in despair. We spend hours and years teaching reading skills to our children and then fail to provide the time in which to use them, either in the home or in the school. SSR is the logical answer.

Originally proposed in the early 1960s by Lyman C. Hunt, Jr., of the University of Vermont, SSR has received its biggest boost from reading experts Robert and Marlene McCracken.[1] Experimenting with a variety of techniques and schools, the McCrackens recommend the following procedures for SSR programs:

1. Children should read to themselves for a *limited* amount of time. Teachers and parents should adapt this to their individual class or family and adjust it with increasing maturity. Ten or fifteen minutes are the frequent choices for the classroom.

2. Each student should select his own book, magazine, or newspaper. No changing during the period is permitted. All materials must be chosen before the SSR period begins.

3. The teacher or parent must read also, setting an example. This cannot be stressed too strongly.

4. No reports are required of the student. No records are kept.

Along with the obvious opportunity to practice reading skills in an informal manner, SSR provides the student with a new perspective on reading—as a form of recreation. There appears to be a desperate need for such an example (see Chapter 1).

Nearly all SSR studies done to date report immediate attitude changes. Junior and senior high schools show significant changes in students' feelings toward the library, voluntary reading, assigned reading, and the importance of reading. While there is no marked improvement in reading skills at this secondary level, there is no decline either, despite the loss of reading instruction time. Since by age 13 children usually have reached their language development peak, attitudes are more apt to improve than are skills during adolescence.[2]

Younger readers, however, show significant improvement in both attitude and skills with SSR.[3] "Poor readers," points out Professor Allington of the State University of New York, "when given 10 minutes a day to read, initially will achieve 500 words and quickly increase that amount in the same period as proficiency grows."

In a School District of Philadelphia–Federal Reserve Bank study made to determine which reading methods "worked," it was shown that among 1,800 Philadelphia fourth-grade students "the more minutes a week of sustained silent reading, the better the pupils achieved." The same study also indicated that the number of minutes a day of reading instruction that might be lost through SSR did not affect pupil achievement.[4]

Martha Efta offers a special example of SSR's worth. Ms. Efta teaches a primary-level class of educable mentally retarded children in Westlake, Ohio. The children, ranging in age from 7 to 10, are frequently hyperactive and nonreaders. When she heard of the SSR procedure in a graduate course, she was cautious about the idea despite the professor's wholehearted support for it. After all, she thought, the experts were talking about normal children, not the retarded.

With some trepidation, she explained the procedures to her students and reshaped the rules to fit her classroom. Because of their short attention spans, she allowed each student to choose as many as three books or magazines for the period. Students were allowed to sit any way and in any place they chose in the room. Ms. Efta initially kept the program to three minutes in length, then gradually increased it to thirteen minutes over a period of weeks. This was the class's limit.

"From the onset [of SSR]," Ms. Efta explains, "the students have demonstrated some exciting and favorable behavior changes—such as independent decision making, self discipline, sharing . . . and broadened reading interests. The enthusiastic rush to select their day's reading materials following noon recess is indicative of the children's interest and eagerness for SSR. The children seem to delight in the adult-like responsibility of selecting their own reading matter." [5]

The McCrackens' extensive studies of SSR show conclusively that best results are achieved when the program is schoolwide, as in the case of Gateway Regional Middle School in Huntington, Massachusetts. This school instituted a twenty-five-minute sustained silent reading program in 1978 on Monday and Friday mornings. During these periods, the entire school (this includes the principals, secretaries, and teachers, as well as the students) puts its "work" aside and picks up something to read. The choice of material is up to the individual.

"We instituted it to show the children just how important and how enjoyable reading is for *everyone*—not just for students," explains principal James Lutat. "Now it's become one of the most popular features of the week. We all look forward to it. We don't allow any work during those twenty-five-minute periods. Why, we don't even answer the phone if we can help it."

At 10:30 a.m. on Mondays and Fridays the only sound in Gateway School is the sound of turning pages—pages that are turned eagerly instead of reluctantly.

The McCrackens report that most of the instances where SSR fails are due to teachers (or aides) who are supervising instead of reading. The other problem area is where classes lack enough SSR materials from which to choose.

Writing in *The Reading Teacher,* the McCrackens called attention to the overwhelming part the teacher plays as a role model in SSR.[6] Teachers reported widespread imitation by students of the teacher's reading habits.

Students in one class noticed the teacher interrupting her reading to look up a word in the dictionary and began doing the same. When a junior-high teacher began to read the daily newspaper each day, the class began doing the same.

But of all the role model examples, the most moving for me was the retarded child in Martha Efta's class. This nonreader found it impossible to settle down with his books until he noticed his friend reading silently and intently. So transfixed was he by his friend's concentration, he spent an entire SSR period just watching the boy scanning the sentences with his finger. Within several days he, too, settled into "reading"—by imitating the behavior of his friend.

When teachers talk about what they are reading or describe a spine-tingling section of their book, students are quick to follow suit and share their reaction. By doing this, the McCrackens write, "they are teaching attitudes and skills; they are teaching children that reading is communication with an author, an assimilation and reaction to an author's ideas."

SSR works as well in the home as in the classroom. The same rules apply, though I recommend they be tailored to fit your family. For children who are not used to reading for more than brief periods of time it is important at first to limit SSR to ten or fifteen minutes. Later, when they are used to reading in this manner and are more involved in books, the period can be extended—often at the child's request. As in the classroom, it is important to have a variety of reading material—magazines, newspapers, novels, picture books. A weekly family trip to the library can do much to solve this need.

The time selected for family SSR is also important. Involve the child in the decision, if possible. Bedtime seems to be the most popular SSR time, perhaps because the child does not have to give up any activity for it except sleeping—and most children gladly surrender that.

9
How to Use
the Treasury

The success we have in helping children become readers will depend not so much on our technical skills but upon the spirit we transmit of ourselves as readers. Next in importance comes the breadth and depth of our knowledge of the books we offer. Only out of such a ready catalogue can we match child and book with the sort of spontaneous accuracy that is wanted time and again during a working day.

> —Aidan Chambers,
> "Talking About Reading,"
> *The Horn Book* (October 1977)

Approximately 2,000 new children's books are published each year. Of that number, 60 percent could be categorized as "fast food for the mind" and of minimum lasting value. Only about 10 percent of the year's crop of books could be rated Grade A.

This is not to say that "fast food" books are worthless. On the contrary, they serve as hors d'oeuvres and build appetites (to say nothing of reading skills) for more nourishing books later. They also serve as valuable transition steps between skillful reading and pleasureful reading. Jacques Barzun, most recently a consultant to the Council for Basic Education, is the author of *Teacher in America* (written while he was professor of history and later provost of Columbia University), in which he comments on so-called junk reading by children: "Let me say at once that all books are good and that consequently a child be allowed to read everything he lays his hands on. Trash is excellent; great works . . . are admirable. . . . The ravenous appetite will digest stones unharmed. Never mind the need to discriminate; it comes in its own time." [1] (In using the word "trash," Barzun was referring to formula fiction like the Hardy Boys and Nancy Drew.)

The reader-aloud, however, offers an alternative for the child, allowing him to sample the "Grade A" books which may be beyond either his skills or his surface appetites. We should, therefore, in reading aloud concern ourselves primarily (though not exclusively) with books that will stimulate children's emotions, minds, and imaginations, stories that will stay with them for years to come, literature that will serve as a harbor light toward which a child can navigate.

Few parents have the time to wade through the vast numbers of newly published books, not to mention the previous years' volumes. Librarians can be a big help in this chore, at least in the picture book category. They know the patrons' favorites from over the years and their story-hour experience is invaluable. But when you are looking for read-aloud novels, the forest begins to thicken and it is much harder to find your way. Not all librarians—and few teachers and parents—have a strong background in this area of read-aloud. It is my hope that the Treasury of Read-Alouds included in this book will help to alleviate this problem.

I make no boast of the Treasury being a comprehensive list. It is intended only as a starter and time-saver. (I'd be willing to wager, in fact, that I've left your all-time favorite off the list.) As much as the list appears to be a potpourri of titles, I do admit to some rhyme and reason for my selections. I required the following for each selection:

1. I must have read and enjoyed the book.
2. The book must have a proven track record of success as a read-aloud with children. I noted the reactions of my own children, neighbors' and friends' children, and school classes.
3. The book must be the kind of book that will inspire children to want to read another one just like it, or even the same book over again.

I did not require that the book be a classic, although some of the books on the list are classics. Nor did I ask that the book be acclaimed previously by the critics, though many on the list own that distinction.

The grade recommendations with each book are meant to be flexible. If you stop to think about it, there is no such thing as a "fourth-grade book" any more than there is a "middle-age book." Many sixth-grade students are fully capable of enjoying the same book a third-grade child is enjoying. The grade numbers are intended only as general read-aloud guidelines, not as rules. In addition to the numbered grade levels, the following codes are included:

> Tod.   Infants and Toddlers up to 3-year-olds
> Pre S.   From 3-year-olds to PreSchoolers
> K   Kindergartners

Wherever possible I have included the names of hardcover and paperback publishers. This information, however, is subject to change as books go out of print or are made available in paperback for the first time. I offer it only as a reference for those readers wishing to obtain a personal copy or, if it is unavailable, a copy through a school or public library. If the book is still in print, it usually can be ordered directly from the publisher. *Children's Books in Print,* available in all libraries, includes a complete listing of publishers' addresses, their different imprint names, and the books that are available. *Paperback Books in Print* does the same for all paperbacks, children and adult. In the Treasury, those books out of print as of 1982 carry (OP) after the publisher's name, though readers should not be discouraged by such a notation—it most probably is still available on library shelves.

In my listing of publishers, the paperback publisher always follows the hardcover publisher, separated by a semicolon, for example: Harper, 1960; Bantam, 1971. Where a particular publisher handles both the hardcover and paperback editions, the notation will be, for example: Harper (both), 1962; 1975.

The Treasury is divided into six categories, arranged as follows: a brief listing of Wordless Books, Picture Books (p), Short Novels (s), Novels (n), Poetry (po), and Anthologies (a). All books in the respective categories are listed alphabetically by title. The Author-Illustrator Index to Treasury (see page 219) will also help you locate books in different categories.

At the end of the book synopses in the Treasury, I often have noted other read-alouds by the same author or referred the reader to related titles listed elsewhere in the Treasury. In these instances, the letter that follows the title—*Ira Sleeps Over* (p)—indicates the section of the Treasury that contains that particular book: (p) for Picture Books. If no letter appears after the recommended title, its synopsis is not available in the Treasury because of space limitations.

In the synopses, I have tried to indicate wherever I thought certain books needed special attention from the reader-aloud. For example, Harry Mazer's *Snow-Bound* is a compelling novel about two teenagers fighting for their lives in a snowstorm. Many of my teacher friends read it to their middle-school classes each year and skip over the occasional four-letter words in the text. The story is one of the children's favorites and it would be a shame to deprive them of its excitement and values because of a dozen strong words. Nevertheless, the reader-aloud should be alerted to the situation.

I have noted "for experienced listeners" to indicate those books I feel would be poor choices for children just beginning the listening experience. These books should be read aloud only after the children's attention and listening spans have been developed with shorter books and stories.

The number of pages noted for each book should indicate to the reader the number of sittings the book requires. A children's book of 32 pages can be completed easily in one session.

All of these books, when they are read aloud in the right manner and with the right attitude by the reader, will go a long way toward turning children into book lovers; they will help to turn on the turned-off reader; and they will reach children in ways far beyond our dreams.

10 Treasury of Read-Alouds

Wordless Books

Picture Books (pages 118–154) are often written and illustrated by the same person. Books marked with an * are described in the Picture Books section of the Treasury.

The Adventures of Paddy Pork, John Goodall (Harcourt, 1968)
Ah-Choo!, Mercer Mayer (Dial, 1976)
Apples, Nonny Hogrogian (Macmillan, 1972)
April Fools, Fernando Krahn (Dutton, 1974)
The Ballooning Adventures of Paddy Pork, John Goodall (Harcourt, 1968)
The Bear and the Fly, Paula Winter (Crown, 1976)
A Birthday Wish, Ed Emberley (Little, Brown, 1977)
Bobo's Dream, Martha Alexander (Dial, 1970)
A Boy, a Dog, and a Frog, Mercer Mayer (Dial, 1967)
Bubble, Bubble, Mercer Mayer (Parents, 1973)
Catch That Car, Fernando Krahn (Dutton, 1978)
Changes, Changes, Pat Hutchins (Macmillan, 1971)

Charlie-Bob's Fan, W. B. Park (Harcourt, 1981)
Creepy Castle, John Goodall (Atheneum, 1975)
The Creepy Thing, Fernando Krahn (Clarion, 1982)
*Deep in the Forest, Brinton Turkle (Dutton, 1976)
Do You Want to Be My Friend?, Eric Carle (Crowell, 1971)
A Flying Saucer Full of Spaghetti, Fernando Krahn (Dutton, 1970)
Frog Goes to Dinner, Mercer Mayer (Dial, 1974)
Frog on His Own, Mercer Mayer (Dial, 1973)
Frog, Where Are You?, Mercer Mayer (Dial, 1969)
The Great Ape, Fernando Krahn (Viking, 1978)
The Great Cat Chase, Mercer Mayer (Four Winds, 1974)
The Hunter and the Animals, Tomie de Paola (Holiday House, 1981)
Jacko, John Goodall (Harcourt, 1972)
Lilly at the Table, Linda Heller (Macmillan, 1979)
Little John and Me, Yutaka Sugita (McGraw-Hill, 1973)
Look What I Can Do, Jose Aruego (Scribner, 1971)
Lost, Sonia Lisker (Harcourt, 1978)
*Max, Giovannetti (Atheneum, 1977)
The Midnight Adventures of Kelly, Dot, and Esmeralda, John Goodall
(Atheneum, 1972)
The Mystery of the Giant Footprints, Fernando Krahn (Dutton, 1977)
Naughty Nancy, John Goodall (Atheneum, 1975)
*Noah's Ark, Peter Spier (Doubleday, 1977)
One Frog Too Many, Mercer Mayer (Dial, 1975)
Out! Out! Out!, Martha Alexander (Dial, 1968)
Paddy Finds a Job, John Goodall (Atheneum, 1981)
Paddy Goes Traveling, John Goodall (Atheneum, 1982)
Paddy Pork's Holiday, John Goodall (Atheneum, 1975)
Paddy's Evening Out, John Goodall (Atheneum, 1973)
Paddy's New Hat, John Goodall (Atheneum, 1980)
Pancakes for Breakfast, Tomie de Paola (Harcourt, 1978)
Peter Spier's Christmas, Peter Spier (Doubleday, 1982)
Peter Spier's Rain, Peter Spier (Doubleday, 1982)
Rosie's Walk, Pat Hutchins (Macmillan, 1968)
The Scribble Monster, Jack Kent (Harcourt, 1981)
Sebastian and the Mushroom, Fernando Krahn (Delacorte, 1976)
The Self-Made Snowman, Fernando Krahn (Lippincott, 1974)
Shrewbettina Goes to Work, John Goodall (Atheneum, 1981)
Shrewbettina's Birthday, John Goodall (Harcourt, 1970)
*The Silver Pony, Lynd Ward (Houghton Mifflin, 1973)
Skates, Ezra Jack Keats (Franklin Watts, 1973)
*The Snowman, Raymond Briggs (Random, 1978)
The Sticky Child, Malcolm Bird (Harcourt, 1981)
Truck, Donald Crews (Greenwillow, 1980)
Two Moral Tales, Mercer Mayer (Four Winds, 1974)
Two More Moral Tales, Mercer Mayer (Four Winds, 1974)

*Up and Up, Shirley Hughes (Prentice-Hall, 1979)
The Wrong Side of the Bed, Edward Ardizzone (Doubleday, 1970)

Picture Books

THE ADVENTURES OF PADDY PORK
by John S. Goodall
Harcourt, 1968
Pre S.–2   60 (small) pages
This is the British counterpart (but more sophisticated in concept) of America's successful Boy and Frog series by Mercer Mayer. It is a series of wordless books that detail the adventures of a naughty pig and his bottomless curiosity. Because of the small format, it is best read with no more than three children at once. Sequels: *Ballooning Adventures of Paddy Pork; Creepy Castle; Jacko; The Midnight Adventures of Kelly, Dot, and Esmeralda; Naughty Nancy; Paddy Finds a Job; Paddy Goes Traveling; Paddy's Evening Out; Paddy's New Hat; Shrewbettina Goes to Work.*

ALEXANDER AND THE TERRIBLE, HORRIBLE, NO GOOD, VERY BAD DAY
by Judith Viorst   •   Illustrated by Ray Cruz
Atheneum (both), 1972; 1976
K and up   34 pages
Everyone has a bad day once in a while but Alexander has the worst of all. Follow him from a cereal box without a prize to a burned-out night light. A modern classic for all ages to chuckle over and admit, "I guess we're all entitled to a terrible, horrible, no good . . ." Sequel: *Alexander Who Used to Be Rich Last Sunday.* Also by the author: *If I Were in Charge of the World and Other Worries* (po); *I'll Fix Anthony* (p).

THE AMAZING BONE
by William Steig
Farrar, 1976; Puffin, 1977
Pre S.–4   28 pages
The fantasy-adventure tale of a magical bone that rescues the book's heroine from the clutches of robbers and a villainous wolf. A Caldecott honor book brimming with suspense. Also by the author: *The Real Thief* (s); *Sylvester and the Magic Pebble* (p).

AMELIA BEDELIA
by Peggy Parrish   •   Illustrated by Fritz Seibel
Harper, 1963; Scholastic, 1970
K–4   24 pages
America's most lovable maid since "Hazel," Amelia is a walking disaster—

thanks to her insistence on taking directions literally. She "dusts the furniture" with dusting powder; "dresses the turkey" in shorts; "puts the lights out" on the clothesline. She makes for a hilarious exploration of homonyms and idioms. Teachers will want to obtain a copy of Fred Gwynne's *The King Who Rained* and *Chocolate Moose for Dinner* and combine them with Amelia for a class on homonyms. Sequels: *Amelia Bedelia and the Surprise Shower; Come Back, Amelia Bedelia; Play Ball, Amelia Bedelia.*

THE AMINAL
by Lorna Balian
Abingdon, 1972
K–5   26 pages
A picture book story of how children's imaginations often run ahead of reality, particularly when accompanied by their fears. Also by the author: *The Sweet Touch* (p); *Humbug Rabbit.* Related books: *How I Hunted the Little Fellows* (p); *Sam, Bangs and Moonshine* (p).

ANDREW HENRY'S MEADOW
by Doris Burn
Coward, 1965 (OP)
K–3   42 pages
Unappreciated at home for his inventions, young Andrew Henry runs away to the big meadow where he is soon joined by other disgruntled children from his neighborhood. Together they build a magical world only a child would create. Also illustrated by the author: *Christina Katerina and the Box; We Were Tired of Living in a House.* Related books: *Henry the Explorer* (p); *No Boys Allowed* (p); *Sleep Out* (p); *Tony's Hard Work Day* (p).

THE BEAR'S TOOTHACHE
by David McPhail
Little, Brown, 1972; Puffin, 1978
Pre S.–2   26 pages
This book deals with children's bedtime fantasies. A little boy is kept awake by the howling of a bear with a toothache outside his bedroom window. Believing he'll never get to sleep until the tooth is fixed, the child invites the bear into the house where, in a struggle to free the tooth, bear and child cause absolute havoc. Also by the author: *Henry Bear's Park* (p); *The Train.* Related books: *The Aminal* (p); *Bedtime for Frances* (p); *The Biggest Bear* (p); *There's a Nightmare in My Closet* (p); *The Beast in the Bed* by Barbara Dillon.

BEDTIME FOR FRANCES
by Russell Hoban • Illustrated by Garth Williams
Harper (both), 1960; 1976
Pre S.–2   28 pages
Frances the badger cannot get to sleep. All the ploys of little children to avoid

bedtime, all the fears of nighttime, are treated with gentle humor here. Sequels: *A Baby Sister for Frances; Best Friends for Frances; A Birthday for Frances; Bread and Jam for Frances* (illustrated by Lillian Hoban). Related books: *The Bear's Toothache* (p); *A Bedtime Story* (p); *Corduroy* (p); *Ira Sleeps Over* (p).

A BEDTIME STORY
by Joan Levine · Illustrated by Gail Owens
Dutton, 1975 (OP)
K–6   26 pages
A funny story about a little girl who hates to go to bed, so her parents switch roles. They let her put them to bed–but first they have to have their snack, brush their teeth, hear a story, and have a glass of water. Related books: *Bedtime for Frances* (p); *Goodnight Moon* (p); *Ira Sleeps Over* (p).

BENJIE
by Joan Lexau · Illustrated by Don Bolognese
Dial, 1964
Pre S.–2   38 pages
When his grandmother loses her earring, Benjie, an overly shy child, attempts to help by going outside and asking others if they have seen it. In doing so, he takes the important first steps in overcoming his shyness and demonstrates his great devotion to his grandmother. In a moving sequel, *Benjie on His Own*, Benjie's grandmother is taken ill and cannot meet him after school as usual. Bravely he finds his way home–only to find his courage challenged further: he must go for help to aid his grandmother. Related books: *My Grandson Lew* (p); *The Stories Julian Tells* (s). *Now One Foot, Now the Other* by Tomie de Paola.

BENNETT CERF'S BOOK OF ANIMAL RIDDLES
by Bennett Cerf · Illustrated by Roy McKie
Random, 1959
Pre S.–2   62 pages
Joke books are an instant favorite with children. Because jokes are easily and willingly committed to memory, they offer the child an opportunity to display his cleverness when he recites them, thus building self-confidence and a sense of humor. Sequels: *Bennett Cerf's Book of Laughs; Book of Riddles; Houseful of Laughter.*

THE BIG RED BARN
by Eve Bunting · Illustrated by Howard Knotts
Harcourt (both), 1979
Gr. 1–4   32 pages
An old family barn serves as an emotional refuge for a little farm boy. He hides there when his mother dies and again later when his dad brings home a new wife. When the barn accidentally burns, the child and his grandfather talk

about new beginnings, and how families and barns can be rebuilt. Related books: *Do You Love Me?* (p); *A Taste of Blackberries* (s); *The Tenth Good Thing About Barney* (p).

THE BIGGEST BEAR
by Lynd Ward
Houghton Mifflin (both), 1952; 1973
K-3   80 pages
Johnny adopts a bear cub fresh out of the woods and its growth presents problem after problem—the crises we invite when we tame what is meant to be wild. Related books: *The Carp in the Bathtub* (p); *Do You Love Me?* (p); *My Friend Mac* (p); *Capyboppy* by Bill Peet.

BLUEBERRIES FOR SAL
by Robert McCloskey
Viking, 1948; Puffin, 1976
Tod.-K   56 pages
While blueberry picking one day, a little girl mistakes a bear for her mother and mom mistakes a bear cub for Sal. A realistic and happy story with bold drawings against a plain white background make this one of the best books for that toddler through kindergarten age group. Also by the author: *Lentil* (p).

THE BOOK OF GIANT STORIES
by David Harrison • Illustrated by Philippe Fix
American Heritage, 1972
K-3   44 pages
Three delightful stories about giants: a giant who throws tantrums (because he can't whistle); a giant who is afraid of butterflies (because he needs glasses); and giants who are frightened by a little boy (because he has measles). To make the "measle" story a bit more accessible for today's child, change the word "measles" to "chicken pox" when reading it aloud. Nowadays few children are aware of the word "measles." Related books: *The Fairy Tale Treasury* (Jack and the Beanstalk) (a); *The Foolish Giant* (p); *Giant Kippernose and Other Stories* (a); *Inside My Feet* (s); *John John Twilliger* by William Wondriska.

THE CARP IN THE BATHTUB
by Barbara Cohen • Illustrated by Joan Halpern
Lothrop, 1972; Dell, 1975
Gr. 1-4   48 pages
When Leah and Harry's mother brings a live carp home (to cook for Passover) and temporarily stores it in the bathtub, she never anticipates their adopting it as their best friend. With bittersweet humor, the story offers a nostalgic view of Passover customs. Also by the author, for older children: *R, My Name Is Rosie* (n); *Benny.* Related books: *The Biggest Bear* (p); *My Friend Mac* (p); *Capyboppy* by Bill Peet.

THE CARROT SEED
by Ruth Krauss • Illustrated by Crockett Johnson
Harper, 1945; Scholastic, 1971
Tod–Pre S. 22 pages
Simple pictures against a plain background depict a child's faith in the carrot seed he plants, despite the fact that no one else believes it will grow. And what a carrot it becomes! Also by the author: *A Hole Is to Dig* (p).

CINDERELLA
Retold by John Fowles • Illustrated by Sheila Beckett
Little, Brown, 1976
Gr. 2–5 32 pages
A highly acclaimed writer for adults has skillfully translated Perrault's classic fairy tale. It is accompanied by 25 exquisite drawings by Sheila Beckett. Related books: *The Fairy Tale Treasury* (a); *Hans Andersen—His Classic Fairy Tales* (p); *Household Stories of the Brothers Grimm* (p).

CLOUDY WITH A CHANCE OF MEATBALLS
by Judi Barrett • Illustrated by Ron Barrett
Atheneum (both), 1978; 1982
Pre S.–5 28 pages
In the fantasy land of Chewandswallow, the weather changes three times a day (at breakfast, lunch, and supper), supplying all the residents with food out of the sky. But suddenly the weather takes a turn for the worse; instead of normal size meatballs, it rains meatballs the size of basketballs; pancakes and syrup smother the streets. Something must be done! Also by the author: *Animals Should Definitely Not Act Like People; Animals Should Definitely Not Wear Clothing; Benjamin's 365 Birthdays; Old McDonald Had an Apartment House.*

THE CONTESTS AT COWLICK
by Richard Kennedy • Illustrated by Marc Simont
Little, Brown, 1975
Pre S.–1 48 pages
When outlaws ride into town one day while the sheriff and his men are off fishing, it falls to little Wally to save the town by arranging an ingenious and amusing series of contests with the outlaws. The scruffy outlaws offer the reader-aloud a wonderful opportunity for loud, grouchy voices. Also by the author: *Inside My Feet* (s); *The Boxcar at the Center of the Universe; Come Again in the Spring; The Rise and Fall of Ben Gizzard.*

CORDUROY
by Don Freeman
Viking, 1968; Puffin, 1976
Tod.–2 32 pages
The story of a teddy bear's search through a department store for a friend. His

quest ends when a little girl buys him with her piggybank savings. Sequel: *A Pocket for Corduroy*. Also by the author: *Norman the Doorman* (p). Related books: *Bedtime for Frances* (p); *Ira Sleeps Over* (p); *David and Dog* by Shirley Hughes.

THE COUNTRY BUNNY AND THE LITTLE GOLD SHOES
by DuBose Heyward • Illustrated by Marjorie Hock
Houghton Mifflin (both), 1939; 1974
Pre S.-3   48 pages
One of the classic holiday stories, this tells of the struggles of a little country bunny to achieve her lifelong dream—to become an Easter Bunny. No one gives her much of a chance, but her persistence and courage carry her not only to her dream but also to the greatest honor a bunny can receive. Related books: *Michael* (p); *Mr. Rabbit and the Lovely Present* by Charlotte Zolotow; *A Rabbit for Easter* by Carol and Donald Carrick.

CRANBERRY THANKSGIVING
by Wende and Harry Devlin
Parents, 1971
K–4   30 pages
The first of a series of mystery-adventure tales set on the cranberry bog shores of Cape Cod. A regular cast of young Becky, her grandmother, and a retired old sea captain are supported by a variety of pratfalling villains and sheriffs, all painted in glowing watercolors by Harry Devlin. If possible, read the series in this order: *Cranberry Thanksgiving; Cranberry Christmas; Cranberry Mystery*.

The Devlins also have done a Halloween picture book series that is excellent for read-aloud: *Old Black Witch; Old Witch and the Polka-Dot Ribbon; Old Witch Rescues Halloween*. Also by the authors: *How Fletcher Was Hatched; The Knobby Boys to the Rescue*.

DEEP IN THE FOREST
by Brinton Turkle
Dutton, 1976
Pre S.-2   30 pages
A wordless book reversing the conventional Goldilocks/Three Bears tale. This time the bear cub visits Goldilocks's family cabin with hilarious and plausible results. Also by the author: *Obadiah the Bold* and sequels (p); *Do Not Open;* for older children, *The Fiddler on High Lonesome*. Related books: *The Three Bears* by Paul Galdone. See also Wordless Books.

DICK WHITTINGTON AND HIS CAT
by Kathleen Lines • Illustrated by Edward Ardizzone
Walck, 1970 (OP)
Gr. 2–5   42 pages
Though embossed by time and legend, this classic folk tale remains essentially

the true story of the impoverished English lad who—with the aid of his cat—
made his fortune and was elected mayor of London. Through his wealth and
high office he became a famous benefactor of the poor and oppressed. This
excellent version relies heavily on fact and very little on legend in portraying
the man and the Middle Ages. Related books: for experienced listeners, *Otto of
the Silver Hand* (n); *Robin Hood* (n); *The Wish at the Top* (p); for younger
children, *Dick Whittington and His Cat* by Marcia Brown.

DON'T FORGET THE BACON
by Pat Hutchins
Greenwillow, 1976; Puffin, 1978
K–5   32 pages
A humorous tale for every child and adult who has ever been sent to the store
to pick up grocery items—only to forget the names of the items along the way.
An excellent listening lesson. Other versions of this tale are: *That Noodle-head
Epaminondas* by Eve Merriam and *The Cat Who Wore a Pot on Her Head* by Jan
Slepian and Ann Seidler.

DO YOU LOVE ME?
by Dick Gackenbach
Seabury, 1975; Dell, 1978
Pre S.–2   46 pages
When young Walter is traumatized by the accidental killing of a hum-
mingbird he tried to capture, his mother eases his pain by showing that not all
creatures want us to love and hug them. A simple book about death, love, and
our fragile relationship with nature. Also by the author: *The Leatherman* (p);
McGoogan Moves the Mighty Rock. Related books: *The Biggest Bear* (p); *My
Friend Mac* (p); *The Tenth Good Thing About Barney* (p).

EAST OF THE SUN AND
WEST OF THE MOON
by Mercer Mayer
Four Winds, 1980
K–6   48 pages
The trouble with most retellings of classic fairy tales is that they tend to sap
the original tale of its strength, leaving the listener with hollow stories. Not so
with this retelling and combination of the Grimms' *Frog Prince* and Norway's
East O' the Sun and West O' the Moon. The author-illustrator has used the
originals only as a seed in bringing forth a magnificent tale of evil, magic, and
courage. See Index to Treasury for other Mercer Mayer books.

EMMETT'S PIG
by Mary Stolz • Illustrated by Garth Williams
Harper, 1959
Pre S.–1   62 pages
Living as he did in a city apartment block, it was impossible for Emmett to

own a pig. But of all the pets he could wish for, a pig was his only choice— much to the concern of his parents. The author treats a childhood obsession realistically and with warmth as we learn that sometimes dreams do come true—in their own time and fashion. Related books: *The Fairy Tale Treasury* (The Three Little Pigs) (a); *Chester the Worldly Pig* by Bill Peet (see Index to Treasury for list of his books); *Don't Ever Wish for a Seven-Foot Bear* by Robert Benton; *This Little Pig* by Miska Miles.

FABLES
by Arnold Lobel
Harper, 1980
Gr. 2–6   42 pages

An award-winning author-artist offers 20 short fables coupled with an equal number of large illustrations, offering both comic and serious commentary on the human condition. Any of these fables is the perfect opening (or closing) note for a school day. If the audience responds to this collection, pick up Ann McGovern's retold *Aesop's Fables* and Eric Carle's *Twelve Tales from Aesop*. Albert Cullum's *Aesop in the Afternoon,* an excellent teacher's guide to 66 fables, shows how easily fables can be made into simple short plays for the classroom. Also by the author: *Frog and Toad Are Friends* (p); *Owl at Home; Uncle Elephant.*

FREDERICK
by Leo Lionni
Pantheon (both), 1966
Pre S. and up   28 pages

Frederick is a tiny gray field mouse. He is also an allegorical figure representing the poets, artists, and dreamers of the world. While his brothers and sisters gather food against the oncoming winter, Frederick gathers the colors and stories and dreams they will need to sustain their hearts and souls in the winter darkness. Also by the author: *Alexander and the Wind-Up Mouse; The Biggest House in the World; Fish Is Fish; Little Blue and Little Yellow; Pezzetino; Swimmy.*

FROG AND TOAD ARE FRIENDS
by Arnold Lobel
Harper (both), 1970; 1979
Pre S.–2   64 pages

Using a simple early-reader vocabulary and fablelike story lines, the author-artist has developed an award-winning series that is a must for young children. Generous helpings of humor and warm personal relationships are the trademarks of the series, each book containing 5 individual stories relating to childhood. Sequels: *Days with Frog and Toad; Frog and Toad All Year; Frog and Toad Together.* Also by the author: *Fables* (p); *Owl at Home; Uncle Elephant.* Related books: Little Bear series (p); *The Empty Squirrel* by Carol Carrick.

THE GIVING TREE
by Shel Silverstein
Harper, 1964
K–4   52 pages
A tender look at friendship, love, and sharing in a simple but unorthodox fashion. Excellent for class discussion about values. Also by the author: *Where the Sidewalk Ends* (po). Related books: see Index to Treasury for Charlotte Zolotow books.

GOODNIGHT MOON
by Margaret Wise Brown
Harper (both), 1947; 1977
Tod.–Pre S.   30 pages
A classic tale for very young children on the bedtime ritual, sure to be copied by every child who hears it. Related books: *Bedtime for Frances* (p); *Goodnight, Fred* by Rosemary Wells; *Goodnight, Goodnight* by Eve Rice.

THE GREAT GREEN TURKEY CREEK MONSTER
by James Flora
Atheneum (both), 1976; 1979
Pre S.–3   32 pages
A mix-up in the seed bin at the general store results in the sprouting of a Great Green Hooligan Vine which wreaks havoc and laughter throughout the town as it grows and grows in a modern "bean stalk" tale. Since the vine is finally subdued by trombone music, one suggestion would be to have a copy of the music of "76 Trombones" from *The Music Man* available to listen to afterwards. Also by the author: *Grandpa's Ghost Stories; Grandpa's Witched-Up Christmas*. Related books: *Mishka* (p); *A Special Trick* (p).

THE GREAT HAMSTER HUNT
by Lenore Blegvad and Erik Blegvad
Harcourt, 1969
K–3   32 pages
When the hamster Tony is taking care of for his friend escapes the night before the friend is due home, the entire family must join in the frantic search. A subtle lesson in responsibility and patience. Related books: *How I Hunted the Little Fellows* (p); *The House Mouse* by Dorothy Harris.

HANS ANDERSEN—HIS CLASSIC FAIRY TALES
Translated by Erik Haugaard   •   Illustrated by Michael Foreman
Doubleday, 1976
K and up   188 pages
This collection of 18 tales taken from Haugaard's *The Complete Fairy Tales and Stories of Hans Christian Andersen* is handsomely illustrated and includes the

most popular stories. (For further discussion on the merits of fairy tales, see Chapter 3.)

The following picture books of his individual stories are recommended:

The Emperor's New Clothes, illustrated by Virginia Lee Burton (Houghton, 1949; Scholastic, 1971), 42 pages.

The Fir Tree, illustrated by Nancy Ekholm Burkert (Harper, 1970), 36 pages.

The Little Match Girl, illustrated by Blair Lent (Houghton, 1968), 44 pages.

The Little Mermaid, translated by Eva Le Gallienne, illustrated by Edward Frascino (Harper, 1971), 50 pages.

The Nightingale, translated by Eva Le Gallienne, illustrated by Nancy Ekholm Burkert (Harper, 1965), 48 pages.

The Snow Queen, adapted by Naomi Lewis, illustrated by Toma Bogdanovic (Scroll, 1968), 30 pages.

The Steadfast Tin Soldier, illustrated by Thomas DiGrazia (Prentice, 1981), 30 pages.

Thumbelina, translated by Richard and Clara Winston, illustrated by Lisbeth Zwerger (Morrow, 1980), 30 pages.

The Ugly Duckling, retold and illustrated by Lorinda Bryan Cauley (Harcourt [both], 1979), 44 pages.

The Wild Swans, retold by Amy Ehrlich, illustrated by Susan Jeffers (Dial, 1981), 40 pages.

For preschool children being introduced to fairy tales for the first time, see Index to Treasury for Paul Galdone books. Other related books: *Cinderella* (p); *The Fairy Tale Treasury* (a); *Household Stories of the Brothers Grimm* (p); *Maid of the North* (feminist fairy tales) (a); *R, My Name Is Rosie* (n).

HARRY AND THE TERRIBLE WHATZIT
by Dick Gackenbach
Seabury, 1977; Scholastic, 1979
Pre S.–3   32 pages

When his mother doesn't return immediately from her errand in the cellar, little Harry is positive she's been captured by the monsters he thinks live down there. A gentle lesson in courage and the need to confront our fears before they get out of hand. Also by the author: *Do You Love Me?* (p); *The Leatherman* (p). Related books: *Where the Wild Things Are* (p); *The Beast in the Bed* by Barbara Dillon; *There's a Nightmare in My Closet* by Mercer Mayer.

HARRY THE DIRTY DOG
by Gene Zion • Illustrated by Margaret B. Graham
Harper (both), 1956; 1976
Tod.–2   28 pages

This little white dog with black spots just might be the most famous dog in all of children's literature. All children identify with Harry—partly for his size, partly for his aversion to soap and water, partly for his escapades. The sentences are simple and expressive but it is the artwork that triumphs in the Harry books. The bold black outline of the characters easily enables very young children to see and understand the progress of the story. Sequels: *Harry and the Lady Next-Door; Harry by the Sea; No Roses for Harry.*

HENRY BEAR'S PARK
by David McPhail
Little, Brown, 1976; Puffin, 1978
Gr. 1–5   48 pages
This story is so original, so dramatic, and so beautifully told and illustrated that few children will forget it. When Henry Bear's well-to-do father leaves suddenly on a ballooning adventure, he leaves Henry in charge of his newly purchased park. Henry, feeling the importance of filling in for his father, moves into the park as superintendent and excels in the position until the loneliness for his father begins to wear him down. In one little book, the author has made some poignant observations about the feelings we all have for "special places," the longing for our loved ones when they are away, the sadness when friends disappoint us, and the joy of being loved.

In the sequel, *Stanley: Henry Bear's Friend,* we are introduced to a little raccoon who eventually becomes Henry's assistant at the park. Driven away from his home by bruising brothers, Stanley sets out to seek his fortune. He runs into a con man, ends up in jail, is vindicated in court, finds a job and a friend and eventually his self-confidence. Here are all the charms of the first book but with even more drama in the story line. Also by the author: *The Bear's Toothache* (p); *The Train.* Related books: *Andrew Henry's Meadow* (p); *Dexter* (s); *My Father's Dragon* (s); *Uncle Elephant* by Arnold Lobel.

HENRY THE EXPLORER
by Mark Taylor • Illustrated by Graham Booth
Atheneum (paperback only), 1976
Pre S.–3   46 pages
Little Henry personifies the need and drive for independence existing in all children. While he climbs mountains, blazes trails, explores jungles, and braves the seas, Henry is Every Child, he is the stuff of which dreams are made. Sequels: *The Case of the Missing Kittens* (a book on Henry's dog Angus); *Henry Explores the Jungle; Henry Explores the Mountains; Henry the Castaway.* Related books: *Andrew Henry's Meadow* (p); Little Tim series (p).

A HOLE IS TO DIG
by Ruth Krauss • Illustrated by Maurice Sendak
Harper, 1952
Tod.–K   44 pages
A little book of little pictures and definitions for little people. The simplicity of the ink drawings against a plain white background as well as that of the text

makes this ideal for toddlers and up. Also by the author: *The Carrot Seed* (p).
Related book: *Where's Spot?* (p).

HOUSEHOLD STORIES OF THE BROTHERS GRIMM
Translated by Lucy Crane • Illustrated by Walter Crane
Dover (paperback only), 1963
K and up   270 pages
This collection of 53 tales contains the Grimms' most popular works in a
translation that is easily read aloud and includes more than 100 illustrations.
The maturity and listening experience of your children should determine their
readiness to handle the subject matter, complexity of plot, and language of
these unexpurgated versions. Among the many picture books of tales of the
Brothers Grimm are:

The Elves and the Shoemaker, retold by Freya Littledale, illustrated by Brinton
   Turkle (Four Winds, 1975; Scholastic, 1977), 30 pages.
Hansel and Gretel, translated by Charles Scribner, Jr., illustrated by Adrienne
   Adams (Scribner [both], 1975; 1978), 28 pages.
King Grisly-Beard, translated by Edgar Taylor, illustrated by Maurice Sendak
   (Farrar, 1973; Puffin, 1978), 22 pages.
Red Riding Hood, retold in rhyming verse by Beatrice Schenk de Regniers,
   illustrated by Edward Gorey (Atheneum [both], 1972; 1977), 44 pages.
Rumpelstiltskin, retold by Edith Tarcov, illustrated by Edward Gorey (Four
   Winds, 1973; Scholastic, 1973), 48 pages.
Sleeping Beauty, retold and illustrated by Trina Schart Hyman (Little, 1977), 48
   pages. See also: *Sleeping Ugly* by Jane Yolen, illustrated by Diane Stanley
   (Coward, 1981).
Snow White, translated by Randall Jarrell, illustrated by Nancy Ekholm Burkert
   (Farrar, 1972), 26 pages.
Tom Thumb, illustrated by Felix Hoffman (Atheneum, 1973), 30 pages.

   For preschool children being introduced to the fairy tale for the first time,
see Index to Treasury for Paul Galdone books. Other related books: *Cinderella*
(p); *The Fairy Tale Treasury* (a); *Hans Andersen—His Classic Fairy Tales* (p);
Maid of the North (feminist fairy tales) (a); *R, My Name Is Rosie* (n).

THE HOUSE ON EAST 88th STREET
by Bernard Waber
Houghton Mifflin (both), 1962; 1975
Pre S.-3   48 pages
When the Primm family discovers a gigantic crocodile in the bathtub of their
new apartment, it signals the beginning of a wonderful picture book series. As
soon as the Primms overcome their fright, they see him as your children will—
as the most lovable and human of crocodiles. Sequels: *Lyle and the Birthday
Party; Lyle Finds His Mother; Lyle, Lyle, Crocodile.* Also by the author: *Ira Sleeps
Over* (p). Related book: *No Fighting, No Biting!* (p).

HOW I HUNTED THE LITTLE FELLOWS
by Boris Zhitkov • Illustrated by Paul O. Zelinsky
Dodd, 1979
Gr. 1–6   48 pages
This is a dramatic and unconventional story that deals with a child's overactive imagination. Forbidden to touch the ship model on his grandmother's mantle, the child begins to imagine there is a tiny crew living aboard the ship. Finally he is so convinced of this that he breaks open the ship to catch them. The unconventional part of the tale is in its ending—it leaves off almost in midair. This edition was translated from the 1930s Russian story by Djemma Bider. The sequel that the author wrote to tie it together was eventually lost. Along with being an excellent book about values, the story offers children the opportunity to imagine what might have happened in the sequel. Related books: *The Aminal* (p); *The Indian in the Cupboard* (n); *The Island of the Skog* (p); *The Littles* (s); *Sam, Bangs and Moonshine* (p).

ICE RIVER
by Phyllis Green • Illustrated by James Crowell
Addison-Wesley, 1975
Gr. 1–5   48 pages
Young Dell is struggling to come to terms with his feelings about his new stepfather, as well as the disappointment he feels toward his seldom-seen real father. One day, he and his friend are involved in a dangerous ice-skating accident on the river that provides an important link between Dell and his stepfather. Also by the author: *Grandmother Orphan* (s); *Wild Violets* (s). Related books: *The Big Red Barn* (p); *A Father Like That* by Charlotte Zolotow (see Index to Treasury for list of her books).

IF I RAN THE ZOO
by Dr. Seuss
Random (both), 1950; 1980
Pre S.–4   54 pages
Little Gerald McGrew finds the animals in the local zoo pretty boring when compared with the wonderfully zany and exotic creatures that populate the zoo of his imagination. Children love to follow in the wake of Gerald's madcap safari around the world in search of Thwerlls, Chuggs, Gussets, Gherkins, and Seersuckers, species so rare only the words and pen of Dr. Seuss could describe them. Be sure to tell your audience that, in real life, Dr. Seuss's father was the zoo director in Seuss's hometown, Springfield, Massachusetts. Sequel: *If I Ran the Circus.*

Dr. Seuss is the best-selling author of children's books for the most deserving of reasons: children love his books. Whether it is because of the verbal gymnastics or the unbounded imagination evident in his drawings, the affection and excitement between child and book is unmistakable. Though Seuss's "limited vocabulary" books like *The Cat in the Hat* are excellent beginning readers, it is his storybooks that should receive the attention of readers-aloud. These include (in rhyming verse): *I Can Lick 30 Tigers Today and Other Stories; I Had Trouble in Getting to Solla Sollew; On Beyond Zebra; Scrambled Eggs Super;* and *Thidwick, the Big-Hearted Moose.* These five, along with *If I Ran the Zoo* and *If I Ran the Circus,* are now available in large-format paperback.

Other Dr. Seuss books which make excellent read-alouds include: *And to Think That I Saw It on Mulberry Street; Bartholomew and the Oobleck; Did I Ever Tell You How Lucky You Are?; Dr. Seuss's Sleep Book; The 500 Hats of Bartholomew Cubbins; How the Grinch Stole Christmas; Horton Hatches the Egg; Horton Hears a Who; The King's Stilts; The Lorax; McElligot's Pool; The Shape of Me and Other Stuff; The Sneetches and Other Stories;* and *Yertle the Turtle.*

Dr. Seuss fans will also enjoy Bill Peet books (see Index to Treasury).

I'LL FIX ANTHONY
by Judith Viorst • Illustrated by Arnold Lobel
Harper, 1969
K–5   30 pages
What every child feels and plans while being plagued by an older brother or sister. Also by the author: *Alexander and the Terrible, Horrible, No Good, Very Bad Day* (p); *If I Were in Charge of the World and Other Worries* (po).

IRA SLEEPS OVER
by Bernard Waber
Houghton Mifflin (both), 1972; 1975
K–6   48 pages
This is a warm, sensitive, and funny look at a boy's overnight visit to a friend's house. The tale centers on the child's personal struggle over whether or not to bring along his teddy bear. It makes for lively discussion about individual sleeping habits, peer pressures, and the things we all hold on to—even as grownups. Also by the author: *The House on East 88th Street* (p). Related books: *Bedtime for Frances* (p); *Corduroy* (p); *David and Dog* by Shirley Hughes.

THE ISLAND OF THE SKOG
by Steven Kellogg
Dial (both), 1973; 1976
Pre S.–2   32 pages
Sailing away from city life, a boatload of mice discover the island of their dreams, only to be pulled up short by the appearance of a fearful monster already dwelling on the island. How imaginations can run away with us and how obstacles can be overcome if we'll just talk with others are central issues in this tale. Also by the author: *Can I Keep Him; The Mysterious Tadpole; The Orchard Cat; Won't Somebody Play With Me?* Related books: *The Aminal* (p); *Harry and the Terrible Whatzit* (p); *How I Hunted the Little Fellows* (p).

JUMANJI
by Chris Van Allsburg
Houghton Mifflin, 1981
Gr. 1–6   28 pages
When a brother and sister bring home the "jungle adventure" board game they found in the park, they have no idea of the bizarre adventure that awaits them once they begin to play it. Their home will be overrun by snakes, monkeys, lions, insects, and flood waters as the game comes to life. The hauntingly lifelike quality of the drawings is explained in detail in the biographical notes on the book's dust jacket and can add a note of art appreciation to the read-aloud process. Winner of the 1982 Caldecott Medal. Also by the author: *Ben's Dream; The Garden of Abdul Gusazi.* Related books: *Grasshopper and the Unwise Owl* (s); *The Indian in the Cupboard* (n); *The Shrinking of Treehorn* (p).

KATY AND THE BIG SNOW
by Virginia Lee Burton
Houghton Mifflin (both), 1943; 1974
Pre S.–2   40 pages
The modern picture book classic about the brave, untiring tractor whose round-the-clock snowplowing saves the blizzard-bound city of Geoppolis. As much as this is the story of persistence, it is also a lesson in civics as Katy assists the local authorities in pursuing their duties. Also by the author: *The Little House* (p); *Mike Mulligan and His Steam Shovel* (p); *Choo Choo—the Runaway Engine.* Related books: *The Little Engine That Could* (p); *Little Toot* (p).

THE LEATHERMAN
by Dick Gackenbach
Seabury, 1977
Gr. 2–5   48 pages
Based on a true story, this book deals with the role of the eccentric in our communities and how we treat him. It portrays a massive, stone-quiet traveler dressed in leather who passes through a town every thirty-four days and a young child's reaction to him. An excellent book about values. Also by the author: *McGoogan Moves the Mighty Rock.* Related books: *Old Mother Witch* (p); *The Snailman* (n); *A Time for Watching* (s); *Apt. 3* by Ezra Jack Keats (see Index to Treasury for list of his books).

LENTIL
by Robert McCloskey
Viking, 1940; Puffin, 1978
Pre S.–6   56 pages
Unable to sing or whistle a note, Lentil picks up the harmonica one day, charms his hometown, and saves the day when the Welcoming Band is sud-

denly unable to play for the returning hometown hero. Harmonica music and a freshly sliced lemon will make perfect visual aids during the reading. Also by the author: *Blueberries for Sal* (p); *Homer Price* (n); *Make Way for Ducklings* (p); *One Morning in Maine* (p); *Burt Dow, Deep-Water Man.*

LITTLE BEAR
by Else Holmelund Minarik   ·   Illustrated by Maurice Sendak
Harper (both), 1957; 1978
Pre S.–1   54 pages
This series of books uses the simple but important elements of a child's life (clothes, birthdays, playing, and wishing) to weave poignant little stories about a child-bear and his family. The series has won numerous awards and is regarded as a classic in its genre. A former first-grade teacher, the author uses a limited vocabulary at no sacrifice to the flavor of the story. The series, which can be read in any order, includes: *Little Bear; A Kiss for Little Bear; Father Bear Comes Home; Little Bear's Friend; Little Bear's Visit.* Also by the author: *No Fighting, No Biting!* (p). Related books: *Frog and Toad Are Friends* (p); *The Empty Squirrel* by Carol Carrick; *Uncle Elephant* by Arnold Lobel.

THE LITTLE ENGINE THAT COULD
by Watty Piper   ·   Illustrated by George and Doris Hauman
Platt, 1961; Scholastic, 1979
Pre S.–2   36 pages
One of the most famous children's picture books of the twentieth century, this is the 1930 story of the little engine that smiled in the face of an insurmountable task and said, "I'm not very big but I'll do my best, and I think I can–I think I can–I think I can." A lesson in positive thinking, self-image, and persistence. This theme is one of the most recurrent in children's literature and can also be found in the following: *The Carrot Seed* (p); *The Contests at Cowlick* (p); *Katy and the Big Snow* (p); *The Little House* (p); *Little Toot* (p); *The Train* by David McPhail; *There's a Train Going by My Window* by Wendy Kesselman.

THE LITTLE HOUSE
by Virginia Lee Burton
Houghton Mifflin (both), 1942; 1978
Pre S.–3   40 pages
This Caldecott Medal winner uses a little turn-of-the-century country house to show the urbanization of America. With each page, the reader/listener becomes the little house and begins to experience the contentment, wonder, concern, anxiety, and loneliness that the passing seasons and encroaching city bring. Many of today's children who daily experience the anxieties of city life will identify with the little house and her eventual triumph. Great use is made of the passing seasons as a means of describing the passage of time and the text is filled with the repetition of word patterns that provides a poetic tone to the

story. Also by the author: *Katy and the Big Snow* (p); *Mike Mulligan and His Steam Shovel* (p). Related books: *Farewell to Shady Glade* and *Wump World* by Bill Peet (see Index to Treasury for list of his books).

LITTLE TIM AND THE BRAVE SEA CAPTAIN
by Edward Ardizzone
Oxford (both), 1936; 1978
Pre S.-3   48 pages
For more than forty years, Little Tim has enchanted and inspired children on both sides of the Atlantic. Each story provides children with the opportunity to achieve all the heroic tasks they dream about. All the books in the series follow Little Tim and one of his friends on a seafaring adventure filled with peril, during which the child overcomes great odds, and after which returns to the warmth and security of home. They are simple adventure stories—stories that are really impossible anywhere but in these books and in children's imaginations. The Little Tim series also includes: *Lucy Brown and Mr. Grimes; Lucy in Danger; Ship's Cook Ginger; Tim All Alone; Tim and Charlotte; Tim and Ginger; Tim's Friend Towser; Tim's Last Voyage; Tim to the Lighthouse.*

Outside of this series, Ardizzone's other picture books include: *Sarah and Simon and No Red Paint* (p); *Johnny the Clockmaker; The Little Girl and the Tiny Doll; Nicholas and the Fast-Moving Diesel; Paul, the Hero of the Fire; Peter the Wanderer;* and *The Wrong Side of the Bed* (wordless).

LITTLE TOOT
by Hardie Gramatky
Putnam (both), 1939; 1978
Pre S.-1   100 (small) pages
There's no boat in American literary history so familiar to American children as this little tugboat and his growing pains as he waits in the watery shadow of a famous father and grandfather. The series can be read in any order after *Little Toot* and includes: *Little Toot on the Grand Canal; Little Toot on the Mississippi; Little Toot on the Thames; Little Toot Through the Golden Gate.* Related books: *The Little Engine That Could* (p); *The Little House* (p).

LIZA LOU AND THE YELLER BELLY SWAMP
by Mercer Mayer
Four Winds, 1976
Gr. 2-5   48 pages
In a style reminiscent of Brer Rabbit, this book tells of a young black girl's adventures in outwitting ghosts, witches, and monsters while crossing the Yeller Belly Swamp on her way to Gramma's house. Related books: *Household Stories of the Brothers Grimm* (Red Riding Hood) (p); *Madeline* (p); *Do Not Open* by Brinton Turkle.

MADELINE
by Ludwig Bemelmans
Viking, 1939; Puffin, 1977
Pre S.–2   54 pages
This series of five marvelous books is about a daring and irrepressible personality named Madeline and her eleven friends who all live together in a Parisian house. Because of the expressive illustrations and the originality of Madeline, the books are among the favorites of children around the world. The author's use of fast-moving verse, daring adventure, naughtiness, and glowing color keep it a favorite in early grades year after year. The other books in the series are: *Madeline and the Bad Hat; Madeline and the Gypsies; Madeline in London; Madeline's Rescue.* Related books: *Henry the Explorer* (p); *Liza Lou and the Yeller Belly Swamp* (p).

THE MAGGIE B.
by Irene Haas
Atheneum, 1975
Pre S.–4   28 pages
One of the most beautiful books published in the 1970s, this is the story of a young girl's wish upon the North Star. Her wish is to sail on a boat of her own. When she wakes in the morning, she and her baby brother are safely aboard the most wonderful boat, filled to overflowing with food, flowers, coziness, and affection. To open the book's pages is to walk in a child's dream world. Related books: *Emmett's Pig* (p); *The Sweet Touch* (p).

MAKE WAY FOR DUCKLINGS
by Robert McCloskey
Viking, 1941; Puffin, 1976
Pre S.–2   62 pages
In this Caldecott Award-winning classic, we follow Mrs. Mallard and her eight ducklings as they make a traffic-stopping walk across Boston to meet Mr. Mallard on their new island home in the Public Garden. For other books by the author, see Index to Treasury.

MATT'S MITT
by Marilyn Sachs   •   Illustrated by Hilary Knight
Doubleday, 1975
Gr. 2–6   30 pages
The story of a boy who grew up with a magical blue baseball mitt—a glove that brought him fame and fortune. This is especially great reading at World Series time or during the first week of the baseball season. Sequel: *Fleet-footed Florence.*

MAX
by Giovannetti
Atheneum, 1977
Pre S.–2   94 pages

Like any of our senses, a sense of humor must be cultivated if it is to grow and flourish. Picture books have long attended to this need, both in picture and in text. This collection of cartoons about an irrepressible hamster offers a special brand of humor—a Chaplinesque approach, if you will. There are no words or captions, just the episodic strips of Max as his childlike curiosity carries him into battle with the world around him: hairdryers, electric shavers, mirrors, pancake irons, ink pens, leaky ice cream cones, and spaghetti. Max represents the curiosity in all of us, and when we laugh at him we learn to laugh at ourselves as well. Because of the need to see clearly the sequence in these cartoon episodes, it is best to read this book with small groups of four or less. Related books: see Wordless Books.

MAX'S FIRST WORD
by Rosemary Wells
Dial, 1979
Tod.   8 pages

This series of four books is intended to be used by the child as well as read to him or her. For this reason, the books are reinforced and all the pages are laminated to stand up to sticky fingers. Short and colorful, the books deal with those subjects close to all children's hearts: family, toys, clothes, and carriages. The series also includes: *Max's New Suit; Max's Ride; Max's Toys*. Related books: *Pat the Bunny* (p); *Where's Spot?* (p); see Index to Treasury for list of Dick Bruna books.

MICHAEL
by Liesel M. Skorpen • **Illustrated by Joan Sandin**
Harper, 1975
Pre S.–3   42 pages

Michael's forgetfulness and lack of responsibility have come under fire lately from his father. So when his newly adopted baby rabbit is suddenly threatened by an electrical storm one night, he remembers his responsibility and heads out into the storm. The rabbit's box is empty! There is a happy ending, though, with a sensitive portrayal of the father-and-son relationship. Also by the author: *Old Arthur* (p); *Bird; Mandy's Grandmother; Outside My Window*.

MIKE MULLIGAN AND HIS STEAM SHOVEL
by Virginia Lee Burton
Houghton Mifflin (both), 1939; 1977
K–4   42 pages

A modern classic, this is the heartwarming story of the demise of the steam shovel and how one shovel found a permanent home. Also by the author: *Katy and the Big Snow* (p); *The Little House* (p). Related books: *Mike's House* (p), the story of a child who loves the Mike Mulligan book so much he won't take any other from the library; *Old Arthur* (p); *Encore for Eleanor* by Bill Peet.

MIKE'S HOUSE
by Julia Sauer
Viking, 1954
Pre S.–2   28 pages
This is the story of a little boy who wants to read one book exclusively: *Mike Mulligan and His Steam Shovel*. The library, in his mind, becomes "Mike's house" because that's where the book lives. His adventures begin when he becomes lost one day on his way to the library and can only tell the policeman that he's on his way to "Mike's house." Related book: *Mike Mulligan and His Steam Shovel* (p).

MISHKA
by Victor Ambrus
Warne, 1978
Pre S.–1   24 pages
In just 20 sentences and 21 colorful pictures, Victor Ambrus enables us to follow young Mishka's rise from obscure violin student on his grandfather's farm to circus violinist extraordinaire. Winner of the Kate Greenaway Award, England's highest annual award for illustration, *Mishka* squeezes a remarkable amount of action into its short length. Listen afterwards to "The Blue Danube" and "Radetzky March," which Mishka plays during the story. It will make this book more memorable. Related music books: *The Great Green Turkey Creek Monster* (p); *Lentil* (p).

MISS NELSON IS MISSING
by Harry Allard   •   Illustrated by James Marshall
Houghton Mifflin, 1977; Scholastic, 1978
Pre S.– 4   32 pages
Poor, sweet Miss Nelson! Kind and beautiful as she is, she cannot control her classroom—the worst behaved children in the school. But when she is suddenly absent, the children begin to realize what a wonderful teacher they had in Miss Nelson. Her substitute is the wicked-looking, strict Miss Viola Swamp, who works the class incessantly. Wherever has Miss Nelson gone and when will she return? A copy of this book should be in the hand of every elementary-level substitute teacher. Sequel: *Miss Nelson Is Back*. Also by the author: *The Stupids Step Out* (p).

MOTHER GOOSE, A TREASURY OF BEST LOVED RHYMES
Edited by Watty Piper   •   Illustrated by Tim and Greg Hildebrandt
Platt (both), 1972
Tod.–2   66 pages
Of the nearly two dozen nursery rhyme books available today, I have two favorites. Since the rhymes are basically the same in most nursery rhyme vol-

umes, the artwork and format distinguish the best from the rest. Tim and Greg Hildebrandt's large-format presentation places present- and olden-day children in the 102 rhymes amidst brightly colored, easily viewed scenes.

Wallace Tripp's *Granfa' Grig Had a Pig and Other Rhymes Without Reason from Mother Goose* (Little, Brown [both], 1976) is one of the cleverest compilations of Mother Goose rhymes and is aimed at an older age group (K–5). Tripp takes 126 verses, many of which were previously incomprehensible to children, and makes obvious sense out of them by sketching them as situation comedies. All the parts are played by Tripp's inimitable animal characters. Also by the illustrator: *Casey at the Bat* (po); *A Great Big Ugly Man Came Up and Tied His Horse to Me: A Book of Nonsense Verse.* You might also want to read from Joan Walsh Anglund's *In a Pumpkin Shell,* in which she uses Mother Goose rhymes to teach the alphabet.

MY FRIEND MAC
by Mary McNeer • Illustrated by Lynd Ward
Houghton Mifflin, 1960
Gr. 1–3   30 pages
When little Baptiste befriends a young moose, he never dreams of the problems he is inviting upon himself and his family. Also by the author: *Little Baptiste.* Also by the illustrator: *The Biggest Bear* (p); *Nic of the Woods; The Silver Pony* (p). Related book: *Do You Love Me?* (p).

MY GRANDSON LEW
by Charlotte Zolotow • Illustrated by William Pène du Bois
Harper, 1974
K–6   32 pages
This is a celebration of the marvelous gift of memory, which enables us to withstand and heal all kinds of adversity—including the death of a loved one. And as long as we have that memory, the person is never completely gone. (See Index to Treasury for list of Charlotte Zolotow books.) Related books: *The Big Red Barn* (p); *Do You Love Me?* (p); *Stone Fox* (s); *The Tenth Good Thing About Barney* (p); *The Accident* by Carol Carrick.

THE MYSTERIOUS TADPOLE
by Steven Kellogg
Dial (both), 1977; 1979
Pre S.–4   30 pages
When little Louis's uncle in Scotland sent him a tadpole for his birthday, neither of them had any idea how much havoc and fun the pet would cause in Louis's home, classroom, and school swimming pool. The tadpole turns out to be a direct descendant of the Loch Ness Monster (but what a cuddly monster this is!). Don't miss the tucked-away name of the junior high school. Also by the author: *The Island of the Skog* (p).

NOAH'S ARK
by Peter Spier
Doubleday (both), 1977; 1981
Tod. and up   44 pages
Only Peter Spier could find new colors and offer new insights to the timeless story of the Great Flood. For this reason, as much as for his art, Spier won the Caldecott Medal for *Noah's Ark.*

Peter Spier's books have a universal appeal. In helping us find beauty in the commonplace or in simplifying the complex, Spier bridges all ages with a variety of perspectives. The 3-year-old looking at the garage scene in *Bored– Nothing to Do!,* where the boys are building a life-size airplane from house scraps, will enjoy the color and fun in the boys' task while a fifth-grade child will see the same page as a dream come true and appreciate the magnitude of the task.

Spier books for all ages: *Bored–Nothing to Do!; Noah's Ark; People; Peter Spier's Christmas; Peter Spier's Rain.*

For toddlers through kindergarten: *Crash! Bang! Boom!; Fast-Slow, High-Low; Gobble, Growl, Grunt.*

Gr. 1–5: *The Cow Who Fell in the Canal* (by Phyllis Krasilovsky); *Erie Canal; Fox Went Out on a Chilly Night; London Bridge Is Falling Down; Oh, Were They Ever Happy; The Star-Spangled Banner.* Because of the minute details of his illustrations, the Spier books are best read to small groups where the art can be appreciated close up.

NOBODY LISTENS TO ANDREW
by Elizabeth Guilfoile
Follett, 1957; Scholastic, 1973
Pre S.–2   28 pages
Knowing what it is like to be ignored by adults, children quickly recognize themselves in this tale of a child who finds an escaped bear in his bed but can't get anyone to listen to his plight. Related book: *Don't Forget the Bacon* (p).

NOBODY STOLE THE PIE
by Sonia Levitin   •   Illustrated by Fernando Krahn
Harcourt (both), 1980
K–5   26 pages
Baking a giant pie in the square is an annual village custom, and working together on the task, the villagers learn that every little bit helps. But one year, after the pie is baked and awaits the evening's festivities, one little nibble leads to another and the villagers learn the hard way that every bit (and bite) *hurts,* as well. Just the story to serve with blueberry or cherry pie.

NO BOYS ALLOWED
by Susan Terris   •   Illustrated by Richard Cuffari
Doubleday, 1976
K–5   40 pages
An 8-year-old boy experiences "men's lib" when he revolts against his four

older sisters' bossing and takes a dangerous trip downtown to go shopping. Related books: Little Tim series (p); *John John Twilliger* by William Wondriska.

NO FIGHTING, NO BITING!
by Else Holmelund Minarik • Illustrated by Maurice Sendak
Harper (both), 1958; 1978
Pre S.-2   64 pages
When a squabbling little brother and sister can't refrain from their constant rivalry, their babysitting cousin makes a striking comparison when she equates them in her story with a squabbling pair of little alligators. The type is large for early readers and the book is divided into 4 chapters. Also by the author: Little Bear series (p). Related books: *Andrew Henry's Meadow* (p); *The House on East 88th Street* (p).

NORMAN THE DOORMAN
by Don Freeman
Viking, 1959; Puffin, 1981
K-3   64 pages
One of the most popular picture books since the late 1950s, this is the tale of Norman, the mouse who sets himself up as a uniformed doorman for visiting mice at the Museum of Art. Norman's adventures inside and the sculpture contest he wins are a wonderful introduction for children to the world of museums. Also by the author: *Corduroy* (p); *Beady Bear; The Night the Lights Went Out; A Pocket for Corduroy.* Related book: *The Island of the Skog* (p).

OBADIAH, THE BOLD
by Brinton Turkle
Viking, 1965; Puffin, 1977
Gr. 1-3   32 pages
This series consists of four books about a 6-year-old boy and his family on colonial Nantucket Island. The adventures deal with friendship, honesty, and bravery while weaving a subtle history lesson. The other three titles are: *The Adventures of Obadiah; Rachel and Obadiah; Thy Friend, Obadiah.* Also by the author: *Deep in the Forest* (wordless); *Do Not Open; Fiddler on High Lonesome; It's Only Arnold;* and the following seasonal books: *Over the River and Through the Wood* (Thanksgiving); *The Elves and the Shoemaker* (Christmas).

OLD ARTHUR
by Liesel M. Skorpen • Illustrated by Wallace Tripp
Harper, 1972
K-5   46 pages
Perhaps because children relate so quickly to animals and because the question of aging is so foreign to children, the author has chosen a dog to carry her

sensitive message on aging to children. Too old to keep the weasels out of the hen house and too slow to hunt rabbits, Old Arthur is about to be put out of his misery when he wanders off into the hands of the dogcatcher. In the animal shelter, Old Arthur is continually passed over for being "too old," until the day someone comes looking, not for a puppy, not for a watchdog, but for a dog who looks you right in the eye and wags his tail, who likes to have his tummy rubbed and will wait long hours for the school bus to come home. That day Old Arthur finds a new home. Related books: *Hurry Home, Candy* (n); *Encore for Eleanor* by Bill Peet (see Index to Treasury for list of his books).

OLD MOTHER WITCH
by Carol and Donald Carrick
Seabury, 1975
Gr. 1–6 32 pages
A group of boys out trick-or-treating on Halloween decide to tease the cranky old woman who lives on their street—only to find a frightening surprise waiting for them. The old woman has suffered a heart attack and is lying unconscious on the porch. A young boy's brush with near tragedy and the sobering effect it has upon him will reach all children, inspiring a new sensitivity to the elderly in their neighborhoods. Also by the authors: *Sleep Out* and sequels (p). Related books: *Old Arthur* (p); *The Snailman* (n); *A Time for Watching* (s).

ONE MORNING IN MAINE
by Robert McCloskey
Viking, 1952; Puffin, 1976
K–5 64 pages
Focusing on a young girl and her family, McCloskey describes the minute-by-minute events that add up to a celebration of family life. From the thrill of a first loose tooth to the shock of losing it in the mud, from the warmth of helping baby sister brush her teeth to the thrill of rowing across the deep harbor with Daddy. For other books by the author, see Index to Treasury. Related books: *The Bear's Toothache* (p); *The Stories Julian Tells* (s).

PAT THE BUNNY
by Dorothy Kunhardt
Golden, 1962
Tod. 18 pages
This book is intended to actively involve the child's senses—patting a bunny picture that has a piece of furry material attached to it; smelling a scented flower picture; lifting a cloth flap on the page to play peek-a-boo with the boy beneath; turning the pages of the tiny book glued to one of the pages. This is a popular and important favorite of very young children. Related books: *Mother Goose Rhymes* (p); *Where's Spot?* (p); see Index to Treasury for list of Dick Bruna books.

PENNY CANDY
by Edward Fenton • Illustrated by Edward Gorey
Holt, 1970 (OP)
Gr. 1-5   48 pages
This is the perfect story to read on the last day of school, since it takes place on such a day; or, almost as good, on Halloween. The plot centers on first-grader Paul, the runt of the neighborhood, who finds a nickel and offers to treat his friends to candy. Since it is his money, he reserves the right to spend it where he pleases. His choice is the dilapidated shop of the mysterious Widow Shinn, whose reputation as a witch has haunted the children of the town for ages. In an effort to prove his courage, Paul leads the reluctant throng into the shop where an unusual piece of penny candy awaits each of them. A special treat with this reading is to have penny candy available—particularly the kind that comes on long strips of paper dotted with tiny pieces of sugar. Related books: *The Chocolate Touch* (s); *The Sweet Touch* (p).

THE POKY LITTLE PUPPY
by Janette S. Lowrey • Illustrated by Gustaf Tenggren
Golden, 1942
Tod.-K   24 pages
One of the all-time best sellers in the Golden Books mass-market line (forty-three-printings through 1979), here is the puppy-dog version of *Peter Rabbit*. The puppy keeps tripping over his curiosity and ends up late or left out of the dessert line at home. Sequels: *The Poky Little Puppy Follows His Nose Home; Poky Little Puppy's First Christmas*. Related books: *The Tale of Peter Rabbit* (p); see Index to Treasury for list of Dick Bruna books.

PRINCE OF THE DOLOMITES
by Tomie de Paola
Harcourt (both), 1980
Gr. 1-5   44 pages
Using the old village storyteller as his narrator, the author recounts the Italian folktale of a young prince who falls in love with a princess from the moon. In today's age of spirited science fiction, the story is far more plausible than centuries ago and de Paola's soft watercolors bring even more life to the story. A longer than usual text for a folktale and a suspenseful plot make this an excellent vehicle for lengthening children's attention spans. Also by the author: *The Clown of God; Four Scary Stories; Francis the Poor Man of Assisi; The Hunter and the Animals* (wordless); *The Lady of Guadalupe; The Legend of Old Befana; Nana Upstairs and Nana Downstairs; Now One Foot, Now the Other; Pancakes for Breakfast; Strega Nona*. Illustrated by the author: *The Night Before Christmas* (po).

REGARDS TO THE MAN IN THE MOON
by Ezra Jack Keats
Four Winds, 1981
Tod.-3   32 pages

When the neighborhood children tease Louie about the junk in his backyard, his father shows him how a little imagination can convert that rubbish into a spaceship that will take him to the farthest galaxies. The next day, Louie and his friend Susie hurtle through space in their glorified washtub and discover that not even gravity can hold back a child's imagination. Related books: *The Aminal* (p); *How I Hunted the Little Fellows* (p); *You Ought to See Herbert's House* (p); for older readers, *R, My Name Is Rosie* (n); and *Wingman* (s); *And to Think That I Saw It on Mulberry Street* by Dr. Seuss; *Bored—Nothing to Do!* by Peter Spier.

Children experiencing the joys and discoveries of early childhood will find themselves cast as the central characters in Ezra Jack Keats's books. The settings for his stories are largely inner-city but the emotions are those of all children in all settings: the pride of learning how to whistle, the excitement of outwitting older children, the warmth that comes in helping a neighbor. As an author or illustrator, Keats has few peers. His works also include: *Apt. 3; Goggles; Hi, Cat; Jenny's Hat; John Henry; A Letter to Amy; Louie; Maggie and the Pirates; Peter's Chair; Pet Show; The Snowy Day; The Trip; Whistle for Willie.*

SAM, BANGS AND MOONSHINE
by Evaline Ness
Holt (both), 1966; 1973
Gr. 1-4   34 pages

A fisherman's young daughter uses her imagination to send her neighbor on a wild-goose chase that almost ends in tragedy. When do daydreams and make-believe become lies? A touching lesson on the thin line between fantasy and reality. Related books: *The Aminal* (p); *How I Hunted the Little Fellows* (p); *You Ought to See Herbert's House* (p).

SARAH AND SIMON AND NO RED PAINT
by Edward Ardizzone
Delacorte, 1965 (OP)
Pre S.-4   48 pages

A disinherited artist and his family are portrayed as they valiantly struggle to survive on his meager sales. Finally there are no more sales, the money runs out, there is not even enough money to buy paint. Sadly, the children sit discussing their woes in a dark corner of their favorite haunt—an old secondhand book store. They are unaware of an eavesdropper on the other side of the shelves, a man who could change their lives immediately if he were so moved. A dramatic and touching tale. Also by the author: Little Tim series (p).

SARAH'S UNICORN
by Bruce and Katherine Coville
Lippincott, 1979
K–2   48 pages
Deep in the forest, Sarah lives happily with her Aunt Meg until the day a spell changes kind-hearted Aunt Meg into cruel-hearted Aunt Meg. Gathering spiders and toads for her aunt one day, Sarah meets a beautiful unicorn that brings sunshine into her life again. Also by the authors: *The Foolish Giant*.

THE SECRET BIRTHDAY MESSAGE
by Eric Carle
Crowell, 1972
Pre S.–2   26 pages
On the night before his birthday, Tim finds a secret message under his pillow, advising him where to find his birthday present. The message leads Tim and the reader through caves, tunnels, and holes. The use of cutout pages to fit the shape of the holes, steps, doors, and caves makes it an exciting journey all the way. Also by the author: *The Very Hungry Caterpillar* (p).

THE SHRINKING OF TREEHORN
by Florence Parry Heide   •   Illustrated by Edward Gorey
Holiday House, 1971; Dell, 1980
Gr. 4–8   60 pages
When a young boy mentions to his social-climbing parents that he's begun to shrink, he's ignored. When he calls it to the attention of his teachers, his words fall on deaf ears. Day by day he grows smaller and day by day the adults continue to talk around him and his problem. Finally he must solve it himself. All children will recognize themselves here, but various age levels will bring different senses of humor and sympathy to the tale. Sequel: *Treehorn's Treasure*. Also by the author: *Giants Are Very Brave People*. Related books: *The Indian in the Cupboard* (n); *Jumanji* (p); *The Magic Finger* (s).

THE SILVER PONY
by Lynd Ward
Houghton Mifflin, 1973
Pre S.–4   176 pages
The classic wordless book, this is the heartwarming story of a lonely farm boy and the flights of fancy he uses to escape his isolation. His imaginative trips take place on a winged pony and carry him to distant parts of the world to aid and comfort other lonely children. Also by the author: *The Biggest Bear* (p); *Nic of the Woods*. Illustrated by the author: *My Friend Mac* (p). Related books: *Henry the Explorer* (p); *The Maggie B.* (p); *Regards to the Man in the Moon* (p); *Up and Up* (p).

SLEEP OUT
by Carol Carrick • Illustrated by Donald Carrick
Seabury (both), 1973, 1982
K-5 30 pages
Christopher and his dog achieve that one great triumph that all children dream of accomplishing: they sleep out alone in the woods one night. This is the first in a series of six books about Christopher and his family. While the books can be enjoyed separately, they work best when read in sequence after *Sleep Out: Lost in the Storm*—Christopher searches for his lost dog after a long night's storm; *The Accident*—Christopher must come to terms with his grief after his dog is killed; *The Foundling*—Christopher adjusts to the idea of starting life anew after the dog's death; *The Washout*—Christopher and his new dog, Ben, rescue Christopher's stranded mother after a storm; *Ben and the Porcupine*—Christopher and his dog confront a neighborhood nuisance.

Other Carrick books involving children include: *Old Mother Witch* (p); *The Climb; The Empty Squirrel; Harald and the Giant Knight; The Highest Balloon on the Common; Paul's Christmas Birthday; A Rabbit for Easter.*

The Carricks also have collaborated on a series of nature picture books for children: *Beach Bird; The Blue Lobster; The Brook; The Clearing in the Forest; The Crocodiles Still Wait; The Dirt Road; Octopus; The Pond; Sand Tiger Shark; The Tree.*

THE SNOWMAN
by Raymond Briggs
Random, 1978
Pre S. and up 30 pages
In this wordless book, a backyard snowman comes to life one night and is brought into a young boy's home. While the child's parents slumber, the boy introduces his visitor to all the comforts and joys of his home—running water, electricity, fireplace and stove, refrigerator and ice cubes, clothes closets, and even a candlelit dinner. The snowman reciprocates with a flying trip around the world before the dawn's heat ends their "dream" relationship. A poignant story illustrated with more than 150 pictures. Also by the author: *Jim and the Beanstalk.* Related books: *Katy and the Big Snow* (p); *The Little House* (p); and *The Snowy Day* by Ezra Jack Keats (see Index to Treasury); *Over and Over* by Charlotte Zolotow (see Index to Treasury).

SNUFFY
by Dick Bruna
Methuen, 1975
Tod.-Pre. S. 24 (small) pages
After Mother Goose, one of Dick Bruna's books should be the next read-aloud for infants and toddlers, even preschoolers who are being introduced to books or read aloud to for the first time. These books also make excellent first readers for children just learning to read. *Snuffy* is typical of Bruna's style: a little dog

canvasses the neighborhood until he finds a neighbor's lost little girl. Simple drawings, bright colors, easily discernible emotions in an uncomplicated story are the ingredients of Bruna's books, which have sold almost 20 million copies across the world. Among his more than thirty titles are: *Animal Book; The Apple; The Christmas Book; Circus; The Egg; The Fish; I Can Count; I Can Count More; I Can Dress Myself; I Can Read; I Can Read More; I Can Read Difficult Words; The King; I Know About Numbers; Lisa and Lynn; The Little Bird; Miffy; Miffy at the Beach; Miffy at the Playground; Miffy at the Zoo; Miffy Goes Flying; Miffy in the Hospital; Miffy in the Snow; Miffy's Birthday; Miffy's Dream; The Sailor; The School; Snuffy and the Fire; When I'm Big.*

A SPECIAL TRICK
by Mercer Mayer
Dial (both), 1970; 1976
Pre S.–5   32 pages
When the magician's houseboy discovers a dictionary of magic spells while he is dusting one day, he can't resist trying his hand at the art. Before he can say, "Sprittle sprattle, nattle tattle," the room is overrun with slithering tooth-gnashing monsters. Fortunately, little Elroy's spunk is up to the challenge. A story told with great color, imagination, and humor. Related books: *The Contests at Cowlick* (p); *The Sweet Touch* (p); *That Terrible Halloween Night* (p); *Where the Wild Things Are* (p); *Do Not Open* by Brinton Turkle; *Pandora's Box* by Paul Galdone.

One of today's most talented and prolific author-artists, Mercer Mayer's books run from simple wordless books to daringly complicated fairy tales. His works are characterized by glowing watercolors and stories with a strong flavor of magic and fantasy.

His wordless books include: *Ah-Choo!; A Boy, a Frog and a Dog* (series); *Bubble, Bubble; Frog Goes to Dinner; Frog on His Own; Frog, Where Are You?; The Great Cat Chase; One Frog Too Many; Two Moral Tales; Two More Moral Tales.*

His picture books for preschoolers to early-elementary grades include: *I Am a Hunter; If I Had; Me and My Flying Machine; There's a Nightmare in My Closet; Terrible Troll; What Do You Do With a Kangaroo?; You're the Scaredy Cat.*

His books for early-elementary to middle-school grades include: *East of the Sun, West of the Moon* (p); *Liza Lou and the Yeller Belly Swamp* (p); *Mrs. Beggs and the Wizard.*

In addition, Mayer has been the illustrator for these books written by others: *Beauty and the Beast* (by Marianna Mayer); *Boy, Was I Mad* (by Kathryn Hitte); *The Crack in the Wall and Other Terrible Weird Tales* (by George Mendoza); *Everyone Knows What a Dragon Looks Like* (by Jay Williams); *Good-Bye Kitchen* (by Mildred Kantrowitz); *Outside My Window* (by Liesel M. Skorpen); *A Reward Worth Having* (by Jay Williams).

Many of Mayer's books are available in both hardcover and paperback.

STAR MOTHER'S YOUNGEST CHILD
by Louise Moeri • Illustrated by Trina Schart Hyman
Houghton Mifflin (both), 1975; 1980
Gr. 4-6   44 pages
A short Christmas fantasy about a reclusive old woman living at the edge of
the forest and a young star in the heavens. The star visits her in the form of an
ugly child on Christmas Eve and together they build a warmth that will last in
children's minds for a long time. Related books: *A Certain Small Shepherd* (s);
The Giving Tree (p); *The Leatherman* (p); *Apt. 3* by Ezra Jack Keats (see Index
to Treasury).

THE STORY OF FERDINAND
by Munro Leaf • Illustrated by Robert Lawson
Viking, 1936; Puffin, 1977
Pre S.-2   68 pages
This world-famous tale of a great Spanish bull who preferred sitting peacefully
among the flowers to fighting gloriously in the bullring is one of early childhood's classics. It is illustrated by Robert Lawson in a simple black and white
style that further enhances children's comprehension of the story about one of
the world's most famous pacifists. Related books: *The Country Bunny and the
Little Gold Shoes* (p); *Ira Sleeps Over* (p); *No Boys Allowed* (p); *William's Doll*
(p); *Oliver Button Is a Sissy* by Tomie de Paola.

THE STUPIDS STEP OUT
by Harry Allard • Illustrated by James Marshall
Houghton Mifflin (both), 1974; 1977
Gr. 1-4   30 pages
The title alone is enough to intrigue children, and the pictures and text will
more than live up to their expectations. The family of Stanley Q. Stupid is
aptly named: when their behavior isn't stupid, it is at the very least silly—and
children will love them. Because of the need to explore the pictures carefully in
search of the humor, small groups are best suited for this read-aloud. Sequels:
The Stupids Die; The Stupids Have a Ball. See also: *Miss Nelson Is Missing* (p).
Related book: *Amelia Bedelia* (p).

THE SWEET TOUCH
by Lorna Balian
Abingdon, 1976
K-5   40 pages
A delightful book about a little girl with a sweet tooth. A plastic ring from
the gumball machine produces a genie who turns everything the child touches
into candy: crayons into candy sticks; her mattress into marshmallow; her
quilt into taffy. It all turns into a mess that will enchant children—and maybe
help cure a sweet tooth or two. Also by the author: *The Aminal* (p). Related

books: *Chocolate Fever* (s); *The Chocolate Touch* (n); *Nobody Stole the Pie* (p); *Penny Candy* (p).

SYLVESTER AND THE MAGIC PEBBLE
by William Steig
Simon & Schuster, 1969; Windmill, 1969
Pre S.–4   30 pages
In this contemporary fairy tale that won the Caldecott Medal, young Sylvester finds a magic pebble that will grant his every wish as long as he holds it in his hand. When a hungry lion approaches, Sylvester wishes himself into a stone. Since stones don't have hands with which to hold pebbles, the pebble drops to the ground and he cannot reach it to wish himself normal again. The subsequent loneliness of Sylvester and his parents is portrayed with deep sensitivity, making all the more real their joy a year later when they are happily reunited. Also by the author: *The Amazing Bone* (p); *The Real Thief* (s). Related books: *The Chocolate Touch* (n); *The Maggie B.* (p); *The Sweet Touch* (p); *The Wingdingdilly* (p); *Don't Ever Wish for a Seven-Foot Bear* by Robert Benton; *The Golden Touch* by Paul Galdone.

TAKE IT OR LEAVE IT
by Osmond Molarsky • Illustrated by Trina Schart Hyman
Scholastic (paperback only), 1980
K–3   64 pages
Chester is the neighborhood's star "swapper." He spends many of his waking moments swapping possessions with his friends, sometimes getting the better of the deal, sometimes not. The story allows us to follow Chester through a typical swapping day in the inner city. Not only will children delight in his shrewd dealing, they'll want to do a little swapping themselves. Related books: *The Sweet Touch* (p); *The Wingdingdilly* (p).

THE TALE OF PETER RABBIT
by Beatrix Potter
Warne, 1902; Dover, 1972
Pre S.–1   58 (small) pages
One of the most famous animal stories of all time, this is the tale of a disobedient rabbit and the consequences he suffers. Children identify with his naughtiness and his sense of adventure, and thrill at his narrow escape from the clutches of the famous Mr. McGregor. All of the author's books are produced in a small format, which makes them particularly attractive for a young child but makes their use somewhat difficult for large groups of children. Nevertheless, Potter's stories are so strong they can carry themselves without pictures, if need be. Among the author's simpler stories: *The Story of a Fierce Bad Rabbit; The Tale of Benjamin Bunny; The Tale of the Flopsy Bunnies; The Tale of Tom Kitten; The Tale of Two Bad Mice.* Her more complicated tales

include: *The Tale of Jemima Puddle-Duck; The Tale of Johnny Town-Mouse; The Tale of Mrs. Tittlemouse.*

THE TENTH GOOD THING ABOUT BARNEY
by Judith Viorst • Illustrated by Erik Blegvad
Atheneum (both), 1971; 1975
K–6   26 pages

One of the simplest and most sensitive treatments of death in modern children's literature. A child and his parents work to cope with the child's sense of loss with the death of his cat, Barney. The boy makes a list of good things about Barney, a list that takes his mind off his grief, a list that becomes a tribute to a devoted friend. This is an affectionate but down-to-earth approach. Related books: *The Big Red Barn* (p); *Do You Love Me?* (p); for older children, *A Taste of Blackberries* (s).

THAT TERRIBLE HALLOWEEN NIGHT
by James Stevenson
Greenwillow, 1980
Pre S.–4   32 pages

When his grandchildren's attempts to frighten him prove fruitless, grandfather explains why: Nothing, he says, could surpass that terrible Halloween night when, as a little child, he approached the haunted house in his neighborhood. He goes on to describe a spooky, event-filled night—with much tongue-in-cheek. Also by the author: *Wilfred the Rat* (p); *Could Be Worse; Howard; The Night After Christmas.* Related book: *Old Mother Witch* (p).

THE THREE LITTLE PIGS
by Paul Galdone
Seabury, 1970; Scholastic, 1970
Tod.–1   36 pages

The classic tale of how the clever and industrious member of the pig family outwitted the wicked wolf. Many of the simpler folktales of Joseph Jacobs, the Brothers Grimm, and Hans Christian Andersen have been made into picture books by author-illustrator Paul Galdone. His versions are not meant as replacements for the originals but merely as introductions to the fairy tale for very young children. Between first and second grades, the child's maturity and listening span should be developed enough to warrant longer, more complicated tales. (See Chapter 3 for a discussion of fairy tales.) Galdone's most popular books include: *Androcles and the Lion; The Bremen Town Musicians; Cinderella; The Frog Prince; The Gingerbread Boy; The Golden Touch; Henny Penny; The House That Jack Built; The Hungry Fox and the Foxy Duck; Little Red Riding Hood; Old Mother Hubbard and Her Dog; Pandora's Box; The Princess and the Pea; Puss in Boots; The Steadfast Tin Soldier; Three Aesop Fox Fables; The*

Three Bears; and *Three Billy Goats Gruff.* Related book: *The Fairy Tale Treasury* (a).

TIKKI TIKKI TEMBO
by Arlene Mosel • Illustrated by Blair Lent
Holt, 1968; Scholastic, 1972
Pre S.–3   40 pages
This little picture book tells the amusing legend of how the Chinese people changed from giving their first-born sons enormously long first names and began giving all children short names. Related book: *Everyone Knows What a Dragon Looks Like* by Jay Williams.

TINTIN IN TIBET
by Hergé
Little, Brown, (paperback only), 1975
Gr. 2–4   62 pages
When you've been in print for fifty years, been translated into twenty-two languages and praised in *The Times* of London and New York, you must be special. Tintin is just that. He's the boy-detective who hopscotches the globe in pursuit of thieves and smugglers. Loaded with humor, adventure, and marvelous artwork (700 pictures in each issue), Tintin's special appeal for parents who want to assist their child in reading is the fact that each Tintin contains more than 8,000 words. Having heard Tintin read aloud, children will want to obtain his other adventures and read them by themselves, oblivious to the fact that they are reading 8,000 words in the process. Because of the size of the pictures, Tintin is best read aloud to no more than two children at a time. There are more than twenty different adventures in the series, sold primarily in select bookstores. The Tintin series also includes: *The Black Island; The Broken Ear; The Calculus Affair; The Castafiore Emerald; Cigars of the Pharaohs; The Crab with the Golden Claws; Destination Moon; Explorers on the Moon; Flight 714; King Ottokar's Sceptre; Land of Black Gold; Prisoners of the Sun; Red Rackham's Treasure; The Red Sea Sharks; The Secret of the Unicorn; The Seven Crystal Balls; The Shooting Star; Tintin and the Picaros.* Related book: *The Adventures of the Black Hand Gang* by Hans Jürgen Press.

TONY'S HARD WORK DAY
by Alan Arkin • Illustrated by James Stevenson
Harper, 1972
Pre S.–2   32 pages
All children dream of building their own nest—be it a fort, hut, castle, or treehouse. They will identify immediately with Tony and his achievement—as fantastic as it might seem. When his family refuses to allow him to help in the renovation of their new home, he sets out to build his own. He digs a cellar, chops down hundreds of trees for the walls, seals the roof with mud and leaves,

and builds a gigantic chimney with thousands of rocks. His family's reaction is the same as your audience's will be. A marvelous opportunity for discussions on work, dreams, and initiative. Related books: *Andrew Henry's Meadow* (p); *Henry the Explorer* and sequels (p); *No Boys Allowed* (p); *Sleep Out* (p).

UP AND UP
by Shirley Hughes
Prentice-Hall, 1979
Pre S.-2   28 pages
In 129 pictures, and without using a single word, Shirley Hughes describes the timeless quest of humanity to fly. A young girl hopelessly pursues her dream of flying until the day she tastes a magic egg. Over the next 28 pages we follow her incredible flight—through her mother's kitchen, past the windows of startled neighbors and classmates, and over the entire village. This is a book that ranks with *The Silver Pony* (p) and *Noah's Ark* (p) in leading the wordless-book field. Also by the author: *Alfie Gets in First; David and Dog; Haunted House; A Throne for Sesame.* Related books: *Bored—Nothing to Do!* by Peter Spier; *Me and My Flying Machine* by Mercer Mayer; see Wordless Books.

THE VERY HUNGRY CATERPILLAR
by Eric Carle
Collins, 1969
Tod.-1   38 pages
What an ingenious book! It is, at the same time, a simple, lovely way to teach a child the days of the week, how to count to five, and how a caterpillar becomes a butterfly. First, this is a book to look at—bright, bright pictures. Then it is something whose pages beg to be turned—pages that have little round holes in them made by the hungry little caterpillar. And as the number of holes grow, so does the caterpillar.

In a slightly more complicated book, *The Grouchy Ladybug,* Carle uses pages in odd sizes to show the passage of time and the growth in size of the ladybug's adversaries. In the middle of it all there's a nice little science lesson. Also by the author: *The Secret Birthday Message* (p).

WHERE'S SPOT?
by Eric Hill
Putnam, 1980
Tod.-2   20 pages
In looking for her missing puppy, Spot's mother searches every corner and niche of the house. As she peeks into closets and pianos, under beds and rugs, the reader and listeners can imitate her search by lifting page flaps to find an assortment of animals in hiding. The flaps are reinforced and the pages durable enough to be handled by young children. The book is an entertaining introduction to household names, animals, and the concept of "No." Sequels: *Spot's*

Birthday Party; Spot's First Walk. Related books: for toddlers, *Pat the Bunny* (p); *The Secret Birthday Message* (p); for preschool and up, *The Very Hungry Caterpillar* (p).

WHERE THE WILD THINGS ARE
by Maurice Sendak
Harper, 1963; Scholastic, 1969
K–3 28 pages
This is the picture book that changed the course of modern children's literature. Sendak creates here a fantasy about a little boy and the monsters that haunt all children. The fact that youngsters are not the least bit frightened by the story, that they love it as they would an old friend, is a credit to Sendak's insight into children's minds and hearts. It was the 1964 winner of the Caldecott Medal. Also by the author: *Higglety Pigglety Pop!; In the Night Kitchen; Maurice Sendak's Really Rosie: Starring the Nutshell Kids;* the Nutshell Library, which includes *Alligators All Around, Chicken Soup with Rice, One Was Johnny, Outside Over There, The Sign on Rosie's Door.* Related books: *The Bear's Toothache* (p); *Harry and the Terrible Whatzit* (p); *The Beast in the Bed* by Barbara Dillon; *Do Not Open* by Brinton Turkle; *There's a Nightmare in My Closet* by Mercer Mayer.

WILFRED THE RAT
by James Stevenson
Greenwillow, 1977; Puffin, 1979
Pre S.–4 30 pages
Quite simply, this is a story about friendship—its joys and sorrows, the crying need in all of us for companionship and affection. Also by the author: *That Terrible Halloween Night* (p); *The Night After Christmas.* Related books: *Dexter* (s); *Frog and Toad Are Friends* (p); *The Giving Tree* (p).

WILLIAM'S DOLL
by Charlotte Zolotow • Illustrated by William Pène du Bois
Harper, 1972
Pre S.–4 32 pages
William's father wants him to play with his basketball or trains; William, to the astonishment of all, wishes he had a doll to play with. "Sissy," say his brother and friends. But William's grandmother says something else—something very important—to William, his father, and his brother. The message is one that all children and their parents should hear. Related books: *The Story of Ferdinand* (p); *Lafcadio, the Lion Who Shot Back* (s); *Oliver Button Is a Sissy* by Tomie de Paola.

One of the most prolific (more than fifty books since 1944) and successful authors for children, Charlotte Zolotow is also one of the most beloved. She writes quiet little books with quiet simple sentences and her work is always illustrated by the best artists available. Few writers have their finger on the pulse of children's emotions as this author does. You'll have no trouble finding the many Zolotow books in your library—she has almost the entire "Z" shelf to herself. Your personal knowledge of your child's or class's emotional maturity should guide you in your Zolotow selections.

Here is a partial listing of her most popular read-alouds: *Big Sister and Little Sister* (siblings); *Do You Know What I'll Do?* (siblings); *A Father Like That* (fatherless boy); *The Hating Book* (anger, friendship); *Hold My Hand* (friendship); *If It Weren't For You* (siblings); *If You Listen* (loneliness); *It's Not Fair* (envy); *Janey* (friend moves away); *May I Visit?* (family, future); *Mr. Rabbit and the Lovely Present* (sharing); *My Friend John* (friendship); *My Grandson Lew* (death); *Over and Over* (seasons, time); *The Quarreling Book* (family friction); *The Sky Was Blue* (family genealogy); *Someone New* (maturing); *The Storm Book* (electrical storms); *The Summer Night* (bedtime, family); *The Unfriendly Book* (jealousy); *Wake Up and Goodnight* (bedtime); *When the Wind Stops* (environmental questions); *The White Marble* (sharing, friendship).

THE WINGDINGDILLY
by Bill Peet
Houghton Mifflin (both), 1970; 1982
Pre S.–5   60 pages
Discontented with his life as a dog, Scamp envies all the attention given to his beribboned neighbor—Palomar the wonder horse. But when a backwoods witch changes Scamp into an animal with the feet of an elephant, the neck of a giraffe, the tail of a zebra, and the nose of a rhinoceros, he gets more attention than he bargained for: he ends up a most unhappy circus freak. Happily, all ends well, and tied into the ending is a subtle lesson for both Scamp and his readers: Be yourself! Related books: *The Bad Times of Irma Baumlein* (n); *Lafcadio, the Lion Who Shot Back* (s); *William's Doll* (p).

Bill Peet is one of the most popular of the contemporary author-illustrators and his picture books never fail to instruct, stimulate, and amuse children. Neither the text (often in rhyming verse) nor the art rests in the shadow of the other—they complement each other beautifully. Though never heavy-handed, many of his books have a fablelike quality. Two of his works—*Wump World* and *Farewell to Shady Glade*—were among the first children's books to call attention to the environmental crises during the 1960s. A sampling of his various themes includes: ambition *(Chester the Worldly Pig)*; arrogance *(Big Bad Bruce)*; aging *(Encore for Eleanor)*; conceit *(Ella)*; courage *(Cowardly Clyde)*; environment *(The Knats of Knotty Pine)*; hope *(The Caboose Who Got Loose)*; loyalty *(Jennifer and Josephine)*; mechanization *(Countdown to Christmas)*; peer pressure *(Fly Homer Fly)*; selfishness *(The Ant and the Elephant)*; timidity *(Merle the High-Flying Squirrel)*.

Other Bill Peet, titles include: *Buford the Little Bighorn; Capyboppy* (short novel); *Cyrus the Unsinkable Sea Serpent; Eli; How Droofus the Dragon Lost His*

Head; Hubert's Hair-Raising Adventure; Huge Harold; Kermit the Hermit; The Luckiest One of All; The Pinkish Purplish Bluish Egg; Randy's Dandy Lions; Smokey; The Spooky Tail of Prewitt Peacock.

Bill Peet fans will also enjoy the Dr. Seuss books; see Index to Treasury. Almost half of Peet's books are available in paperback.

THE WISH AT THE TOP
by Clyde Robert Bulla • Illustrated by Chris Conover
Crowell, 1974
Gr. 1-5   32 pages
In the Middle Ages, a tiny village barricades itself behind high walls to avoid the evil bandit who roams the hillsides. In this village, the wife of a poor blacksmith carries a heavy burden in her heart: for ten years the threat of the outlaw band has prevented her from seeing her parents. One day when her son hears the legend that whoever rubs the top of the church steeple will receive any wish of his choosing, he conceives of a plot to help his mother. A dramatic and spellbinding tale. Also by the author: *Dexter* (s); *Shoeshine Girl* (s); *A Lion to Guard Us; The Moon Singer.* Related books: *Dick Whittington and His Cat* (p); for older children, *Otto of the Silver Hand* (n); *Robin Hood* (n); *Search for Delicious* (n); *Stone Fox* (s).

WOLFIE
by Janet Cheney • Illustrated by Marc Simont
Harper, 1969
K-2   64 pages
Wolfie is a wolf spider, safely captured in Harry's box. He's the pride of Harry and George's clubhouse and the subject of Polly's growing curiosity. Through their combined efforts to keep the spider alive and well fed, the children learn some valuable science lessons about one of childhood's most fascinating nemeses: spiders. The boy-girl clubhouse rivalry, Polly's tenacity, and frequent touches of humor make this an entertaining as well as informative book.

YOU OUGHT TO SEE HERBERT'S HOUSE
by Doris Lund • Illustrated by Steven Kellogg
Franklin Watts, 1973
K-4   28 pages
The old story of "Can you top this?" takes a novel twist when Herbert visits his pal Roger's house. Everything Roger has, Herbert has better at home. Or so he says. Herbert's imagination and bragging get the better of him—until he learns that it's best to face reality and to enjoy what you have. Related books: *The Aminal* (p); *How I Hunted the Little Fellows* (p); *Ira Sleeps Over* (p); *Sam, Bangs and Moonshine* (p); *Take It or Leave It* (p).

Short Novels

AMONG THE DOLLS
by William Sleator
Dutton, 1975
Gr. 4–6   70 pages
A spooky psychological thriller about a girl who receives an old doll house for a birthday present, and finds herself drawn into the house and tormented by the very dolls she'd mistreated the day before. A spellbinder. Also by the author: *Run*. Related books: *The Indian in the Cupboard* (n); *Inside My Feet* (s); *Prisoners at the Kitchen Table* (n); *Against Time* by Roderick Jefferies.

THE BEARS' HOUSE
by Marilyn Sachs
Doubleday, 1971
Gr. 4–6   82 pages
A perfect vehicle for a discussion of values in the classroom, this novel deals with a 10-year-old girl whose mother is ill and can no longer care for the family after the father deserts. The girl decides to tend the family, all the while suffering the taunts of classmates because she sucks her thumb, wears dirty clothes, and smells. To escape, she retreats to the fantasy world she has created in an old doll house in her classroom. The need for greater understanding and patience among classmates is an inherent part of this read-aloud. Related books: *Burnish Me Bright* (s); *The Gumdrop Necklace* (s); *J.T.* (s).

THE BEST CHRISTMAS PAGEANT EVER
by Barbara Robinson
Harper, 1972; Avon, 1973
Gr. 2–6   80 pages
What happens when the worst-behaved family of kids in the town—the ones no mother would think of allowing her kids to play with—comes to Sunday school and muscles into all the parts for the Christmas pageant? The results are zany and heartwarming; a most unusual Christmas story. Related book: *Star Mother's Youngest Child* (p).

BRAVE JIMMY STONE
by Elliott Arnold
Scholastic (paperback only), 1975
Gr. 3–5   92 pages
A young boy and his father are on a hunting trip. A sudden fall breaks the

father's leg and a blinding blizzard almost keeps the child from finding help. A beautiful love story between father and son, as well as a lesson in persistence and courage. The father and mother in the book are on the edge of divorce, living apart, and the hunting incident brings the family back together. Related books: *Ice River* (p); *The Long Journey* (n); *Stone Fox* (s).

BURNISH ME BRIGHT
by Julia Cunningham
Pantheon, 1970; Dell, 1980
Gr. 4-7   80 pages

A once-famous pantomimist, now retired and living on the edge of poverty, meets an orphaned mute boy who yearns to learn the art of mime. The subsequent sharing between man and boy cuts away the loneliness that enshrouded their lives. Filled with living definitions of love, friendship, and courage, it is also an excellent introduction to the art of pantomime. Sequels: *Far in the Day; The Silent Voice.* Related books: *The Cay* (n); *A Certain Small Shepherd* (s); *Child of the Silent Night* (n); *The Half-A-Moon Inn* (s).

CALL IT COURAGE
by Armstrong Sperry
Macmillan (both), 1940; 1971
Gr. 2-6   94 pages

Set in the South Seas before the traders or missionaries arrived, this story describes the struggle of a boy to overcome his fear of the sea. Finally the taunts of his peers drive him into open confrontation with his fears. A Newbery Award–winning study of fear and courage. Related book: *The Cay* (s).

A CERTAIN SMALL SHEPHERD
by Rebecca Caudill • Illustrated by William Pène du Bois
Holt (both), 1965; 1971
Gr. 2-6   48 pages

A mute child, assigned to the role of a shepherd in the school Christmas pageant, is heartbroken when a blizzard cancels the pageant. However, two visitors during the storm stir the depths of the child's soul and bring the story to a dramatic and touching end. Related books: *Burnish Me Bright* (s); *Child of the Silent Night* (n); *The Half-A-Moon Inn* (s).

CHOCOLATE FEVER
by Robert K. Smith
Dell (paperback only), 1978
Gr. 1-5   94 pages

Henry Green is a boy who loves chocolate—he's insane over it. He even has chocolate sprinkles on his cereal and chocolate cake for breakfast. He thus becomes a prime candidate to come down with the world's first case of chocolate fever. Zany but with a subtle message on moderation in our eating habits. Also by the author: *Jelly Belly*. Related books: *The Chocolate Touch* (n); *The Sweet Touch* (p).

DEXTER
by Clyde Robert Bulla
Crowell, 1973
Gr. 2-5   68 pages
One of the best of the author's more than fifty books, this is the story of a promise between two friends—friends who are eventually parted by neighbors and distance but never separated in their hearts. One boy promises to take care of the other's horse until he is able to return. Despite the threats of neighbors and the pains of winter storms, the boy clings to the promise—and to the hope his friend will someday return. Also by the author: *Shoeshine Girl* (s); *The Wish at the Top* (p); *Almost a Hero; Daniel's Duck; A Lion to Guard Us*.

THE FALLEN SPACEMAN
by Lee Harding
Harper, 1980; Bantam, 1982
Gr. 2-5   86 pages
An alien object drops to the earth's surface in view of two young brothers playing in the woods. The Army's efforts to deal with the aliens are complicated when one of the brothers wanders inside the object and encounters an alien child. A dramatic and touching science fiction tale, a rare treat for this age level. Related book: *Science Fiction Tales* (a).

FAMILY SECRETS:
FIVE VERY IMPORTANT STORIES
by Norma Shreve   •   Illustrated by Richard Cuffari
Knopf, 1979
Gr. 3-7   56 pages
Five stories about a boy and his family as they encounter the death of a pet, the suicide of a neighbor, an aging grandparent, a relative's divorce, and cheating in math class. Five fragile moments in a child's life, written with sensitivity, compassion, and hopefulness.

FRECKLE JUICE
by Judy Blume
Four Winds, 1971; Dell, 1971
Gr. 2-5   32 pages
Andrew wishes he had freckles. Everyone else seems to have them. Thus, when his classmate Sharon sells him a recipe for freckles, he quickly swallows it— much to his stomach's dismay. Class rivalries, peer pressure, mixed with many

laughs. Also by the author: *Tales of a Fourth Grade Nothing* and its sequel, *Superfudge*.

GRANDMA DIDN'T WAVE BACK
by Rose Blue
Franklin Watts, 1972; Dell, 1976
Gr. 4–6   62 pages
Touching story of a 10-year-old girl who slowly realizes that her grandmother's memory is deteriorating and that she may have to go to a nursing home. The closeness between the child and the grandparent over the years is beautifully described, making the parting all the more touching. Related books: *Gramp* (see *Luke's Garden and Gramp)* (s); *My Grandson Lew* (p); *Stone Fox* (s); *Now One Foot, Now the Other* by Tomie de Paola.

GRANDMOTHER ORPHAN
by Phyllis Green
Nelson, 1977
Gr. 5–6   76 pages
A tough little girl with a chip on her shoulder is sent to visit her grandmother after being caught shoplifting. But this grandmother is like none you've read about lately—she's a tough-as-nails, truck-driving granny. But her heart is pure marshmallow. Honesty, adoption, and family life are central themes in this tender story. Also by the author: *Ice River* (p); *Wild Violets* (s). Related books: *Luke Was There* (s); *The Pinballs* (n); *Shoeshine Girl* (s).

GRASSHOPPER AND THE UNWISE OWL
by Jim Slater
Holt, 1979
Gr. 1–5   88 pages
Here's a bundle of fascinating science lessons wrapped around the adventures of a young boy who is mistakenly reduced to the size of a mouse. Attempting to save his mother from an unscrupulous landlord, the shrunken child encounters a host of threatening animals and insects, each of whom he converts to his aid by capitalizing on their various natural characteristics. Exciting fantasy-adventure with just the right blend of humor. Related books: *The Chocolate Touch* (s); *The Flight of the Fox* (n); *Hans Andersen—His Classic Fairy Tales* (Thumbelina) (p); *The Indian in the Cupboard* (n); *The Littles* (s); *Mr. Popper's Penguins* (n); *The Shrinking of Treehorn* (p).

THE GUMDROP NECKLACE
by Phyllis LaFarge
Knopf, 1967 (OP)
Gr. 2–5   54 pages
In this remarkably sensitive story, we follow young Jake in his great leap from loneliness to friendship. As we watch him being smothered in spitefulness by a guardian aunt (who runs the neighborhood candy store), we too begin to feel

his desperation as life threatens to pass him by. Finally, there is a ray of hope. Jake, who fears he hasn't a friend in the world, receives his first invitation to a birthday party—from the nicest girl in class. When his aunt refuses to let him earn the money for a gift, Jake desperately reaches into his dreams for a gift. Your listeners will be touched as deeply as his classmate was by his choice. Related book: *Wild Violets* (s).

THE HALF-A-MOON INN
by Paul Fleischman
Harper, 1980; Scholastic, 1982
Gr. 2-6   88 pages
A chilling fantasy-adventure story about a mute boy separated from his mother by a blizzard and later kidnapped by the wicked proprietress of a village inn. Fast-moving, white-knuckle reading. Also by the author: *The Birthday Tree*. Related books: *Among the Dolls* (s); *Burnish Me Bright* (s); *A Certain Small Shepherd* (p); *Child of the Silent Night* (n).

THE HAYBURNERS
by Gene Smith
Delacorte, 1974 (OP)
Gr. 4-6   64 pages
A well-to-do family is influenced by the selflessness of a retarded man they hire to do chores one summer. A touching lesson on the mentally handicapped, a lesson that breaks many of the stereotypes children hold about the mentally ill. Also by the author: *The Visitor* (s). Related book: *Ironhead* (n).

HEART OF ICE
by Benjamin Appel   •   Illustrated by James Lambert
Pantheon, 1977
Gr. 1-6   58 pages
Originally written in France during the 1700s, this is the fairy tale story of a young prince and princess who each have spells placed upon them by wicked fairies in their respective kingdoms. The boy is never allowed to grow to full stature and the girl's heart is imprisoned atop a mountain of ice at the North Pole. Destiny places the boy on a dangerous and thrilling journey which eventually leads to the ice mountain and the princess. The tale is filled with enchantment, bandits, beasts, combat, and triumph—everything one expects from a classic fairy tale. Related books: *The Fairy Tale Treasury* (a); *Hans Andersen—His Classic Fairy Tales* (p); *The Hero from Otherwhere* (n); *Household Stories of the Brothers Grimm* (p).

HELP! I'M A PRISONER IN THE LIBRARY
by Eth Clifford
Houghton Mifflin, 1979; Dell, 1981
Gr. 1-4   106 pages
When their father's car runs out of gas in a blizzard, Mary Rose and Jo-Beth

are told to stay in the car while Dad goes for help. The two sisters, however, soon leave in search of a bathroom and end up mysteriously locked into an empty old stone library. Before long, the lights go out, the phone goes dead, and a threatening voice cries out "Off with their heads!" Dreadful moans emanate from the second floor. The dilemmas are all neatly solved when the girls find an old librarian who has fallen and hurt herself on the second floor. Together, the three of them begin to plan their escape. The author's blend of humor and mystery makes this a super read-aloud. Sequel: *The Dastardly Murder of Dirty Pete.* Related books: *Brave Jimmy Stone* (s); *The Leatherman* (p); *Old Mother Witch* (p); *Day of the Blizzard* by Marietta Moskin.

"HEY, WHAT'S WRONG WITH THIS ONE?"
by Maia Wojciechowska
Harper, 1969
Gr. 3-6   96 pages
The wacky and hilarious adventures of three brothers who tire of their widowed father's reluctance to find a new wife. Taking matters into their own hands, they decide to find one for him. Amid the hilarity, some tender moments. Related books: *Grandmother Orphan* (s); *Ice River* (p).

THE HUNDRED DRESSES
by Eleanor Estes
Harcourt (both), 1944; 1974
Gr. 3-6   78 pages
Wanda Petronski comes from the wrong side of the tracks and is the object of the class jokes until her classmates sadly realize their awful mistake and cruelty. But by then it's too late. Related books: *Call It Courage* (s); *Meaning Well* (s); *Wild Violets* (s).

INSIDE MY FEET: THE STORY OF A GIANT
by Richard Kennedy
Harper, 1979
Gr. 3-5   72 pages
In an age of *Star Wars* and revivals of *King Kong,* it is a rare story that can chill middle-graders, especially a story about a giant. But this tale of a frightened but determined child's battle to rescue his parents from an invisible giant will have children on the edge of their seats. This giant is no pushover—he's mean, conniving, and awesome—yet he carries a heavy heart, burdened with a bitter question: "What became of the child that I was?" Also by the author: *The Contests at Cowlick* (p). Related books: *Among the Dolls* (s); *The Leopard's Tooth* (s); *Nightmares* (po); *The Phantom Fisherboy* by Ruth Ainsworth.

JACOB TWO-TWO MEETS THE HOODED FANG
by Mordecai Richler
Knopf, 1975; Bantam, 1977
Gr. 3-5   84 pages
For the crime of insulting a grownup, Jacob is sent to Children's Prison where

he must confront the infamous Hooded Fang. A marvelous tongue-in-cheek adventure story, sure to delight all. Related books: *Chocolate Fever* (s); *Nightmares* (po).

LAFCADIO, THE LION WHO SHOT BACK
by Shel Silverstein
Harper, 1963
Gr. 2–6   90 pages
Lafcadio decides he isn't satisfied being a lion—he must become a marksman and man-about-town and painter and world traveler and . . . Well, he tries just about everything and anything in hopes of finding happiness. If only he'd try being himself. A witty and thought-provoking book. Also by the author: *The Giving Tree* (p); *Where the Sidewalk Ends* (po); *A Light in the Attic.* Related books: *William's Doll* (p); *The Wingdingdilly* (p).

THE LEOPARD'S TOOTH
by William Kotzwinkle
Houghton Mifflin, 1976; Avon, 1978
Gr. 5–7   96 pages
In the darkest jungles of Africa, a 1911 anthropological expedition shudders under the hex of a native witch doctor. Both the story's readers and characters drift back and forth between believing and disbelieving the jungle magic. There is no doubt, however, in the effectiveness of the author's tale and his ability to bring alive the sights, sounds, and smells of the jungle. A tale of courage and of the unknown, for experienced listeners. Related books: *Among the Dolls* (s); *The Dog Days of Arthur Cane* (n); *Inside My Feet* (s); *Jumanji* (p); *The Wonderful Story of Henry Sugar* (s).

THE LITTLES
by John Peterson
Scholastic (paperback only), 1970
Gr. 1–4   80 pages
Children have always been fascinated with the idea of "little people"—from leprechauns to Lilliputians, from Thumbelina to hobbits. Unfortunately, much of the famous fantasy literature is often too sophisticated for reading aloud to young children. The Littles series is the exception—short novels that provide fast-paced reading. While not great literature, they serve as excellent introductions to the notion of "chapters" in books, and are ideal springboards to more complicated literature.

The series centers on a colony of six-inch people who live inside the walls of the Bigg family's home. Their dramatic escapades with gigantic mice, cats, gliders, and telephones, while keeping their existence a secret, are a stimulant for reading appetites. The Littles are an obvious takeoff on the critically acclaimed Borrowers series. Unfortunately, the latter is too slowly paced and a bit stilted in its dialogue for good reading aloud to this age group.

The Littles series also includes: *The Littles and the Big Storm; The Littles and*

Their Friends (a guidebook to the series, complete with maps and anecdotes); *The Littles and the Trash Tinnies; The Littles Have a Wedding; The Littles' Surprise Party; The Littles to the Rescue; Tom Little's Great Halloween Scare.* Related books: *Hans Andersen—His Classic Fairy Tales* (Thumbelina) (p); *Household Stories of the Brothers Grimm* (Tom Thumb) (p); *The Indian in the Cupboard* (n).

THE LUCKY STONE
by Lucille Clifton • Illustrated by Dale Payson
Delacorte, 1979
Gr. 2–6   62 pages
A young black girl narrates the dramatic tale of how a tiny stone has brought luck to four generations of young black women, dating back to the time of slavery. Related books: *Roll of Thunder, Hear My Cry* (n); *The Stories Julian Tells* (s); *Sylvester and the Magic Pebble* (p).

LUKE'S GARDEN AND GRAMP
by Joan Tate
Harper, 1981
Gr. 3–7   *Luke's Garden:* 84 pages; *Gramp:* 52 pages
There are two short novels included in this one volume. The first, *Luke's Garden,* is a moving portrait of a boy who marches to a different drummer than his classmates. He is quiet and sensitive, tends to be a loner yet feels comfortable in the company of the community's handicapped or rejected. In a senseless flash of intolerance, a small group of his classmates turn on him and the story comes to a startling and moving climax. Related books: *Call It Courage* (s); *Grey Cloud* (n); *The Hundred Dresses* (s); *Meaning Well* (s); *The Snailman* (n); *The Story of Ferdinand* (p); *William's Doll* (p); *Oliver Button Is a Sissy* by Tomie de Paola.

   In the second story, *Gramp,* a young boy rebels against the indifference of his parents in an effort to save his beloved grandfather's dignity and self-worth. Related books: *Grandma Didn't Wave Back* (s); *Old Mother Witch* (p); *The Snailman* (n); *Stone Fox* (s); *A Time for Watching* (s); *Encore for Eleanor* by Bill Peet.

LUKE WAS THERE
by Eleanor Clymer
Holt, 1973
Gr. 3–5   92 pages
A story presenting the problems that lonely, uncared-for children have in finding someone they can trust. A boy running away from a shelter home in New York City and away from the burdens of responsibility is portrayed in a simple but touching manner. Also by the author: *My Brother Stevie* (s); *Me and*

the Eggman. Related books: *Grandmother Orphan* (s); *Ice River* (p); *J.T.* (n); *The Pinballs* (n); *Slake's Limbo* (n); *Wingman* (s).

THE MAGIC FINGER
by Roald Dahl • Illustrated by William Pène du Bois
Harper, 1966
Gr. 2–6   40 pages
A short fantasy about an irate 8-year-old girl who puts the "magic finger" on people and turns them into . . . Well, that would be giving away too much of the story. Also by the author: *James and the Giant Peach* (n).

MEANING WELL
by Sheila R. Cole
Franklin Watts, 1974
Gr. 5–7   64 pages
A study of friendship—what it should be and what it should not be. This book shows in a very dramatic fashion the peer pressures within a sixth-grade classroom. Related books: *The Hundred Dresses* (s); *Luke's Garden* (s); *Wild Violets* (s); *Wilfred the Rat* (p); *Wingman* (s).

MY BROTHER STEVIE
by Eleanor Clymer
Holt, 1967
Gr. 3–6   94 pages
In this story of inner-city life, a young girl grows increasingly worried about her younger brother's delinquent behavior. With only an aging grandmother as his guardian, the boy has no role model—until he takes on a daily chore for his teacher, who lives in the neighborhood. His behavior improves and all is well until a family emergency suddenly calls the teacher out of town. Trouble quickly surfaces for the boy, forcing his sister to begin a desperate search for the teacher. Also by the author: *Luke Was There* (s); *Me and the Eggman.* Related books: *Four Miles to Pinecone* (n); *J.T.* (n); *Roll of Thunder, Hear My Cry* (n).

MY FATHER'S DRAGON
by Ruth S. Gannett
Random, 1948; Dell, 1980
K–2   78 pages
Here is a three-volume series bursting with fantasy, hair-raising escapes, and evil creatures. The tone is dramatic enough to be exciting for even mature preschoolers but not enough to frighten them. The narrator relates the tales as adventures that happened to his father when he was a boy. This is an excellent transition series for introducing children to longer stories with fewer pictures.

The series, in order, also includes: *Elmer and the Dragon; The Dragons of Blueland.* Related books: *The Reluctant Dragon* (s); *A Book of Dragons* by Ruth Manning-Sanders; *How Droofus the Dragon Lost His Head* by Bill Peet.

OWLS IN THE FAMILY
by Farley Mowat
Little, Brown, 1961; Bantam, 1981
Gr. 2–6   108 pages
No child should miss this experience of reliving with the author his rollicking boyhood on the Saskatchewan prairie, raising dogs, gophers, rats, snakes, pigeons, and—most dramatically of all—owls. It is an era we will never see again; the next best thing is to bask in it secondhand through this piece of nostalgia, filled with childhood's laughter and adventure. Also by the author: *Lost in the Barrens.* Related books: *Gentle Ben* (n); *Storm Boy* (s); *Capyboppy* by Bill Peet.

PETER POTTS
by Clifford Hicks
Dell (paperback only), 1979
Gr. 2–4   106 pages
The zaniest kid in town! From do-it-yourself tooth-pulling to April Fools, from soapbox derbies to spelling bees—this is a favorite of every child. Also by the author: *The Marvelous Inventions of Alvin Fernald* (series). Related books: *Me and Caleb* (n); *Owls in the Family* (s); *Ramona the Pest* (n); *Room 10* (s).

THE REAL THIEF
by William Steig
Farrar, 1973
Gr. 3–5   58 pages
The author uses animals here (as he does in most of his books) to act out a story of theft, guilt, friendship, and pride. Standing up and admitting our mistakes is dealt with here in a touching manner. For experienced listeners. Also by the author: *The Amazing Bone* (p); *Sylvester and the Magic Pebble* (p). Related books: *The Bad Times of Irma Baumlein* (n); *Grandmother Orphan* (s); *Mandy* (n).

THE RELUCTANT DRAGON
by Kenneth Grahame   •   Illustrated by Ernest H. Shepard
Holiday House, 1953
Gr. 3–5   54 pages
The author of the classic *Wind in the Willows* offers us here a simple tale: simple in size (just an oversized short story); and simple in scope (a dragon, a boy, and a knight). But for all its simplicity, it is deep in charm. The dragon is not a devouring dragon but a reluctant dragon who wants nothing to do with violence. The boy is something of a local scholar, well versed in dragon lore

and torn mightily between his desire to view a battle between the dragon and the knight and his desire to protect his friend the dragon. And the knight— he's no simple knight at all. He's the one and only St. George the Dragon Killer. This 1938 story is a charming introduction to a legendary time and place. For experienced listeners. Related books: *The Story of Ferdinand* (p); *Weird Henry Berg* (n); in *A Wonder Book* (a): "The Gorgon's Head" and "The Chimaera" (these are Greek myths for experienced listeners); *Everyone Knows What a Dragon Looks Like* by Jay Williams.

ROOM 10
by Agnes McCarthy
Doubleday, 1971 (OP)
Gr. 1–4   70 pages
A warm and funny story describing a year in the life of a typical grade-school class as it survives its pet show, class trip, costume party, new kid, class play, substitute teacher, et cetera. Related books: *Me and Caleb* (n); *Miss Nelson Is Missing* (p); *Peter Potts* (s); *Ramona the Pest* (n).

SHOESHINE GIRL
by Clyde Robert Bulla
Crowell, 1975; Scholastic, 1977
Gr. 2–4   84 pages
A spoiled and greedy little girl learns something about life, money, and friendship when she becomes a shoeshine girl. Also by the author: *Dexter* (s); *The Wish at the Top* (p). Related books: *Grandmother Orphan* (s); *Stone Fox* (s).

THE SMARTEST MAN IN IRELAND
by Mollie Hunter
Rand McNally, 1965 (OP)
Gr. 3–6   96 pages
You can't help but love Patrick Kentigern Keenan—perhaps the smartest man in Ireland but certainly the laziest. But along with loving him, you'll learn to understand him and root for him as he battles the "little people" of Ireland in this fairy tale. Under the cover of darkness, fierce battles of wits and fist are waged over golden spoons and necklaces, silver bridles, a life-giving stone, and last but not least, Patrick's right to boast that he's "the smartest man in Ireland." A magnificent fairy tale by a contemporary author. Also by the author: *A Stranger Came Ashore* (n). Related books: *James and the Giant Peach* (n); *The Lion, the Witch and the Wardrobe* (n); *Weird Henry Berg* (n).

SOUP
by Robert Newton Peck
Knopf, 1974; Dell, 1979
Gr. 4–6   96 pages
Two Vermont pals share a genius for getting themselves into trouble. The

stories are set in the rural 1930s when life was simpler and the days were longer. But the need for a best friend was just as great then as now. Sequels: *Soup and Me; Soup for President; Soup on Wheels; Soup's Drum.* Also by the author: for older children, *A Day No Pigs Would Die* (n). Related books: *Dexter* (s); *The Hayburners* (s); *Me and Caleb* (n); *Owls in the Family* (s); *Ida Early Comes over the Mountain* by Robert Burch.

STONE FOX
by John R. Gardiner
Crowell, 1980
Gr. 3–6   96 pages
Here is a story that, like its 10-year-old hero, never stands still. It is filled to the brim with action and determination, the love of a child for his grandfather, and the loyalty of a great dog for his young master. Based on a Rocky Mountain legend, the story describes the valiant efforts of young Willy to save his ailing grandfather's farm by attempting to win the purse in a local bobsled race. The figure of Stone Fox, the towering favorite for the race, is an unusual departure from the Indian stereotype in children's literature. Pulsing with action, emotion, and originality. Related books: *Caddie Woodlawn* (n); *Gramp* (see *Luke's Garden and Gramp)* (s); *My Grandson Lew* (p); *Storm Boy* (s); *Toliver's Secret* (n); *Where the' Red Fern Grows* (n).

THE STORIES JULIAN TELLS
by Ann Cameron
Pantheon, 1981
Gr. K–3   72 pages
The author takes six short stories involving little Julian and his family and weaves them into a fabric that glows with the mischief, magic, and imagination of childhood. Though centered on commonplace subjects like desserts, gardens, loose teeth, and new neighbors, these stories of family life are written in an uncommon way that will both amuse and touch young listeners.

Don't miss the opportunity to incorporate related activities into these readings: everyone can enjoy pudding while listening to the dessert story, or make pudding afterwards; order seeds from a catalog or plant a garden after the garden story; measure everyone's height after the birthday fig tree story. Related books: *Benjie* (p); *The Lucky Stone* (s).

STORM BOY
by Colin Thiele   •   Illustrated by John Schoenherr
Harper, 1978
Gr. 3–6   64 pages
The story of an Australian hermit and his son who live an idyllic life in a shack by the sea. It is also the story of the loyal little pelican they adopt, train, and lose to thoughtless hunters. There is a haunting quality to the story that will

have you licking your lips to taste the salt and wiping your eyes to clear the tears. Also by the author: *Fire in the Stone*. Related books: *Gentle Ben* (n); *Stone Fox* (s); *Capyboppy* by Bill Peet.

A TASTE OF BLACKBERRIES
by Doris B. Smith • Illustrated by Charles Robinson
Crowell, 1973; Scholastic, 1976
Gr. 4-7 52 pages
One of the first of contemporary authors to look at death from the child's point of view, Ms. Smith allows us to follow the narrator's emotions as he comes to terms with the death of his best friend, who died as a result of an allergic reaction to bee stings. The sensitivity with which the attendant sorrow and guilt are treated makes this an outstanding book. It blazed the way for many others which quickly followed, but few have approached the place of honor that this one holds. Eight short chapters. Related books: *The Big Red Barn* (p); *The Tenth Good Thing About Barney* (p); *Where the Red Fern Grows* (n); *The Accident* by Carol Carrick.

A TIME FOR WATCHING
by Gunilla Norris
Random, 1969 (OP)
Gr. 3-6 82 pages
"An idle mind is the devil's workshop," goes the adage, and 10-year-old Joachim appears to do his best to prove it true in this book. He moves from one disaster to another in search of himself. As his curiosity runs wild, so does his carelessness: he ruins his sister's doll, frightens away a farmer's chickens, dismantles his postmaster-father's scale, sneaks down the coal chute of the neighborhood eccentric. Each incident becomes less humorous and more dangerous as the boy's frustrations grow and we are led to the moment when Joachim and his family discover his true self. Here is a child whose hands literally cry out to be used, who cannot sit idle, who must find the "whys" behind every lock. The author has put her finger on the very heartbeat of this child—a child that many a classmate, teacher, and parent will recognize. This is a powerful and important story in understanding and self-awareness. Related books: *J.T.* (n); *The Midnight Fox* (n); *My Brother Stevie* (s).

TWENTY AND TEN
by Claire H. Bishop
Viking, 1952; Puffin, 1978
Gr. 3-6 76 pages
Set in occupied France during World War II, this book depicts the courage and ingenuity of twenty fifth-graders in hiding ten Jewish refugee children. The story is filled with high drama and history. Adult readers might give a brief explanation of the ration card system—both as a control system in peacetime

(gas rationing) and wartime (food)—before reading the novel to children. Related books: *The Man in the Box* (n); *Sing Down the Moon* (n); *Waiting for Mama* (s).

WAITING FOR MAMA
by Marietta Moskin
Coward, 1975
Gr. 2–4   92 pages
Fleeing the persecution of the Czar at the end of the century, a family of Russian Jews comes to America—but not a complete family. Because of the sudden illness of her baby, the mother must remain in Russia. After arriving in the tenement on New York's Lower East Side, the family begins the dual task of starting a new life and saving enough money to pay for the mother and child's passage. The author presents the two-year struggle through the eyes of young Becky. The anguish of the immigrant is still with us today, eighty years after this story takes place. It will touch base in many classrooms. Though simple in its construction and language, this book's sensitivity to age-old hopes and fears is very deep. Also by the author: *Adam and the Wishing Charm; Day of the Blizzard.* Related books: *Cinderella* (p); *J.T.* (n); *Simon and Sarah and No Red Paint* (p); *Twenty and Ten* (s); *The Witch of Fourth Street* (s).

WARTON AND MORTON
by Russell Erickson   •   Illustrated by Lawrence Di Fiori
Morrow, 1976; Dell, 1977
Gr. 1–4   60 pages
Combining adventure, brotherhood, and a sense of humor, here is a series of books that children will cherish. Two domesticated brother toads, Morton and Warton, display very different approaches to life and adventure. In all the stories there is the recurrent theme of adventure and facing adversity with a sense of courage, along with the warming bonds of brotherhood. The series also includes: *A Toad for Tuesday; Warton and the Castaways; Warton and the King of the Skies; Warton and the Traders; Warton's Christmas Eve Adventure.*

THE WEREFOX
by Elizabeth Coatsworth
Macmillan (paperback only), 1975
Gr. 3–6   70 pages
Something about Johnny's new neighbor and best friend is disturbing. Johnny's suspicions grow until he discovers the truth—his friend becomes a fox by night. A powerful story of fantasy and friendship. I suggest, however, omitting the first chapter from read-aloud because it gives too much of the story away too soon. (Published originally in hardcover under the title *Pure Magic.*) Related books: *Among the Dolls* (s); *The Dog Days of Arthur Cane* (n); *Inside My Feet* (s); *The Magic Finger* (s); *Sylvester and the Magic Pebble* (p).

WIGGER
by William Goldman
Dell (paperback only), 1977
Gr. 1-5   80 (small) pages
Every child who has ever had a security blanket or favorite stuffed animal will identify with this story. Wigger is a tattered pink blanket, but to orphaned Susanna it is a no-nonsense friend who keeps her spirits up. But suddenly Wigger is stolen and Susanna's courage—even her will to live—begins to fail. How they are reunited is a tender story that will captivate and charm many grade levels. Related books: *The Indian in the Cupboard* (n); *Ira Sleeps Over* (p); *David and Dog* by Shirley Hughes.

WILD VIOLETS
by Phyllis Green
Nelson, 1977; Dell, 1980
Gr. 3-6   104 pages
While the rags-to-riches, riches-to-rags theme may not be new to children's literature, it is hard to imagine it being done any better than this little story. Cornelia is the richest, prettiest, and most popular girl in her fourth-grade class. Ruthie is the homeliest, poorest, and least popular. Fate draws them together in friendship and then, through Cornelia's father's illness and Ruthie's father's good fortune, their roles are reversed. Also by the author: *Grandmother Orphan* (s); *Ice River* (p). Related books: *The Gumdrop Necklace* (s); *The Hundred Dresses* (s); *Meaning Well* (s); *The Secret Garden* (n); *Wingman* (s); *Sara Crewe* by Frances Hodgson Burnett.

WINGMAN
by Daniel Manus Pinkwater
Dodd, 1975; Dell, 1976
Gr. 3-6   64 pages
A poor Chinese boy in New York City rejects school for his comic book collection. The story shows how fantasy provides a protective covering from hurts and prejudices. Also by the author: *The Big Orange Splot; Lizard Music*. Related books: *The Bears' House* (s); *How I Hunted the Little Fellows* (p); *J.T.* (n); *Slake's Limbo* (n); *Waiting for Mama* (s).

THE WITCH OF FOURTH STREET
by Myron Levoy
Harper (paperback only), 1972
Gr. 2-5   110 pages
What a glorious collection of read-aloud short stories! Both its readability and subject matter make it must reading in every classroom and home. All the stories are set among the tenements of New York's Lower East Side during the early 1900s and deal with the daily crises, hopes, fears, laughter, and customs of

a neighborhood melting pot of Russian, Polish, Irish, Italian, German, Protestant, Catholic, and Jewish families. Eight stories in all, approximately 13 pages each. Related books: *Mama's Bank Account* (n); *Waiting for Mama* (s); *Wingman* (s); *Ike and Mama and the Once-a-Year Suit* (series) by Carol Snyder.

THE WONDERFUL STORY OF HENRY SUGAR & SIX MORE
by Roald Dahl
Knopf, 1977; Bantam, 1979
Gr. 4–7   226 pages
Here is a seven-story collection by Roald Dahl for experienced listeners. Two stories—"Lucky Break" and "A Piece of Cake"—are not good read-alouds. However, the other five pieces are excellent, especially the title story. Also by the author: *James and the Giant Peach* (n).

Novels

THE ADVENTURES OF PINOCCHIO
by Carlo Collodi
Macmillan, 1963; Scholastic, 1978
Gr. 1–5   252 pages
Unfortunately, whatever familiarity the modern child may have with this 1892 classic most often comes from having seen it emasculated in the movie version. Treat your children to the real version of the poor woodcarver's puppet who faces all the temptations of childhood, succumbs to most, learns from his follies, and gains his boyhood by selflessly giving of himself for his friends. The original is divided into 36 chapters, most as short as 2 pages. A well-condensed retelling is available in a Scholastic edition (64 pages). Related books: *The Bad Times of Irma Baumlein* (n); *Mandy* (n); *The Real Thief* (s).

THE BAD TIMES OF IRMA BAUMLEIN
by Carol Ryrie Brink
Macmillan (both), 1972; 1974
Gr. 3–6   134 pages
Irma, the new girl in school, tells a lie to impress her classmates, and before she knows it the lie steamrolls out of control. A witty and perceptive novel on truth, peer pressure, and friendship. Related books: *The Adventures of Pinocchio* (n); *Mandy* (n); *Meaning Well* (s); *The Real Thief* (s); *Wild Violets* (s).

A BAG OF MARBLES
by Joseph Joffo
Houghton Mifflin, 1974
Gr. 6 and up   244 pages
As the Nazis tighten their grip on Paris in 1941, a Jewish father sends his two

young sons on a journey that will cover three years and nearly cost their lives. This is a true story, filled with all the fear and courage, heartbreak and triumph that characterize an oppressed, proud people. Joffo does not soften the harshness of his tale except for the wit that is the boys' personality, so the reader may expect an occasional four-letter word. This book may be filed with adult fiction. For experienced listeners. Related books: *The Foxman* (n); *The Man in the Box* (n); *Sing Down the Moon* (n); *Twenty and Ten* (s).

BLACK AND BLUE MAGIC
by Zilpha Keatley Snyder
Atheneum (paperback only), 1972
Gr. 4–6   186 pages
Any child who has ever wondered what it would be like to fly can find the answer in 12-year-old Harry Marcos, who grew wings one summer. The ensuing adventures also help him to grow a new self-image. An amusing and impressive story for experienced listeners. Related books: *Grasshopper and the Unwise Owl* (s); *The Silver Pony* (p) and *Up and Up* (p), two wordless books.

THE BLACK STALLION
by Walter Farley
Random (both), 1944; 1977
Gr. 2–6   188 pages
When Walter Farley began writing this book as a Brooklyn high-school student, he could never have dreamed he was creating what *The New York Times* subsequently called "the most famous fictional horse of the century." He would go on to write more than fifteen sequels and see the stallion portrayed in a widely acclaimed motion picture. *The Black Stallion* is a novel with all the qualities of a thoroughbred—fast-paced, sleek in line, strong in character, dramatic in its turns. Among the sequels: *Black Stallion and Satan; Black Stallion Mystery; Black Stallion Returns.*

BRIDGE TO TERABITHIA
by Katherine Paterson
Crowell, 1977; Avon, 1979
Gr. 4–7   128 pages
Few novels for children have dealt with so many emotions and issues so well: sports, school, peers, friendship, death, guilt, art, and family. A Newbery Award winner, this book deserves to be read or heard by everyone. Also by the author: *The Great Gilly Hopkins.* Related book: *Where the Red Fern Grows* (n).

THE BUTTON BOAT
by Glendon and Kathryn Swarthout
Doubleday, 1969 (OP)
Gr. 3–6   160 pages
A brother and sister (two of the sweetest, poorest, and smelliest kids you'll

ever meet) star in this old-time thriller-chiller-killer-diller of a story. It comes complete with bank robbers, a daredevil hero, a villain, a beer-drinking dog, a hateful stepfather, and an old-fashioned happy ending. Related books: *The Half-A-Moon Inn* (s); *Humbug Mountain* (n); *Prisoners at the Kitchen Table* (n); *Toliver's Secret* (n).

CADDIE WOODLAWN
by Carol Ryrie Brink
Macmillan (both), 1935, 1970; 1973
Gr. 4–6   286 pages
You take *The Little House on the Prairie;* I'll take *Caddie Woodlawn.* Ten times over, I'll take this tomboy of the 1860s with her pranks, her daring visits to Indian camps, her one-room schoolhouse fights and her wonderfully believable family. The 1935 edition was illustrated by Kate Seredy. Try to pick up the 1973 revised edition with Trina Schart Hyman's sensitive illustrations. For experienced listeners. Sequel: *Magical Melons.* For an interesting comparative study, see *Introducing Shirley Braverman* (n).

THE CALL OF THE WILD
by Jack London
Grosset, 1965; Bantam, 1969; Scholastic, 1970; Penguin, 1981
Gr. 6 and up   126 pages
This 1903 dog story, set amidst the rush for gold in the Klondike, depicts the savagery and tenderness between man and his environment in unforgettable terms. For experienced listeners. Related books: *Hurry Home, Candy* (n) for younger readers; *Lassie Come Home* (n); *Where the Red Fern Grows* (n); *Lost in the Barrens* by Farley Mowat.

CAPTAIN GREY
by Avi
Pantheon, 1977; Scholastic, 1982
Gr. 4–7   142 pages
A swashbuckling pirate story told in the classic adventure style, it deals with a young boy's determination to free himself from a band of pirates based on the New Jersey shoreline just after the Revolutionary War. For experienced listeners. Also by the author: *Emily Upham's Revenge* (n); *The History of Helpless Harry.* Related book: *Sarah Bishop* (n).

THE CASE OF THE BAKER STREET IRREGULAR
by Robert Newman
Atheneum, 1978; Bantam, 1981
Gr. 4–8   216 pages
This finely crafted mystery novel is an excellent introduction for young readers to the world of Sherlock Holmes. A young orphan is suddenly pitted against the dark side of turn-of-the-century London when his tutor-guardian is kid-

napped. Complete with screaming street urchins, sinister cab drivers, bombings, murder, back alleys, and a child's-eye view of the great sleuth himself—Sherlock Holmes. For experienced listeners. Sequels: *The Case of the Somerville Secret; The Case of the Threatened King; The Case of the Vanishing Corpse.*

CATCH A KILLER
by George Woods
Harper, 1972 (OP)
Gr. 6 and up   248 pages
This is one of my family's all-time favorite read-aloud novels. When a young teenager runs away from home, hoping to give his widowed mother a temporary scare, he runs smack into a killer. A psychological suspense story that probes the disturbed mind in a moving manner. Related books: *Collision Course* (n); *Five Were Missing* (n); *Killing Mr. Griffin* (n).

THE CAY
by Theodore Taylor
Doubleday, 1969; Avon, 1977
Gr. 2-6   144 pages
An exciting adventure about a blind white boy and an old black man shipwrecked on a tiny Caribbean island. The first chapters are slow but it builds with taut drama to a stunning ending. Related books: *Burnish Me Bright* (s); *Call It Courage* (s); *Child of the Silent Night* (n); *The Long Journey* (n); *Stone Fox* (s).

CHARLOTTE'S WEB
by E. B. White • Illustrated by Garth Williams
Harper (both), 1952
Gr. 2-4   184 pages
One of the most universally acclaimed books in contemporary children's literature, it is loved as much by adults as by children. The tale centers on the barnyard life of a young pig who is slated to be butchered in the fall. The animals of the yard (particularly a haughty gray spider named Charlotte) conspire with the farmer's daughter to save the pig's life. While there is a lot of humor in the novel, the author brings in wisdom and pathos in developing his theme of friendship within the cycle of life. Also by the author: *Stuart Little*. Related books: *The Cay* (n); *Cricket in Times Square* (n); *The Cricket Winter* (n); *Wild Violets* (s); *Wilfred the Rat* (p).

CHILD OF THE SILENT NIGHT:
THE STORY OF LAURA BRIDGMAN
by Edith Fisher Hunter
Houghton Mifflin, 1963
Gr. 3-5   124 pages
When Charles Dickens visited the United States in 1842, the person he most

wished to see was a 13-year-old girl in Boston named Laura Bridgman. And no wonder. This child's story is an inspiration to all who heard it then or hear it now. It was the triumphant efforts of this child and her teachers that eventually paved the way for another deaf, dumb, and blind child nearly forty years later—Helen Keller. One cannot read or hear Laura's inspiring biography without having one's own sensitivity heightened for that wonderful gift so often taken for granted—language. Related books: *Burnish Me Bright* (s); *The Half-A-Moon Inn* (s); *Our John Willie* (n).

THE CHOCOLATE TOUCH
by Patrick Skene Catling
Morrow, 1979; Bantam, 1981
Gr. 1-4   122 pages
Here is a new and delicious twist to the old King Midas story. Young John learns a dramatic lesson in self-control when everything he touches with his lips turns to chocolate—toothpaste, bacon and eggs, water, pencils, trumpet. What would happen, then, if he kissed his mother?

Either before or after reading this story, read or tell the original version, "The Golden Touch," which details King Midas's bout with greed and regret. For fifth grade and up, the tale is included as one of the stories in Hawthorne's *A Wonder Book* (a). Younger readers will enjoy Paul Galdone's picture book version, *The Golden Touch*. Related books: *Chocolate Fever* (s); *Penny Candy* (p); *The Sweet Touch* (p); *Jelly Belly* by Robert K. Smith.

COLLISION COURSE
by Nigel Hinton
Nelson, 1977; Dell, 1979
Gr. 7 and up   172 pages
In this young-adult novel, a teenager goes to great lengths to cover his footsteps after he has accidentally struck and killed a woman with his motorcycle. As the story progresses, so too does his sense of guilt and anxiety—forcing him, like Raskolnikov in *Crime and Punishment,* into suspicious eccentricities. Fast-paced, sympathetic, and totally believable. For experienced listeners. Related books: *Catch a Killer* (n); *Killing Mr. Griffin* (n).

CRICKET IN TIMES SQUARE
by George Selden   •   Illustrated by Garth Williams
Farrar, 1960; 1970
Gr. 3-6   156 pages
The fanciful story of a cat and mouse living in Times Square, where they discover the world's most talented cricket. Friendship and personal sacrifice are central issues. Related books: *Charlotte's Web* (n); *The Cricket Winter* (n); *The Indian in the Cupboard* (n).

THE CRICKET WINTER
by Felice Holman
Norton, 1967; Dell, 1973 (both OP)
Gr. 3–5   112 pages
A lonely and inventive 9-year-old boy, using Morse code, begins to communicate with a cricket and soon finds himself immersed in the problems of that cricket and his winter neighbors. A sensitive presentation of the idea that sometimes we do the right thing, not for the praise we'll receive but because it is the right thing to do. Also by the author: *At the Top of My Voice* (po); *Slake's Limbo* (n). Related books: *Charlotte's Web* (n); *Cricket in Times Square* (n).

DANNY THE CHAMPION OF THE WORLD
by Roald Dahl
Knopf, 1978; Bantam, 1979
Gr. 3–6   196 pages
This is the exciting and tender story of a motherless boy and his father—"the most wonderful father who ever lived"—and their great adventure together. Teachers and parents should explain the custom and tradition of "poaching" in England before going too deeply into the story. Also by the author: *James and the Giant Peach* (n); *The Magic Finger* (s); *The Wonderful Story of Henry Sugar* (s); *Charlie and the Chocolate Factory; The Enormous Crocodile; The Fantastic Mr. Fox.*

A DAY NO PIGS WOULD DIE
by Robert Newton Peck
Knopf, 1972
Gr. 6 and up   150 pages
Set among Shaker farmers in Vermont during the 1920s, this poignant story deals with the author's coming of age at 13, his adventures, fears, and triumphs. As a novel of life and death, it should be read carefully by the teacher or parent before it is read aloud to children. A very moving story by the author of the Soup series (s). For experienced listeners. Related books: *Bridge to Terabithia* (n); *The Foxman* (n); *Where the Red Fern Grows* (n); *Words by Heart* (n).

THE DOG DAYS OF ARTHUR CANE
by T. Ernesto Bethancourt
Holiday House, 1976; Bantam, 1980
Gr. 5–8   160 pages
When an affluent high-school boy is mysteriously transformed into a mongrel dog, he discovers exactly what is meant by the expression "a dog's life." Surviving on the streets of New York by his wits and the skin of his teeth, Arthur faces all the modern canine perils—dogcatchers, poisoned meat, speeding cars, even the gas chamber. Though the book has its humorous moments,

much of its strength is in sheer drama. Readers may want to be alert to an occasional four-letter word. Related books: *The Call of the Wild* (n); *Lassie Come Home* (n).

DOWN THE LONG HILLS
by Louis L'Amour
Bantam (paperback only), 1968
Gr. 4 and up   150 pages
An Indian massacre leaves a 7-year-old boy and 3-year-old girl with only a horse and a knife to face the limitless prairie, savage outlaws, and marauding Indians. Originally written for the adult western market, its compelling drama and authentic tone hold children's attention just as well. Related books: *My Brother, the Wind* (n); *Sing Down the Moon* (n); *Snow-Bound* (n).

THE 18th EMERGENCY
by Betsy Byars
Viking, 1973; Puffin, 1981
Gr. 4–6   126 pages
Benjie has made the mistake of angering the toughest boy in school. What to do when you fear the bully is waiting for you around every corner? Sooner or later, one must face the consequences of one's actions, as Benjie does here. Also by the author: *The Midnight Fox* (n); *Trouble River* (n); *Summer of the Swans*; *The Winged Colt of Casa Mia*. Related books: *Call It Courage* (s); *Into the Painted Bear Lair* (n); *Introducing Shirley Braverman* (n).

EMILY UPHAM'S REVENGE
by Avi
Pantheon, 1978; Avon, 1979
Gr. 4–6   172 pages
Here's a book that is plain fun, an adventure story to help children realize that reading doesn't have to be connected with the tedium of workbooks. Written in a style that is reminiscent of an old-time silent movie and set in 1875, it is peopled with little lost Emily from a proper Boston family, an unscrupulous banker, crooks, frauds, and the fabulous 11-year-old Seth Marple. What a joy to read aloud!

Written in the same style is Avi's *The History of Helpless Harry*, 40 fast-paced, spoofy, very short chapters. Also by the author: *Captain Grey* (n). Related books: *The Button Boat* (n); *Humbug Mountain* (n).

THE ENORMOUS EGG
by Oliver Butterworth
Little, Brown, 1956; Dell, 1978
Gr. 3–6   188 pages
When a New Hampshire farm lad's diligence in caring for an oversized egg in

the henhouse is rewarded with the birth of a prehistoric triceratops, his life takes a dramatic turn. Scientists, commercial entrepreneurs, reporters, and television cameramen descend on the little farm, all hoping to exploit the child and his famous "find." It is a book filled with humor—both warm and bittersweet. What was included in 1956 as some gentle satire on the media and Washington politics now in the 1980s reads more accurately than satirically. Sequel: *The Narrow Passage*. Related book: *Grasshopper and the Unwise Owl* (s).

FIRE STORM
by Robb White
Doubleday, 1979
Gr. 4–8   112 pages
The awesome fury and devastation of a forest fire are depicted in this story about a hard-nosed forest ranger and his teenage prisoner—the suspected arsonist. The fire traps the two and the ensuing drama finds them battling the flames as hotly as they battle each other. Readers may wish to omit the occasional four-letter word. Related books: *The Cay* (n); *Ironhead* (n); *Almost Too Late* by Elmo Wortman.

FIVE WERE MISSING
by Lois Duncan
New American Library (paperback only), 1972
Gr. 5 and up   144 pages
Published ten years before the *real* California school-bus kidnapping case made headlines in the 1970s, this novel has all the tense human drama of today's headlines. Five bus-riding high-school students are kidnapped and begin a minute-to-minute fight to survive. For experienced listeners. This book was published in hardcover under the title *Ransome*. Also by the author, for older children, *Killing Mr. Griffin* (n). Related books: *Catch a Killer* (n); *Prisoners at the Kitchen Table* (n).

THE FLIGHT OF THE FOX
by Shirley Rousseau Murphy
Atheneum, 1978
Gr. 3–6   168 pages
The captivating story of an energetic young boy who joins ranks with a roguish kangaroo rat to rid a local airport of a dangerous flock of starlings. Combining fantasy with realism, the author confronts problems in modern technology, offers various plausible solutions, and stimulates the listener's imagination. The book provides many opportunities for class projects: rats, lemmings, starlings, airport problems, model airplanes. Also by the author: *Elmo Doolan and the Search for the Golden Mouse*. Related books: *The Cricket Winter* (n); *Grasshopper and the Unwise Owl* (s); *Mrs. Frisby and the Rats of NIMH* (n).

FOUR MILES TO PINECONE
by Jon Hassler
Warne, 1977
Gr. 4-7   118 pages
Working his grocery store summer job, Tom recognizes one of the two youths who robbed and assaulted his employer. He wrestles with the dilemma of whether or not to tell the police about his friend. A taut drama on family and peer relationships and personal responsibility. Related books: *The Foxman* (n); *Grey Cloud* (n); *Killing Mr. Griffin* (n).

THE FOXMAN
by Gary Paulsen
Nelson, 1977
Gr. 5-8   126 pages
Two cousins lost in a snowstorm stumble upon the cottage of a recluse. The old man is in hiding because of hideous facial wounds suffered during World War I. As repulsive as his face is, one of the boys begins a friendship with the man that will reach the deepest parts of a reader's or listener's heart. There are several sexual references which the reader may wish to omit. Related books: *A Bag of Marbles* (n); *Four Miles to Pinecone* (n); *The Snailman* (n); *A Time for Watching* (s); *Boris* by Jaap ter Haar.

GENTLE BEN
by Walt Morey
Dutton, 1965; Avon, 1976
Gr. 3-6   192 pages
A young boy adopts a huge brown bear and brings to his family in Alaska all the joys and tears attendant to such a combination. Though the struggle to save animals from ignorant but well-intentioned human predators is one that has been written many times over, Morey's handling of characters, plot, and setting makes an original and exciting tale. He supports the pace of his story with many lessons in environmental science—from salmon runs to hibernation. Related books: for younger readers, *The Biggest Bear* (p), *My Friend Mac* (p), and *Capyboppy* by Bill Peet; for older readers, *Call of the Wild* (n) and *Storm Boy* (s).

GOOD OLD BOY
by Willie Morris
Harper, 1971; Avon, 1974 (both OP)
Gr. 5-8   128 pages
If Tom Sawyer had lived in the 1940s, this would have been the story that Mark Twain wrote. Willie Morris and his pals fill this novel with humor,

legend, and suspense. Long chapters can be easily divided into smaller ones by the reader. For experienced listeners. Related book: *Pinch* (n).

GREY CLOUD
by Charlotte Graeber
Four Winds, 1979
Gr. 4–8   124 pages
This is a book about being the new kid in school, about befriending the class oddball, about carrier pigeon racing, and about peer pressure. Its descriptions of pigeon racing alone make it fascinating reading, but combined with all its other facets, it is a book that is must reading for children at the age when their emotions are so fragile. Related books (on peer pressure): *Four Miles to Pinecone* (n); *Killing Mr. Griffin* (n); *Meaning Well* (s).

HANG TOUGH, PAUL MATHER
by Alfred Slote
Lippincott, 1973; Avon, 1975
Gr. 5–7   156 pages
A moving sports story about a boy with leukemia and his struggle to win— against both his disease and his baseball opponents. After reading this aloud, encourage your listeners to read on their own the many other Alfred Slote sports books. Related books: *It's a Mile From Here to Glory* (n); *Thank You, Jackie Robinson* (n); *Winning Kicker* (n); *Benny* by Barbara Cohen.

THE HERO FROM OTHERWHERE
by Jay Williams
Archway (paperback only), 1980
Gr. 5–7   190 pages
A fast-paced fantasy–science fiction story of two boys who are sent to the principal's office for fighting, only to discover two men waiting for them in the office. The two men, from a parallel world on Earth, ask the two boys to help in a dangerous quest to save their worlds. A soaring piece of imaginative writing. Related books: *The Fallen Spaceman* (s); *Mrs. Frisby and the Rats of NIMH* (n); *Science Fiction Tales* (a); *The Twenty-One Balloons* (n).

HOMER PRICE
by Robert McCloskey
Viking, 1943; Penguin, 1976
Gr. 2–5   160 pages
A modern classic, this is a hilarious collection of stories about a small-town boy's neighborhood dilemmas. Whether it's the story of Homer's foiling the bank robbers with his pet skunk or the tale of his uncle's out-of-control doughnut maker, these six Homeric tales will long be remembered. Sequel:

Centerburg Tales. Related books: *Humbug Mountain* (n); *Me and Caleb* (n); *Peter Potts* (s); *Pinch* (n); *Soup* (s).

HUMBUG MOUNTAIN
by Sid Fleischman
Little, Brown, 1978; Scholastic, 1980
Gr. 4–6   172 pages
Overflowing with humor, suspense, and originality, here are the captivating adventures of the Flint family as they battle outlaws, crooked riverboat pilots, ghosts, and their creditors on the banks of the Missouri River in the late 1800s. Very reminiscent of Mark Twain. Also by the author: *By the Great Horn Spoon; Chancy and the Grand Rascal; The Ghost in the Noonday Sun; The Ghost on Saturday Night; Longbeard the Wizard; Me and the Man on the Moon-eyed Horse; Mr. Mysterious and Company.* Related books: *The Button Boat* (n); *Emily Upham's Revenge* (n); *Pinch* (n).

HURRY HOME, CANDY
by Meindert DeJong
Harper (both), 1953
Gr. 2–6   244 pages
With a childlike sense of wonder and pity, this book describes the first year in the life of a dog—from the moment she is lifted from her mother's side, through the children, adults, punishments, losses, fears, friendships, love, and trust that flesh out this moving story. Related books: for Gr. 5 and up, *The Dog Days of Arthur Cane* (n); *Lassie Come Home* (n); *Stone Fox* (s); *Where the Red Fern Grows* (n).

INCIDENT AT HAWK'S HILL
by Allan W. Eckert
Little, Brown, 1971; Dell, 1972
Gr. 6 and up   174 pages
An extremely timid 6-year-old who wandered away from his family's farm in 1870 is adopted by a ferocious female badger, à la Mowgli in the Jungle Books. The boy is fed, protected, and instructed by the badger through the summer until the family manages to recapture the now-wild child. Definitely for experienced listeners. Reading this aloud, I would paraphrase a large portion of the slow-moving prologue. Related books: *The Dog Days of Arthur Cane* (n); *Ironhead* (n); *The Pond* (n).

THE INDIAN IN THE CUPBOARD
by Lynne Reid Banks
Doubleday, 1981
Gr. 2–6   182 pages
A witty, exciting, and poignant fantasy tale of a 9-year-old English boy who accidentally brings to life his three-inch plastic Indian toy. Once the shock of

the trick wears off, the boy begins to realize the immense responsibility involved in feeding, protecting, and hiding a three-inch human being from another time (1870s) and culture. An excellent values clarification model. Readers-aloud should note beforehand that the miniature cowboy in the story occasionally uses the word "damn" in his exclamations. Related books: *The Flight of the Fox* (n); *Grasshopper and the Unwise Owl* (s); *The Littles* (s).

INTO THE PAINTED BEAR LAIR
by Pamela Stearns • Illustrated by Ann Strugnell
Houghton Mifflin, 1976
Gr. 3–6   154 pages
This outrageously witty, touching, and unconventional fantasy–fairy tale concerns a young boy who can't find his way back to the toy store from whence he entered this strange land, a female knight named Sir Rosemary who is involved in a dangerously chilling mission, and a ferocious bear named Bear who would like nothing more than to devour the boy and the knight. And yet, for all its seeming foolishness, this is a novel of beautiful prose and dramatic dialogue showing that life is a succession of choices, and that the amount of happiness in our lives depends on how we handle those choices. Not the least of those choices, the author demonstrates, is friendship and the value we place on it. The fantasy will bring the reader and listener to new heights of imagination. Related books: *The Hero from Otherwhere* (n); *The Lion, the Witch and the Wardrobe* (n); *Search for Delicious* (n).

INTRODUCING SHIRLEY BRAVERMAN
by Hilma Wolitzer
Farrar, 1975; Dell, 1981
Gr. 3–5   154 pages
This novel covers slightly less than a year in the life of a Brooklyn, N.Y., girl during World War II. In 22 short, fast-paced chapters, we glimpse family life as it is affected by the war (air-raid practices, letters from soldier neighbors, telegrams from the War Department, the triumphant return of peace) and family life as it is usually lived: spelling bee competitions, visiting grandpa in the nursing home, curing your little brother of his timidity, facing down the neighborhood bully, and dress-up games on rainy days. This book makes a sensitive and enlightening comparative study with *Caddie Woodlawn*. Many similar family and community situations appear in the two novels and the nearly 100-year difference in their settings offers a unique social and cultural study. Other related books: *Mama's Bank Account* (n); *Me and Caleb* (n); *Ramona the Pest* (n); *Ida Early Comes over the Mountain* by Robert Burch.

IRONHEAD
by Mel Ellis
Archway (paperback only), 1970
Gr. 4–7   152 pages
Seventeen-year-old Doug searches for a legendary rattlesnake which, if cap-

tured, will provide him with enough reward money to pay for his father's medical care. The father is suffering from a mental breakdown but cannot afford treatment. Set in the Florida Everglades, the book is a close-up study of nature, courage, and persistence. For experienced listeners. Related books: *Fire Storm* (n); *Incident at Hawk's Hill* (n); *The Pond* (n).

IT'S A MILE FROM HERE TO GLORY
by **Robert C. Lee**
Little, Brown, 1972; Tempo, 1979
Gr. 4–7   150 pages
An inspiring sports story about an antagonistic farm boy who gains a new sense of self-worth and insight into those around him while competing on his school track team. Guaranteed to spur an interest in running. Related books: *Hang Tough, Paul Mather* (n); *Winning Kicker* (n).

JAMES AND THE GIANT PEACH
by **Roald Dahl**   •   **Illustrated by Nancy Ekholm Burkert**
Knopf, 1961; Bantam, 1978
Gr. 1–6   120 pages
Young James, orphaned, is sent to live with his mean aunts and appears resigned to spending the rest of his life as their humble servant. It is just about then that a giant peach begins growing in the backyard. Waiting inside that peach is a collection of characters that will captivate your audience as well they did James. Few books hold up over six grade levels as well as this one does. It's my all-time favorite. Also by the author: *Danny the Champion of the World* (n); *The Magic Finger* (s); *The Wonderful Story of Henry Sugar* (s); *The Enormous Crocodile*; *Fantastic Mr. Fox*; *George's Marvelous Medicine*.

JOURNEY OUTSIDE
by **Mary Q. Steele**
Puffin (paperback only), 1979
Gr. 3–7   144 pages
This Newbery honor winner is a book of many layers. The most obvious one is the adventure story: the recounting of a boy's escape from a subterranean, almost prehistoric, world where his people ride an endless river in search of a better world. As the first of his people to see the outside world in nearly a hundred years, he is dazzled by its sights and confronted with challenge after challenge. It also works as an allegory: the endless monotony of the subterranean world symbolizes the womb/family out of which the child steps—into a dazzling world of dilemmas and decisions. For experienced listeners. Related books: *The Hero from Otherwhere* (n); *The Pond* (n); *Sarah Bishop* (n); *Slake's Limbo* (n).

J.T.
by Jane Wagner • Photographs by Gordon Parks
Dell (paperback only), 1971
Gr. 3–5   124 pages
J.T. is an inner-city black child, harassed by neighbors and teenagers and the despair of his mother. He is, in fact, tottering on the brink of delinquency when an old, one-eyed alley cat brings out his sensitivity and responsibility. Excellent book about inner-city life, individual responsibility, life and death. Related books: *Luke Was There* (s); *My Brother Stevie* (s); *Roll of Thunder, Hear My Cry* (n); *The Stories Julian Tells* (s); *A Time for Watching* (s); *Wingman* (s).

KILLING MR. GRIFFIN
by Lois Duncan
Little, Brown, 1978; Dell, 1980
Gr. 7 and up   224 pages
This young-adult story offers a chilling dissection of peer pressure and group guilt. Because of the subject matter and occasional four-letter words, care should be used in its presentation. The story deals with five high-school students who attempt to scare their unpopular English teacher by kidnapping him. When their carefully laid plans slowly begin to unravel towards a tragic catastrophe, they find themselves unable to handle the situation. For a discussion of this book's use in the classroom, see Chapter 3. For experienced listeners. Also by the author: *Five Were Missing* (n). Related books: *Catch a Killer* (n); *Collision Course* (n).

LASSIE COME HOME
by Eric Knight
Holt, 1940, 1971 (revised); Dell, 1972
Gr. 4 and up   200 pages
This is one of the greatest dog stories you could ever hope to read. It reads so easily, the words ring with such feeling, that you'll find yourself coming back to it year after year. As is the case with most dog stories, there are the usual sentiments of loss, grief, courage, and struggle. But here these feelings are presented in such a way that most other dog stories pale by comparison. Set between the Scottish Highlands and Yorkshire, England, in the early 1900s, the novel describes the triumphant struggle of a collie dog to return the 100 miles to her young master. Unfortunately, Hollywood and television have badly damaged the image of this story with their tinny, affected characterization. This is the original Lassie story. Related books: *The Call of the Wild* (n); *The Dog Days of Arthur Cane* (n); *Hurry Home, Candy* (n); *Stone Fox* (s); *Where the Red Fern Grows* (n).

THE LION, THE WITCH AND THE WARDROBE
by C. S. Lewis
Macmillan (both), 1950; 1970
Gr. 3–6   186 pages

Four children discover that the stuffy wardrobe closet in an empty room leads to the magic kingdom of Narnia—a kingdom filled with heroes, witches, princes, and intrigue. The first of seven enchanting books called the Narnia Chronicles. The sequels, in order, are: *Prince Caspian; The Voyage of the "Dawn Treader"; The Silver Chair; The Horse and His Boy; The Magician's Nephew;* and *The Last Battle.* Related books: *The Hero from Otherwhere* (n); *Into the Painted Bear Lair* (n); *Search for Delicious* (n).

THE LONG JOURNEY
by Barbara Corcoran
Atheneum (paperback only), 1970
Gr. 3–6   188 pages

In a desperate effort to aid her stricken grandfather, 13-year-old Laurie sets off on horseback in search of her uncle at the other end of Montana. Skirting cities and towns for fear of trouble, this gritty heroine encounters both unexpected danger and friendship in a fast-paced contemporary story. Related books: *The Hero from Otherwhere* (n); *Toliver's Secret* (n); *Trouble River* (n); *Chancy and the Grand Rascal* by Sid Fleischman.

LOUIE'S LOT
by E. W. Hildick
David White, 1965
Gr. 4–7   146 pages

Without a doubt, this is one of the greatest read-alouds imaginable. Louie is a milkman in England—the toughest, most exacting, most respected, and most professional of all milkmen. The "Lot" refers to the lot of those boys who work for him. The story tells of one boy's struggle against savage dogs, milk-money thieves, competitors, and Louie in order to win a vacant spot in Louie's Lot. Great humor and magnificent language.

MAMA'S BANK ACCOUNT
by Kathryn Forbes
Scholastic (paperback only), 1975
Gr. 4–6   126 pages

This is the 1948 best-seller that became a Broadway play (twice) and the television hit, *I Remember Mama.* Its 17 chapters recalling turn-of-the-century San Francisco and a loving Norwegian-American family are perfect lessons about values, each one offering conflicts and alternatives. But at the heart of every chapter is the mother whose love towers over the entire book like a beacon light. For experienced listeners. Related books: *Waiting for Mama* (s); *The Witch of Fourth Street* (s).

MANDY
by Julie Andrews Edwards
Harper, 1971; Bantam, 1973
Gr. 3-6   196 pages
Ten-year-old Mandy climbs the orphanage wall one day to explore the woods—and finds a deserted cottage. A book dealing with the pitfalls of "little white lies," as well as love and friendship. For experienced listeners. Related books: *The Bad Times of Irma Baumlein* (n); *Grandmother Orphan* (s); *The Secret Garden* (n); *Wild Violets* (s).

THE MAN IN THE BOX: A STORY FROM VIETNAM
by Mary Lois Dunn
McGraw-Hill, 1968; Dell, 1975
Gr. 4-6   120 pages
An American airman is brought as a captive to a Vietnamese village by the Vietcong and held prisoner in a wooden box. A village youth recalls how his own father had been tortured in just such a way and vows to find a way to free the American. A gripping story of the punishment war wreaks on all sides. Related books: *A Bag of Marbles* (n); *The Foxman* (n); *Otto of the Silver Hand* (n); *Sing Down the Moon* (n); *Boris* by Jaap ter Haar.

ME AND CALEB
by Franklyn Mayer
Scholastic (paperback only), 1982
Gr. 4-6   160 pages
Don't miss this collection of adventures. The escapades of two brothers make entertaining as well as tender reading. The book's chapters are divided by months; thus the subjects match the seasons. Sequel: *Me and Caleb Again*. Related books: *Introducing Shirley Braverman* (n); *Peter Potts* (s); *Soup* (s).

THE MIDNIGHT FOX
by Betsy Byars
Viking, 1968; Penguin, 1981
Gr. 4-6   160 pages
From the very beginning, young Tommy is determined he'll hate his aunt and uncle's farm where he must spend the summer. His determination suffers a setback when he discovers a renegade black fox. His desire to keep the fox running free collides with his uncle's wish to kill it, and the novel builds to a stunning moment of confrontation and courage. An excellent book about values and superb character development. Also by the author: *The 18th Emergency* (n); *The Pinballs* (n); *Trouble River* (n); *Summer of the Swans*. Related books: *Gentle Ben* (n); *Stone Fox* (s); *Storm Boy* (s); *Weird Henry Berg* (n); *My Boy John That Went to Sea* by James Vance Marshall.

MR. POPPER'S PENGUINS
by Richard and Florence Atwater • Illustrated by Robert Lawson
Little, Brown, 1938; Dell, 1978
Gr. 2–4   140 pages
When you add twelve penguins to the family of Mr. Popper the house painter, you've got immense food bills, impossible situations, and a freezer full of laughs. Extra-short chapters that will keep your audience hungry for more. Related books: *Grasshopper and the Unwise Owl* (s); *Owls in the Family* (s); *Peter Potts* (s); *Ramona the Pest* (n).

MRS. FRISBY AND THE RATS OF NIMH
by Robert C. O'Brien
Atheneum (both), 1971
Gr. 4–6   232 pages
A fantasy–science fiction tale that can only be described as "unforgettable." A group of rats have become super-intelligent through a series of laboratory injections. Though it opens with an almost fairy-tale softness, it grows into a taut and frighteningly realistic tale. Also by the author: *The Silver Crown* (n). Related books: *The Cricket Winter* (n); *The Enormous Egg* (n); *The Flight of the Fox* (n); *The Hero from Otherwhere* (n); *The Twenty-One Balloons* (n); *The Walking Stones* (n).

MY BROTHER, THE WIND
by G. Clifton Wisler
Doubleday, 1979
Gr. 6 and up   184 pages
Set in the post–Civil War west, this is the story of a 7-year-old orphan boy taken captive by Indians and later sold to a mountain man. Their life together for the next ten years is depicted with all the legend, color, cruelty, and excitement that characterized the twilight years of the frontier. Readers should be cautioned that though there is no unnecessary violence in the story, it is depicted with great realism. Such descriptions can be skipped if necessary without losing the story's effectiveness. More than an adventure novel, this is an accurate historical picture and a story of personal sacrifice and love. This book was nominated for the National Book Award in 1979 and most likely will be found in the adult fiction section of public libraries. For experienced listeners. Related books: *Down the Long Hills* (n); *Sarah Bishop* (n); *Sing Down the Moon* (n); *Baker's Hawk* by Jack Bickham; *The Spirit of Cochise* by Elliott Arnold; *Where the Buffaloes Begin* by Olaf Baker.

OTTO OF THE SILVER HAND
by Howard Pyle
Scribner, 1954; Dover, 1967
Gr. 5–8   132 pages
First published in 1888 and written by one of the leading figures of American

children's literature, this book is an ideal introduction to the classics. Set in the Middle Ages, the narrative spins the tale of a young boy's joy and suffering as he rises above the cruelty of the world. Though the language may be somewhat foreign to the listener at the start, it soon adds to the flavor of the narrative. The story literally rings with the clash of armored knights and the solemn knell of monastery bells. For experienced listeners. Also by the author: for older children, *Men of Iron*. Related books: *A Bag of Marbles* (n); *The Man in the Box* (n); *Robin Hood* (n); *The Wish at the Top* (p); *Boris* by Jaap ter Haar.

OUR JOHN WILLIE
by Catherine Cookson
Bobbs-Merrill, 1974; New American Library, 1975
Gr. 4-8   192 pages
A gothic novel set in the mine country of northern England, this book portrays the unselfish love between two orphaned brothers (one is a deaf-mute). Add to this the forbidding figure of Miss Peamarsh, the village mystery woman, and you have a gripping historical novel set in the 1850s. Teachers and parents should note pages 152-53, which mention a child born out of marriage. For experienced listeners. This book usually is filed with adult fiction. Related books: *Burnish Me Bright* (s); *Child of the Silent Night* (n); *The Half-A-Moon Inn* (s).

THE PINBALLS
by Betsy Byars
Harper, 1977; Scholastic, 1979
Gr. 5-7   136 pages
Brought together under the same roof, three foster children prove to each other and the world that they are *not* pinballs to be knocked around from one place to the next; they have a choice in life—to try or not to try. The author has taken what could have been a maudlin story and turned it into a hopeful, loving, and very witty book. Very short chapters with easy-to-read dialogue. No wonder 58,000 school children in Georgia voted it their favorite in 1979. Also by the author: *The 18th Emergency* (n); *The Midnight Fox* (n); *Trouble River* (n); *Summer of the Swans; The Winged Colt of Casa Mia*. Related books: *Grandmother Orphan* (s); *Luke Was There* (s); *Slake's Limbo* (n).

PINCH
by Larry Callen
Little, Brown, 1976
Gr. 4-6   180 pages
Pinch, a boy growing up in the country, becomes involved with a pig he trains to hunt and a mean, crafty neighbor who teaches Pinch the art of trickery. The story deals with family and community relationships and personal honesty with a sense of drama and humor. Sequels: *The Deadly Mandrake; The Muskrat*

War. Also by the author: *Dashiel and the Night.* Related books: *Good Old Boy* (n); *Homer Price* (n); *Me and Caleb* (n); *Soup* (s); *Take It or Leave It* (p).

THE POND
by Robert Murphy
Dutton, 1964; Avon, 1965 (both OP)
Gr. 6 and up   254 pages
In my opinion, this is one of the finest juvenile novels ever written. I've yet to meet someone who has read it and not been deeply moved. It's about history: urban and suburban life in America in 1917. It's about nature: the mutual effects and affections between mankind and a patch of Virginia backwoods with its giant bass, wild turkeys, mink, and squirrels. It's about human nature: a young boy's coming of age as he realizes his own capacity for good and evil— whether through the gun he carries into the woods or through the kindness he carries into others' lives. The winner of numerous awards, *The Pond* has often been compared to *The Yearling* and *Rascal;* as a read-aloud, it wins any such comparison hands down. For experienced listeners. Related books: *A Day No Pigs Would Die* (n); *Incident at Hawk's Hill* (n); *Ironhead* (n); *My Brother, the Wind* (n).

PRISONERS AT THE KITCHEN TABLE
by Barbara Holland
Houghton Mifflin, 1979
Gr. 3–6   122 pages
Two neighborhood friends (a timid boy and boisterous girl) are pitted against a bickering husband-and-wife kidnapping team, a creepy, secluded farmhouse, and a week of waiting—waiting for food, waiting for ransom, waiting for a chance to escape. Along with a nice blend of humor and suspense, the author provides us with an excellent study of character development. Your listeners will think twice before accepting a ride with strangers after hearing this story. Also by the author: *The Pony Problem.* Related books: *The Adventures of Pinocchio* (n); *The Button Boat* (n); *Captain Grey* (n); *Five Were Missing* (n); *The Half-A-Moon Inn* (s); *Sing Down the Moon* (n); *The Wolves of Willoughby Chase* (n).

RAMONA THE PEST
by Beverly Cleary
Morrow, 1968; Dell, 1982
Gr. K–4   144 pages
Not all of Beverly Cleary's books make good read-alouds. A prolific writer for the early reader, her books sometimes move too slowly to hold read-aloud interest. But that's not so with *Ramona the Pest,* which follows the outspoken young lady through her early months in kindergarten. All children will smile in recognition at Ramona's encounters with the first day of school, show and tell, seat work, a substitute teacher, Halloween, young love—and dropping out of kindergarten. Long chapters can easily be divided. Sequels: *Ramona and Her*

Father; Ramona and Her Mother; Ramona Quimby, Age 8; Ramona the Brave.
Early grades should have some listening experience with read-alouds before
tackling these books. Related books: for older children, *Caddie Woodlawn* (n);
for younger children, *Freckle Juice* (s); *Madeline* (p); *The Magic Finger* (s); *Peter
Potts* (s); *Room 10* (s).

R, MY NAME IS ROSIE
by Barbara Cohen
Lothrop, 1978; Scholastic, 1980
Gr. 4-6   188 pages
In this book, the author offers us two complete stories, neatly intertwined. The
first is that of Rosie—11 years old, fat, and forgotten. Her widowed mother
manages the inn where Rosie and her brother and sister live, and in Rosie's
eyes, she also manages to overlook Rosie's potential. The second story (90
pages long) runs intermittently through the book, in the form of a serialized
fairy tale created by Rosie and her friend the bartender during their daily
meetings. Young listeners will recognize both Rosie's insecurities and her need
for a fantasy world to which she can retreat. And they will cheer her eventual
triumph both at home and in the other world. This book is a gentle reminder
to children of the need for fantasy in their lives and the purpose it serves. Try
reading some of the original Andersen and Grimm fairy tales after this book.
Also by the author: *Thank You, Jackie Robinson* (n); *Benny*. Related books: *The
Fairy Tale Treasury* (a); *Into the Painted Bear Lair* (n); *Introducing Shirley Braverman* (n).

ROBIN HOOD—PRINCE OF OUTLAWS
by Bernard Miles   •   Illustrated by Victor Ambrus
Rand McNally, 1979
Gr. 3-6   124 pages
Of the more than 700 books written on the famous outlaw of Sherwood
Forest, this is one of the most ambitious and most successful of contemporary
efforts. Relying as much as possible on fact and personal observation of the
historic English locale, the author has humanized Robin while retaining his
medieval flavor. His updating of the language to nearer present-day usage
brings the story within the listening bounds of children as young as third
grade. The book's format is large and allows for brilliant full-color illustrations
on every page. For experienced listeners. Also by the author and illustrator:
Favorite Tales From Shakespeare. Related books: *Otto of the Silver Hand* (n);
Search for Delicious (n); *The Wish at the Top* (p).

ROLL OF THUNDER, HEAR MY CRY
by Mildred Taylor
Dial, 1976
Gr. 5 and up   276 pages
Filled with the lifeblood of a black Mississippi family during the Depression,
this novel throbs with the passion and pride of a family that refuses to give in

to threats and harassments by white neighbors. The story is told through daughter Cassie, age 9, who experiences her first taste of social injustice and refuses to swallow it. She, her family, her classmates and neighbors will stir listeners' hearts and awaken many children to the problems of minorities in our society. Winner of the Newbery Award. For experienced listeners. Sequel: *Let the Circle Be Unbroken*. Related books: *A Bag of Marbles* (n); *The Lucky Stone* (s); *Sing Down the Moon* (n); *Words by Heart* (n).

SARAH BISHOP
by Scott O'Dell
Houghton Mifflin, 1980; Scholastic, 1982
Gr. 5 and up   184 pages
Based on an actual historical incident, this is the story of a courageous and determined young girl who flees war-torn Long Island after her father and brother are killed at the outbreak of the Revolutionary War. In the Connecticut wilderness, she takes refuge in a cave where she begins her new life. It is a story of constant courage, as well as a historical account of a time that shaped our nation's destiny. *Sarah Bishop* makes an interesting comparative study with two other read-aloud novels dealing with children running away: *Slake's Limbo* (n) and *Journey Outside* (n). Each approaches the subject from a different point in time but each poses the same question: Is any man or woman really an island unto themselves? For experienced listeners. Also by the author: *Sing Down the Moon* (n); *The King's Fifth*. Related books: for younger children, *The Long Journey* (n); *Toliver's Secret* (n); for older children, *The Witch of Blackbird Pond* (n).

THE SEARCH FOR DELICIOUS
by Natalie Babbitt
Farrar, 1969; Avon, 1974
Gr. 3–7   160 pages
Here is a small masterpiece: fantasy and the English language as they were meant to be written. After a nasty argument among the King, Queen, and their court over the correct meaning of the word "delicious," the Prime Minister's adopted son is dispatched to poll the kingdom and determine the choice of the people. The foolishness of man, his pettiness and quarrelsome nature are suddenly aroused by the poll: Everyone has a different personal definition of "delicious" and civil war looms. An excellent book about values that is guaranteed to challenge every child's sense of the word "delicious." Also by the author: *Tuck Everlasting* (n). Related books: *Chocolate Fever* (s); *The Chocolate Touch* (n); *Robin Hood* (n); *The Wish at the Top* (p).

THE SECRET GARDEN
by Frances Hodgson Burnett   •   Illustrated by Tasha Tudor
Lippincott, 1962; Dell, 1971
Gr. 2–5   256 pages
Few books spin such a web of magic about its readers (and listeners) as does

this children's classic (first published in 1911) about the contrary little orphan who comes to live with her cold, unfeeling uncle on the windswept English moors. Wandering the grounds of his immense manor house one day, she discovers a secret garden, locked and abandoned. This leads her to discover her uncle's invalid child hidden within the mansion, her first friendship, and her own true self. For experienced listeners. Also by the author: *Little Lord Fauntleroy; A Little Princess; The Lost Prince; Sara Crewe* (an earlier, shorter version of *A Little Princess*). Related books: *Bridge to Terabithia* (n); *Wild Violets* (s).

SING DOWN THE MOON
by Scott O'Dell
Houghton Mifflin, 1970; Dell, 1973
Gr. 3-6   138 pages
Through the first-person narrative of a 14-year-old Navaho girl, we follow the plight of the American Indian in 1864 when the U.S. government ordered the Navahos out of their Arizona homeland and marched them 300 miles to Fort Sumner, New Mexico, where they were imprisoned for four years. Known as "The Long Walk," it is a journey that has since become a part of every Navaho child's heritage. The injustices and the subsequent courage displayed by the Indians should be known by all Americans. The novel also provides a detailed account of daily Indian life during the period. Short chapters are told with the vocabulary and in the style appropriate to a young Indian child. Also by the author: *Sarah Bishop* (n). Related books: *Annie and the Old One* by Miska Miles; *The Indian in the Cupboard* (n); *The Man in the Box* (n); *Roll of Thunder, Hear My Cry* (n); *Where the Buffaloes Begin* by Olaf Baker. After reading *Sing Down the Moon* you might follow up with an article, "The Navajos," from the December 1972 *National Geographic,* for an updated view of the Navajo nation.

SLAKE'S LIMBO
by Felice Holman
Scribner, 1974; Dell, 1977
Gr. 5-8   117 pages
A 15-year-old takes his fears and misfortunes into the New York City subway one day, finds a hidden construction mistake in the shape of a cave near the tracks, and doesn't come out of the system for 121 days. The story deals simply but powerfully with the question: Can anyone be an island unto himself? It is as much a story of survival as it is a tale of personal discovery. This book makes an interesting comparative study with two other books which discuss running away, hiding, and personal discovery: *Journey Outside* (n) and *Sarah Bishop* (n). For experienced listeners. Other related books: *The Cay* (n); *J.T.* (n); *Luke Was There* (s); *Snow-Bound* (n).

THE SNAILMAN
by Brenda Sivers
Little, Brown, 1978
Gr. 3–6   118 pages
When a lonely young boy adopts the village's homely eccentric as his friend, he must stand against intense family and peer pressure to do otherwise. A novel that deals with overcoming loneliness. Related books: *The Leatherman* (p); *Old Mother Witch* (p); *A Time for Watching* (s); for older readers, *The Foxman* (n) and *The Witch of Blackbird Pond* (n).

SNOW-BOUND
by Harry Mazer
Delacorte, 1973; Dell, 1975
Gr. 5–8   146 pages
Two teenagers, a boy and a girl, marooned by a car wreck during a severe snowstorm, fight off starvation, frostbite, wild dogs, broken limbs, and personal bickering in order to survive. An excellent example of people's lives being changed for the better in overcoming adversity. Adults should be advised of occasional four-letter words in the dialogue. Related books: *The Call of the Wild* (n); *The Cay* (n); *Fire Storm* (n); *The Foxman* (n); *Slake's Limbo* (n); *Almost Too Late* by Elmo Wortman.

A STRANGER CAME ASHORE
by Mollie Hunter
Harper (both), 1975; 1977
Gr. 4–7   163 pages
The handsome stranger who claims to be the sole survivor of a shipwreck off the Scottish coast is really the Great Selkie, come to lure the Henderson family's beautiful daughter to her death at the bottom of the sea. Here is a novel brimming with legend and suspense. Also by the author: *The Smartest Man in Ireland* (s); *The Walking Stones* (n); *The Kelpie's Pearls*.

TALES OF A FOURTH GRADE NOTHING
by Judy Blume
Dutton, 1972; Dell, 1976
Gr. 3–5   120 pages
A perennial favorite among schoolchildren, this story deals with the irksome problem of a kid brother and his hilarious antics with his fourth-grade brother, Peter. Sequel: *Superfudge* (Readers-aloud should be cautioned that this book deals with the question: Is there or is there not a Santa Claus?). Also by the author: *Freckle Juice* (s). Related books: *Chocolate Fever* (s); *The Chocolate Touch* (n); *Humbug Mountain* (n); *Me and Caleb* (n); *Peter Potts* (s); *Ramona the Pest* (n).

THANK YOU, JACKIE ROBINSON
by Barbara Cohen
Lothrop, 1974
Gr. 5-7   126 pages
Set in the late 1940s, this is the story of young Sam Green, one of that rare breed known as the True Baseball Fanatic and a Brooklyn Dodger fan. His widowed mother runs an inn and when she hires a 60-year-old black cook, Sam's life takes a dramatic turn for the better. They form a fast friendship and begin to explore the joys of baseball in a way that the fatherless boy has never known. A tender book that touches on friendship, race, sports, personal sacrifice, and death. Also by the author: *R, My Name Is Rosie* (n); *Benny*. Related books: *The Cay* (n); *The Foxman* (n).

TOLIVER'S SECRET
by Esther Wood Brady
Crown, 1976; Avon, 1979
Gr. 3-5   166 pages
During the Revolutionary War, 10-year-old Ellen Toliver is asked by her ailing grandfather to substitute for him and carry a secret message through the British lines to a waiting courier. What he estimates to be a simple plan is complicated by Ellen's exceptional timidity and an unforeseen shift in the British plans. As much as this fast-paced historical novel is a study of the Revolutionary period, it is also a portrait of one child's personal growth in self-esteem and courage. Each chapter includes at least one heart-stopping crisis. In her second novel, *The Toad on Capitol Hill,* Brady views the War of 1812 and the burning of the Capitol through the eyes of another young girl—this time a fiercely independent one. Related books: *Call It Courage* (s); *The Long Journey* (n); *Prisoners at the Kitchen Table* (n); *Sing Down the Moon* (n); *Stone Fox* (s); *Boris* by Jaap ter Haar.

TROUBLE RIVER
by Betsy Byars
Viking, 1969; Penguin, 1972
Gr. 3-6   158 pages
A pioneer lad takes his cantankerous grandmother downriver on his makeshift raft to avoid an Indian attack. Forty miles later, they have learned much about each other's resolve and courage. Also by the author: *The Midnight Fox* (n). Related books: *Gramps* in the volume *Luke's Garden and Gramps* (s); *Sing Down the Moon* (n); *Stone Fox* (s); *The Walking Stones* (n); *Weird Henry Berg* (n).

TUCK EVERLASTING
by Natalie Babbitt
Farrar, 1975; Bantam, 1976
Gr. 4-7   124 pages
A young girl stumbles upon a family that has found the "Fountain of Youth,"

and in the aftermath there is a kidnapping, a murder, and a jailbreak. Touching and well written, this story suggests a sobering answer to the question: What would it be like to live forever? For experienced listeners. Also by the author: *The Search for Delicious* (n). Related books: *The Big Red Barn* (p); *A Taste of Blackberries* (s); *The Tenth Good Thing About Barney* (p).

THE TWENTY-ONE BALLOONS
by William Pène du Bois
Viking, 1947; Dell, 1969
Gr. 4–6   180 pages
Here is a literary smorgasbord; there are so many different and delicious parts one hardly knows which to mention first. The story deals with a retired teacher's attempts to sail by balloon across the Pacific in 1883, his crash landing and pseudo-imprisonment on the island of Krakatoa and, finally, his escape. The book is crammed with nuggets of science, history, humor, invention, superior language, and marvelous artwork. Winner of the Newbery Medal. For experienced listeners. Related books: *The Hero from Otherwhere* (n); *Mrs. Frisby and the Rats of NIMH* (n). You might follow up the Pène du Bois by reading "Mount St. Helens," in the January 1981 issue of *National Geographic*—an in-depth study of volcanoes.

THE WALKING STONES
by Mollie Hunter
Harper (paperback only), 1970
Gr. 3–6   144 pages
In a battle of the ancient versus the modern, an old wise man in the Scottish Highlands vows to stop the electric power company flooding the valley for a new power supply. The author's descriptions of the tender conspiracy between the old hermit and his young pupil will leave your listeners with a new feeling for the word "magic." Also by the author: *The Smartest Man in Ireland* (s); *A Stranger Came Ashore* (n). Related books: *The Cay* (n); *The Snailman* (n); *Stone Fox* (s); *Weird Henry Berg* (n).

WEIRD HENRY BERG
by Sarah Sargent
Crown, 1980; Dell, 1981
Gr. 4–6   114 pages
Twelve-year-old Henry is content to play the role of class weirdo and family recluse until the family heirloom he inherited from his grandfather hatches into a dragon. That's when Henry begins to change. That is also the moment when the dragon's relatives in Wales send an emissary to Henry's hometown in search of the newborn member of the clan. Henry's subsequent adventures with Millie, the town's elderly eccentric, in pursuit of the dragon are filled with a happy blend of mystery, humor, and fantasy. Related books: *The Half-*

A-Moon Inn (s); *The Indian in the Cupboard* (n); *The Reluctant Dragon* (s); *The Walking Stones* (n).

WHERE THE RED FERN GROWS
by Wilson Rawls
Doubleday, 1961; Bantam, 1974
Gr. 3–7   212 pages
A 10-year-old boy growing up in the Ozark mountains, praying and saving for a pair of hounds, finally achieves his wish. He then begins the task of turning the hounds into first-class hunting dogs. It would be difficult to find a book that speaks more definitively about perseverance, courage, family, sacrifice, work, life and death. Long chapters are easily divided. Related books: *Bridge to Terabithia* (n); *A Day No Pigs Would Die* (n); *The Dog Days of Arthur Cane* (n); *Lassie Come Home* (n); *Stone Fox* (s).

WINNING KICKER
by Thomas J. Dygard
Morrow, 1978
Gr. 6–8   190 pages
A hard-nosed football coach at the end of a long and successful career is jolted in his final season when a girl makes his high-school team as a place-kicker, potentially turning the season into a three-ring circus. The author offers a liberated and sensitive view of the family, school, and community pressures which attend such an occurrence. Sure to stir the interest of both sexes and make for lively class discussion. Also by the author: *Outside Shooter; Point Spread; Quarterback Walk-On; Running Scared; Soccer Duel.*

THE WITCH OF BLACKBIRD POND
by Elizabeth George Speare
Houghton Mifflin, 1958; Dell, 1972
Gr. 6 and up   250 pages
This Newbery Award–winning novel portrays an impetuous 16-year-old girl's struggles and growth in a Puritan community of Connecticut Colony. After being raised in a free-thinking tropical home, Kit balks at the narrow-minded ways of her aunt and uncle with whom she goes to live after the death of her grandfather. Seeking a port in her emotional storm, she wanders into friendship with a lonely old woman who is suspected by villagers of being a witch—a suspicion that is eventually pinned on the rebellious Kit as well. Particularly well drawn is the community's peer pressure and ostracism of the old woman because of her independent and unconventional ways. An excellent novel about values for experienced listeners. Also by the author: *Calico Captive*. Related books: *The Foxman* (n); *The Leatherman* (p); *Old Mother Witch* (p); *The Snailman* (n); *A Time for Watching* (s).

THE WOLVES OF WILLOUGHBY CHASE
by Joan Aiken
Doubleday, 1962; Dell, 1981

Gr. 3–6   168 pages

Here is Victorian melodrama in high gear: a great English estate surrounded by hungry wolves, two young girls mistakenly left in the care of a wicked, scheming governess, secret passageways and tortured flights through the snow in the dark of night. For experienced listeners. Sequels: *Black Hearts in Battersea; The Cuckoo Tree; Nightbirds on Nantucket; The Stolen Lake.*

THE WONDERFUL WIZARD OF OZ
by L. Frank Baum
Dover (paperback only), 1960; Ballantine, 1980

Gr. 1–5   260 pages

Before your children are exposed to the movie version, treat them to the magic of this 1900 book many regard as the first American fairy tale, as well as early American science fiction. (Incidentally, the book is far less terrifying for children than the film version.) The magical story of Dorothy and her friends' harrowing journey to the Emerald City is but the first of 14 books on the Land of Oz by the author. If your audience already has seen the movie, introduce them to one of the sequels: *Dorothy and the Wizard of Oz; The Emerald City of Oz; Glinda of Oz; The Lost Princess of Oz; The Magic of Oz; The Marvelous Land of Oz; Ozma of Oz; The Patchwork Girl of Oz; Rinkitink of Oz; The Road to Oz; The Scarecrow of Oz; Tik-tok of Oz; The Tin Woodman of Oz.*

WORDS BY HEART
by Ouida Sebestyen
Little, Brown, 1979; Bantam, 1981

Gr. 5 and up   162 pages

A young girl and her family must summon all their courage and spirit in order to survive as the only black family in this 1910 Texas community. The child's spunk, her father's tireless patience, and the great faith in God he leaves with her make this an unforgettable book. For experienced listeners. The slow-moving first chapter can be edited with prereading. Related books: *A Bag of Marbles* (n); *Roll of Thunder, Hear My Cry* (n); *Sing Down the Moon* (n).

Poetry

AT THE TOP OF MY VOICE
by Felice Holman
Scribner, 1970

Gr. K–6   56 pages

In these 18 poems, the author takes us on a witty and sprightly excursion into childhood with all of its triumphs, pretensions, wonders, disasters, and fears.

Also by the author: *The Cricket Winter* (n); *Slake's Limbo* (n). Related book: *If I Were in Charge of the World and Other Worries* (po).

THE BEST LOVED POEMS OF THE AMERICAN PEOPLE
Edited by Hazel Felleman
Doubleday, 1936
Gr. 3 and up   648 pages
As editor of the Queries and Answers page of *The New York Times Book Review,* Hazel Felleman was fully aware of the nation's tastes in poetry. By keeping track of the *Times*'s readers' poetry correspondence, she was able to compile the most often requested poems. Parents and teachers could not have been better served, especially when she arranged her anthology under various themes, thereby easing the burden of those who go in search of a poem to fit a particular child or occasion. Here are poems that tell a story (the best loved by children), poems of friendship, inspiration, home and motherhood, childhood, patriotism, humor, and animals. Usually filed in the poetry section of your library, most of these 575 poems are for experienced listeners.

CASEY AT THE BAT
by Ernest Thayer   •   Illustrated by Wallace Tripp
Coward, 1978
Gr. 2 and up   28 pages
This should be part of every child's poetic heritage. It describes a small-town baseball game and local hero. The color has neither changed nor faded from the game and its fans in the one hundred years since this poem was first written. The illustrations imbue the poem with a fablelike quality by casting it with animal characters wearing the fashions of 1888. When children have been treated to *Casey at the Bat,* they'll enjoy follow-up readings of lesser-known sequels: *Casey's Revenge* by James Wilson and *Casey: 20 Years Later* by S. P. McDonald, both included in *The Best Loved Poems of the American People* (po).

THE COVERED BRIDGE HOUSE
by Kaye Starbird   •   Illustrated by Jim Arnosky
Four Winds, 1979
Gr. 1–6   53 pages
A collection of 35 narrative poems about such whimsical children as the girl who hops on her horse one day and rides from New York to Vermont without leaving word with a soul; the leg-in-a-cast girl who becomes the world's highest jumper; sly little Beverly who becomes the scourge of Camp Blue Sky; and Artie Dole who can't control his imagination. There is also a new slant on why chickens cross the road.

THE GOLDEN TREASURY OF POETRY
Edited by Louis Untermeyer · Illustrated by Joan Walsh Anglund
Golden, 1959
Pre S. and up   324 (large) pages
One of the most ambitious poetry anthologies (and one of the best buys), this collection offers a wide variety of styles from the world's most respected poets and carries introductory comments by Untermeyer for most of the 379 selections. Collected especially for children, the poetry is divided into 12 sections, including animals, rhymes, people, stories, humor, and seasons.

HAILSTONES AND HALIBUT BONES
by Mary O'Neill · Illustrated by Leonard Weisgard
Doubleday (both), 1961; 1973
Pre S.–6   60 pages
Twelve poems which explore the spectrum of colors in the world around us and the feelings aroused by those colors. Mary O'Neill takes the commonplace object and shows us the glowing colors we've been taking for granted or missing.

HONEY, I LOVE
by Eloise Greenfield · Illustrated by Diane and Leo Dillon
Crowell, 1978
Pre S.–3   42 pages
Here are 16 short poems about the things and people children love: friends, cousins, older brothers, keepsakes, mother's clothes, music, and jump ropes. Set against an urban background, the poems elicit both joyous and bittersweet feelings.

A HOUSE IS A HOUSE FOR ME
by Mary Ann Hoberman · Illustrated by Betty Fraser
Viking, 1978; Puffin, 1982
Pre S.–6   44 pages
On the surface this book is a rhyming picture book about the variety of dwelling places people, animals, and insects call home. Below the surface it is an ingeniously entertaining study of metaphor: "cartons are houses for crackers," "a rose is a house for a smell," "a throat is a house for a hum." Such imagination-expanding thoughts can be easily developed after the book is finished. Encourage the class or child to compile their own list of houses. Also by the author: *Bugs; I Like Old Clothes; Nuts to You and Nuts to Me; The Raucous Auk; Yellow Butter Purple Jelly Red Jam Black Bread.*

IF I RAN THE ZOO
by Dr. Seuss
See page 130.

IF I WERE IN CHARGE OF THE WORLD
AND OTHER WORRIES
by Judith Viorst
Atheneum, 1981
Gr. 3 and up   56 pages
If the meter or rhyme in these 41 poems is occasionally imperfect, it is easily
overlooked in light of their perfect pulse and timing. In prescribing these short
verses "for children and their parents," this contemporary American humorist
offers a two-point perspective: Children reading these poems will giggle, then
recognize themselves, their friends and enemies, and think "That's really the
way it is!" Parents will recognize in the poems the child they used to be.
Witty, introspective, sometimes bittersweet poems on children's hopes, fears,
and feelings. Also by the author: *Alexander and the Terrible, Horrible, No Good,
Very Bad Day* (p); *I'll Fix Anthony* (p); *The Tenth Good Thing About Barney*
(p); *Alexander Who Used to Be Rich Last Sunday; My Mama Says There Aren't
Any Zombies, Ghosts, Vampires, Creatures, Demons, Monsters, Fiends, Goblins or
Things; Rosie and Michael.*

IS SOMEWHERE ALWAYS FAR AWAY?
by Leland B. Jacobs   •   Illustrated by John E. Johnson
Holt, 1967
Pre S.-4   42 pages
One of America's leading authorities on children's literature, Jacobs is also one
of our best children's poets. In this collection of 41 short poems, he applies his
gentle touch and wit to the magical though everyday charms children find in
the city or the country, in making believe, and right in their own homes. Also
by the author: *Hello, People!; Hello, Pleasant Places!; Hello, Year!; Teeny-Tiny.*
Also edited by the author: *Funny Bone Ticklers in Verse and Rhyme; Poetry for
Chuckles and Grins; Poetry of Witches, Elves and Goblins.*

MOTHER GOOSE,
A TREASURY OF BEST LOVED RHYMES
See page 137.

MY TANG'S TUNGLED AND
OTHER RIDICULOUS SITUATIONS
Collected by Sara and John Brewton, and G. Meredith Blackburn III
Crowell, 1973
Gr. 1 and up   112 pages
These 122 poems are a wonderful celebration of the ridiculous and the hi-
larious. No mercy is shown and no one escapes unscathed as some of our finest
poets take aim at friends, food, family, and schools. The opening 24 poems are
rhyming tongue-twisters that will challenge every reader-aloud and delight
children. Also collected by the Brewtons: *Laughable Limericks; Shrieks at
Midnight.*

THE NIGHT BEFORE CHRISTMAS
by Clement Moore • Illustrated by Tomie de Paola
Holiday House (both), 1980
Pre S.–6   30 pages

One of the most beloved American poems, it is still attracting the efforts of new artists 150 years after its creation. Using his own hundred-year-old farmhouse in a small New Hampshire village as a model and bordering each of the large-format pages with brightly colored New England quilt patterns, de Paola has created one of the most memorable editions of the classic. Also by the author-illustrator: *The Prince of the Dolomites* (p); *The Clown of God; Helga's Diary; The Hunter and the Animals* (wordless); *Nana Upstairs and Nana Downstairs; Now One Foot, Now the Other; Oliver Button Is a Sissy; Pancakes for Breakfast* (wordless).

NIGHTMARES: POEMS TO TROUBLE YOUR SLEEP
by Jack Prelutsky • Illustrated by Arnold Lobel
Greenwillow, 1976
Gr. 4 and up   40 pages

Here are a dozen poems to make your children squirm but never lose interest. The poet's haunting imagery brings out the worst of bogeymen, vampires, dragons of death, trolls, and ogres. Beneath the cobwebs and gloom, young listeners will find a crackling sense of humor. Sequel: *The Headless Horseman Rides Tonight*. Also by the author: for younger children, *Circus; It's Halloween; The Mean Old Hyena; The Pack Rat's Day and Other Poems; The Queen of Eene; The Snopp on the Sidewalk; The Wild Baby* (po). Related book: *Scary Stories to Tell in the Dark* (a).

NOW WE ARE SIX
by A. A. Milne • Illustrated by Ernest H. Shepard
Dutton, 1927; Dell, 1975
K and up   104 pages

This best-selling classic celebrates the dreams and nonsense of childhood in 31 narrative poems: stories of good children and naughty children, foolish kings, and imaginary friends. For experienced listeners. Also by the author: *The House at Pooh Corner; When We Were Very Young* (poetry); *Winnie-the-Pooh*.

OH, SUCH FOOLISHNESS
Collected by William Cole • Illustrated by Tomie de Paola
Lippincott, 1978
Gr. 1–6   70 pages

One of our most prolific anthologists, William Cole offers here 57 poems—some long, some short, some spooky, some spoofy, but all decidedly humorous. Other anthologies by the author: *Beastly Boys and Ghastly Girls; A Book of Animal Poems; The Book of Giggles; Good Dog Poems; Knock Knocks: The Most*

Ever; Knock Knocks You've Never Heard Before; Oh, That's Ridiculous; Oh, What Nonsense.

OUT IN THE DARK AND DAYLIGHT
by Aileen Fisher • Illustrated by Gail Owens
Harper, 1980
Pre S.–5 152 pages
This award-winning poet's specialty is polishing the drab, taken-for-granted things in a child's life in such a way that we see colors and dimensions we've never observed before. Only Aileen Fisher would ask if rabbit ears hear better than horses' ears, or if basset ears hear better than robins'. Only she would ask what kind of debt a caterpillar owes for all of his nibbles, or if parks grow lonely in the winter. In asking such questions, she stirs a child's sense of wonder. These 140 short poems are arranged chronologically by seasons and holidays for easy reference. Other poetry by the author: *Anybody Home?; Cricket in a Thicket; Do Bears Have Mothers, Too?; Easter; Going Barefoot; In One Door and Out the Other; I Stood Upon a Mountain; My Cat Has Eyes of Sapphire Blue.*

PIPER, PIPE THAT SONG AGAIN
Collected by Nancy Larrick
Random, 1965
Pre S.–6 84 pages
An often-cited anthology that touches all bases of childhood. The verse is short, light, highly readable, and represents many of the best poets in its 76 selections. Also collected by the author: *Piping Down the Valleys Wild; Poetry for Holidays* and *More Poetry for Holidays; Room for Me and a Mountain Lion.*

SEE MY LOVELY POISON IVY
by Lilian Moore • Illustrated by Diane Dawson
Atheneum, 1975
Pre S.–4 48 pages
If a witch's child asked her mother to tell her a story these 35 poems would be just what she wanted. Filled with tongue-in-cheek drama and eeriness, they touch upon shadows, cats, trolls, ghouls and ghosts, monsters, haunted houses, ogres, and witches. Typical of Moore's light touch is the poem about a child who has misplaced his head and is worried because everything he needs is in it.

WHERE THE SIDEWALK ENDS
by Shel Silverstein
Harper, 1974
K–8 166 pages
This is, without question, the best-loved collection of poetry for children. (It sold 1 million copies during its first eight years in print.) When it comes to knowing children's appetites Silverstein is pure genius. The titles alone are

enough to bring children to rapt attention: "Bandaids"; "Boa Constrictor"; "Crocodile's Toothache"; "The Dirtiest Man in the World"; "If I Had a Brontosaurus"; "Recipe for a Hippopotamus Sandwich." Here are 130 poems that will either touch children's hearts or tickle their funny bones. Equally marvelous is Silverstein's second book of poetry, *A Light in the Attic*. Also by the author-illustrator: *The Giving Tree* (p); *Lafcadio, the Lion Who Shot Back* (s).

THE WILD BABY
by Barbro Lindgren • **Illustrated by Eva Eriksson**
Greenwillow, 1981
Pre S.–5   22 pages
Adapted from the Swedish by American poet Jack Prelutsky, this rhyming narrative follows a mischievous child whose naughty exploits never dampen his mother's love for him. Also by Prelutsky: *Nightmares* (po). Related books: *Deep in the Forest* (p); *The Giving Tree* (p); *Henry the Explorer* (p).

THE WINGDINGDILLY
by Bill Peet
See page 153.

Anthologies

THE AMERICAN SPIRIT
Compiled by Reader's Digest
Berkley–Reader's Digest (paperback only), 1981
Gr. 7 and up   260 pages
This collection of 57 articles is pure Americana: here is the wit, the enthusiasm, the genius, and the spirit that shaped a nation; America at war and peace, yesterday and today, laughing and crying—from baseball stories and campaign buttons to the night the Martians landed. Its authors include Martin Luther King, Jr., writing on fear, John Steinbeck on his neighbors, Russell Baker on John Alden, and Mark Twain on Ben Franklin. Most of the selections average four pages in length and are ideal for introducing the listening experience and a little history to older children.

ANIMALS CAN BE ALMOST HUMAN
Compiled by Reader's Digest
Reader's Digest, 1979
Gr. 3 and up   416 pages
This collection of 82 true-to-life animal stories offers something for everyone and every moment: from rib-ticklers to heart-stoppers, from parakeets to porcupines, from the jungles to Jersey, from the long to the short. Beautifully

illustrated throughout. Also by Reader's Digest: *The American Spirit* (a); *Drama in Real Life* (a); *Unforgettable Characters* (a); *Animals You Will Never Forget.*

A BOOK OF MAGIC ANIMALS
by Ruth Manning-Sanders
Dutton, 1974
Gr. 2–7   128 pages
The author has spent a lifetime combing the world for magic and collecting it in more than a dozen books, each brimming with international folk and fairy tales. Each volume is written in a style that is easily read aloud and contains as many as 21 tales. The series also includes: *A Book of Cats and Creatures; A Book of Charms and Changelings; A Book of Devils and Demons; A Book of Dragons; A Book of Dwarfs; A Book of Ghosts and Goblins; A Book of Giants; A Book of Kings and Queens; A Book of Mermaids; A Book of Monsters; A Book of Ogres and Trolls; A Book of Princes and Princesses; A Book of Sorcerers and Spells; A Book of Spooks and Spectres; A Book of Witches; A Book of Wizards.*

CRICKET'S CHOICE
Edited by Clifton Fadiman and Marianne Carus
Open Court, 1974
Pre S.–4   290 pages
This is one of the most versatile collections of children's read-aloud stories ever assembled: poetry and pictures, scary stories and funny stories, fiction and nonfiction, folk tales, fairy tales, and tall tales. The collection is based upon stories that have appeared in *Cricket: The Magazine for Children* (see Chapter 6).

DRAMA IN REAL LIFE
Compiled by Reader's Digest
Berkley–Reader's Digest (paperback only), 1980
Gr. 6 and up   260 pages
This volume includes 50 inspiring true stories of human courage, ingenuity, and endurance in the face of terror and tragedy. These fast-moving accounts (each averaging 6 pages in length) are ideal for introducing older children to the listening experience and exposing them to some extraordinary role models. Also compiled by Reader's Digest: *The American Spirit* (a); *Unforgettable Characters* (a).

THE FAIRY TALE TREASURY
Collected by Virginia Haviland · Illustrated by Raymond Briggs
Coward, 1972; Dell, 1980
Pre S.–4   191 pages
While head of the children's book section of the Library of Congress, Virginia Haviland selected 32 of the most popular fairy tales of all time, including favorites from Andersen, Grimm, Jacobs, and Perrault. Her choices range from

the short and simple "Henny Penny" to the more complex "Snow White." Presented in large format with full-color illustrations in both hardcover and paper.

FREE TO BE YOU AND ME
Edited by Carole Hart, Letty C. Pogrebin, Mary Rodgers, and Marlo Thomas
McGraw-Hill (paperback only), 1974
Pre S.-3   116 pages
This is a liberated collection of stories, songs, poems, drawings, and photos aimed at encouraging children to the highest goals regardless of sex or race. With humor and sensitivity, many contemporary stereotypes are challenged and subdued here by a variety of authors for children, including: Judy Blume, Lucille Clifton, Carol Hall, Betty Miles, Carl Reiner, Mary Rodgers, Shel Silverstein, Judith Viorst, and Arnold Lobel. A record of the book's songs is also available through libraries and record stores.

GIANT KIPPERNOSE AND OTHER STORIES
by John Cunliffe
Deutsch, 1972
Gr. 1–4   112 pages
This collection of the author's short stories for primary-grade youngsters (an area that is largely ignored in the short-story field) has everything this age group demands in its books: originality, suspense, humor, ferocious villains, and happy endings. Typical is the giant in the title story: When Kippernose comes to town, people flee the streets, bolt the doors, and lock their windows—despite his tearful pleadings that he only wants to be their friend. Unbeknownst to Kippernose, it is not his size they fear—it is his smell. He hasn't taken a bath, changed his socks, or brushed his teeth in a hundred years. But who has the nerve (or the nose) to instruct a giant on personal hygiene? Other collections by the author: *The Adventures of Pip; The Great Dragon Competition and Other Stories; Riddles and Rhymes and Rigmaroles.*

THE MAID OF THE NORTH
by Ethel Johnston Phelps
Holt, 1981
Gr. 2 and up   174 pages
In an effort to balance a field that is top-heavy with heroes, this collection of fast-moving folk and fairy tales offers us twenty-one heroines from seventeen different ethnic cultures. Like their counterparts of the opposite sex, they are resourceful, clever, confident, with a clear sense of self-worth, sometimes physically attractive but always morally attractive. These tales have the perfect balance of compassion, humor, and conflict. They will appeal to boys as well as girls, and each can be read in a single sitting. Also by the author: *Tatterhood*

and Other Tales. Related books: *Into the Painted Bear Lair* (n); *R, My Name Is Rosie* (n).

PAUL HARVEY'S THE REST OF THE STORY
by Paul Aurandt
Doubleday, 1977; Bantam, 1978
Gr. 6 and up   234 pages

These collections of broadcaster Paul Harvey's five-minute radio show, *The Rest of the Story,* are perfect for teachers and parents trying to win older students to the art of listening. Nearly all of these pieces deal with famous people past and present. The person's name is saved for the last few lines of the tale and serves as an O. Henry punch. The 81 stories average 2 pages in length. Sequel: *More of Paul Harvey's The Rest of the Story.* Related books: *Drama in Real Life* (a); *Unforgettable Characters* (a).

SCIENCE FICTION TALES:
INVADERS, CREATURES, AND ALIEN WORLDS
Edited by Roger Elwood
Rand McNally (both), 1973
Gr. 3–6   124 pages

These 7 tales are an excellent science fiction sampler for middle-grade young people, an age level that is largely overlooked in sci-fi publishing. Sequel: *More Science Fiction Tales.* Related books: *The Fallen Spaceman* (s); *The Hero from Otherwhere* (n); *Baleful Beasts and Eerie Creatures* edited by Roger Elwood.

SCARY STORIES TO TELL IN THE DARK
Collected by Alvin Schwartz   •   Illustrated by Stephen Gammell
Lippincott, 1981
Gr. 5 and up   112 pages

Dipping into the folk vaults of the past and present, the author presents 29 American "horror" stories and songs guaranteed to make your listeners cringe. The text includes suggestions for the reader-aloud on when to pause, when to scream, even when to turn off the lights. The selections run the gamut from giggles to gore and average 2 pages in length. In addition, a source section briefly traces each tale's origin in the U.S. Discretion is advised because of the subject matter. Related book: *Nightmares* (po).

A SPECIAL KIND OF COURAGE:
PROFILES OF YOUNG AMERICANS
by Geraldo Rivera
Simon & Schuster, 1976; Bantam, 1977
Gr. 6 and up   274 pages

Written by an award-winning television reporter, here are 11 true stories about 11 children of our time who chose to be extraordinarily brave in character or heart: the lone survivor of a gigantic jetliner crash fighting for his 11-year-old life and winning the hearts of an entire city; Bernard Carabello, mistakenly assigned to one of the nation's worst mental institutions, struggling to let the world know there has been a terrible mistake; Henry Schwartz, knifed to death when he refused to let two neighborhood teenagers steal a young boy's bike.

In only one of the stories does the author slacken his fast pace. In telling the story of Gail Etienne, the first black child to be integrated into a New Orleans public school, he becomes bogged down in a long description of the political-legislative history preceding the child's first day in school. This may leave some listeners restless unless the reader-aloud does some editing beforehand. Another note of caution: While Rivera's subjects will wrench your children's hearts, their language may burn your tongue. Rivera pulls no punches and you may want to read the stories ahead of time to make any adjustments you deem necessary. Each of the stories is approximately 20 pages in length. Related book: *Drama in Real Life* (a).

UNFORGETTABLE CHARACTERS
Compiled by Reader's Digest
Berkley–Reader's Digest (paperback only), 1980
Gr. 6 and up   244 pages
This collection profiles the lives of 36 people and the qualities in their lives that brought joy, inspiration, and love to those fortunate enough to know them. They include famous figures like Robert Frost, Babe Ruth, Helen Keller, Albert Einstein, and Booker T. Washington, as well as comparative unknowns. Fast-moving stories that average 6 pages in length, they are ideal for introducing the listening experience to older children. Related books: *The American Spirit* (a); *Drama in Real Life* (a); *Paul Harvey's The Rest of the Story* (a); *A Special Kind of Courage* (a).

WITH A DEEP SEA SMILE:
STORY HOUR STRETCHES FOR LARGE
OR SMALL GROUPS
by Virginia Tashjian   •   Illustrated by Rosemary Wells
Little, Brown, 1974
Pre S.–3   129 pages
Here's a potpourri of stories, poems, chants, finger games, riddles, jokes, and tongue twisters that will charm even the most restless child. The selections are short, filled with good humor, and most invite audience participation with vocal responses. Also by the author: *Juba This and Juba That.*

A WONDER BOOK
by Nathaniel Hawthorne
Airmont, 1966; Grosset, 1967
Gr. 4–8   160 pages
Fearing that the classical tone of the ancient myths would frighten future

generations of children away from these great stories, Nathaniel Hawthorne produced this collection in 1851. Translating the classical language into modern romantic, he used a keen ear that was carefully tuned to children. Sadly, the book is not well known by today's parents and educators.

The book is divided into six chapters, each treating a different myth. The stories are supposedly told by a college student to his cousins, and his conversations with them serve as transitions between the various tales. These conversations are the least successful and the least necessary parts of the book, and I recommend that you skip them entirely.

Many everyday expressions and symbols have their roots in these myths, and children will gain a new appreciation for such expressions after hearing them. The myths include: "The Gorgon's Head," a marvelous monster story; "Paradise of Children," the story of Pandora's box; "The Golden Touch," the story of King Midas; "The Three Golden Apples," the story of Hercules; "The Miraculous Pitcher," the rewards of a charitable heart; "The Chimaera," the story of Pegasus, the winged horse. Of the six tales I find "The Three Golden Apples" to be the least successful for reading aloud. For experienced listeners.

WORLD TALES
Collected by Idries Shah
Harcourt, 1979
Gr. 5 and up   259 pages
The brotherhood of nations and the intimate nature of the family of man is never more obvious than in this collection of 65 fairy tales and myths, all pointing to the "extraordinary coincidence of stories told in all times, in all places." Supported by his thirty-five years of research into the world's oral and written heritage of tales, the author introduces each tale with a brief but fascinating description of its ancestry. For example, in presenting the tale of Cinderella as told by the Algonquin Indians, he notes the appearance of more than 300 Cinderella tales throughout the world, including one in China dating back to the ninth century. With a cross section of world cultures represented, this is an ideal volume to read aloud to world history or geography classes. The volume includes more than 100 full-color paintings by 37 popular illustrators working in diverse styles. For experienced listeners.

YOU'RE DUMBER IN THE SUMMER
by Jim Aylward
Holt, 1980
Gr. 6 and up   64 pages
This is the perfect book for those who have only a minute or two to spare for read-aloud. This collection of little-known but fascinating facts is addictive— once you've started them, you don't want to stop. You'll find answers to the following questions: how many windows are broken by baseballs each year? what does the bump on your nose mean? how many other people in the world share your birthday? what is America's favorite food and dessert? how often

does the average person lose his temper each week? which kills more people—bee stings, lightning, or snake bites? what is the third most popular name in the Manhattan phone directory? Related books: *Amazing Real Life Coincidences* by Douglas Colligan; *FACTS-ination* by Florence H. Munat.

ZLATEH THE GOAT AND OTHER STORIES
by Isaac B. Singer • Illustrated by Maurice Sendak
Harper, 1966
Gr. 3–6   90 pages
The magic of one of the world's great storytellers and winner of the Nobel Prize for literature is seen in these seven folk tales. Derived from the Eastern European Jewish oral tradition, the captivating blend of humor, fantasy, and devilry in these stories has become a Singer trademark. For experienced listeners.

Notes

CHAPTER 1

1. Courtney B. Cazden, *Child Language and Education* (New York: Holt, Rinehart and Winston, 1972).
2. U.S. Office of Education, "Adult Performance Level Project," 1975. See also *The New York Times* article on the Ford Foundation study on the vastness of American illiteracy, September 9, 1979, p. 1.
3. Harry F. Waters, "What TV Does to Kids," *Newsweek,* February 21, 1977, p. 63.
4. John Steinbeck, *The Acts of King Arthur and His Noble Knights* (New York: Farrar, Straus and Giroux, 1976), p. 3.
5. *The New York Times,* August 11, 1981, p. C6.
6. Chow Loy Tom, "What Teachers Read to Pupils in the Middle Grades," (Dissertation, Ohio State University, 1969), p. 174. See also: Chow Loy Tom, "Paul Revere Rides Ahead: Poems Teachers Read to Pupils in the Middle Grades," *Library Quarterly,* vol. 43 (January 1973), pp. 27–38.
7. California State Department of Education, "Student Achievement in California Schools, 1979–80 Annual Report" (Sacramento, Calif., 1980).
8. Richard Allington, "If They Don't Read Much, How They Gonna Get Good?" *Journal of Reading,* October 1977, pp. 57–61. See also: Richard Allington, "Sustained Approaches to Reading and Writing," *Language Arts,* September 1975, pp. 813–15.
9. Bruno Bettelheim, *The Uses of Enchantment: The Meaning and Importance of Fairy Tales* (New York: Knopf, 1976), pp. 3–6.

10. Robert Penn Warren, "Why Do We Read Fiction," *Saturday Evening Post,* October 20, 1962, pp. 82–84.

11. Dorothy Cohen, "The Effect of Literature on Vocabulary and Reading Achievement," *Elementary English,* vol. 45 (February 1968), pp. 209–213, 217. See also: Bernice Cullinan, Angela Jaggar, and Dorothy Strickland, "Language Expansion for Black Children in the Primary Grades: A Research Report," *Young Children,* vol. 29 (January 1974), pp. 98–112.

CHAPTER 2

1. These remarks were made during a half-hour interview (September 3, 1979) with Dr. Brazelton conducted by John Merrow for *Options in Education,* a co-production of National Public Radio and the Institute for Educational Leadership of the George Washington University. See note 7 below.

2. Dorothy Butler, *Cushla and Her Books* (Boston: The Horn Book, 1980).

3. Anthony Brandt, "Literacy in America," *The New York Times,* August 25, 1980, p. 25.

4. Benjamin Bloom, *Stability and the Change in Human Characteristics* (New York: Wiley, 1964), p. 72.

5. Martin Deutsch, "The Disadvantaged Child and the Learning Process," in *Education in Depressed Areas,* ed. A. Harry Passow (New York: Teachers College, 1963), pp. 168–78.

6. Jerome Kagan, "The Child: His Struggle for Identity," *Saturday Review,* December 1968, p. 82. See also: Steven R. Tulkin and Jerome Kagan, "Mother-Child Interaction in the First Year of Life," *Child Development,* March 1972, pp. 31–41.

7. A complete transcript of this interview is available by writing: *Options in Education,* 2025 M Street, N.W., Washington, D.C., 20036.

8. Further examples of "concept–attention span" can be found in Jerome Kagan, "The Child: His Struggle for Identity," p. 82.

9. Dolores Durkin, *Children Who Read Early* (New York: Teachers College, 1966). See also: Anne D. Forester, "What Teachers Can Learn from 'Natural Readers,'" *Reading Teacher,* November 1977, pp. 160–66; Margaret M. Clark, *Young Fluent Readers* (London: Heinemann, 1976).

10. *The New York Times,* March 22, 1959, Section IV, p. 9.

11. Paula Fox's comments are reported by Augusta Baker in a biographical note on Fox for *Newbery and Caldecott Medal Books 1966–1975* (Boston: The Horn Book, 1975), pp. 124–25.

CHAPTER 3

1. Clifton Fadiman, *Empty Pages: A Search for Writing Competence in Schools and Society* (Belmont, Calif.: Fearon Pitman, 1979), p. 157.

2. Barbara Cass-Beggs, *Your Baby Needs Music* (New York: St. Martin's, 1980). A poignant example of this phenomenon is described by Barry Farrell in *Pat and Roald* (New York: Random, 1969), p. 22. When actress Patricia Neal (wife of author Roald Dahl) was struck by a series of near-fatal strokes, she suffered a total loss of language memory. While her loss of language was complete and required more than a year's recovery, she never lost the language or memory of the songs she learned as a child. Her first words after twenty-two days of total silence were the words to a childhood song.

3. Bruno Bettelheim, *The Uses of Enchantment: The Meaning and Importance of Fairy Tales* (New York: Knopf, 1976), pp. 17–18.

4. Kornei Chukovsky, *From Two to Five,* trans. Miriam Morton (Berkeley, Calif.: University of California, 1963), pp. 7, 9.

5. Eli M. Bower, "The Magic Symbols," *Today's Education,* vol. 57 (January 1968), pp. 28–31.

6. Bruno Bettelheim, *The Uses of Enchantment,* pp. 3–19.

7. Donald Barr, *Who Pushed Humpty Dumpty? Dilemmas in American Education Today* (New York: Atheneum, 1971), p. 69.

8. Richard Abrahamson, "An Analysis of Children's Favorite Picture Storybooks," *Reading Teacher,* November 1980, pp. 167–70. *Children's Choices* is an annual publication of the International Reading Association in conjunction with the Children's Book Council. Its purpose is to publicize the favorite books of school children across the U.S., and a copy may be obtained by sending an SASE (first-class postage for 2 ounces) to Children's Book Council, 67 Irving Place, New York, N.Y., 10003.

9. William F. Coughlin, Jr., and Brendan Desilets, "Frederick the Field Mouse Meets Advanced Reading Skills as Children's Literature Goes to High School," *Reading Journal,* December 1980, pp. 207–11.

10. Robert C. O'Brien, "Newbery Award Acceptance," *Newbery and Caldecott Medal Books 1966–1975* (Boston: The Horn Book, 1975), pp. 83–89.

11. Daniel N. Fader and Elton B. McNeil, *Hooked on Books: Program and Proof* (New York: Berkley, 1968), pp. 65–67.

12. Katherine Paterson, "National Book Award Acceptance," *The Horn Book,* August 1979, pp. 402–3.

13. Bernice E. Cullinan, with Mary K. Karrer and Arlene M. Pillar, *Literature and the Child* (New York: Harcourt Brace Jovanovich, 1981), p. 250.

14. Donald Barr, *Who Pushed Humpty Dumpty?,* pp. 313–14.

15. Arthur Schlesinger, Jr., "Advice From a Reader-Aloud-to-Children," *The New York Times Book Review,* November 25, 1979.

16. Emma Halstead Swain, "Using Comic Books to Teach Reading and Language Arts," *Journal of Reading,* December 1978, pp. 253–58. See also: Larry Dorrell and Ed Carroll, "Spider-Man at the Library," *School Library Journal,* August 1981, pp. 17–19.

CHAPTER 5

1. C. S. Lewis, "On Three Ways of Writing for Children," *The Horn Book,* October 1963, pp. 459–69.
2. Edward W. Rosenheim, Jr., "Children's Reading and Adults' Values," *Library Quarterly,* January 1967, p. 3.

CHAPTER 6

1. Lester Del Rey, *Early Del Rey* (Garden City, N.Y.: Doubleday, 1975), pp. 3–4.

CHAPTER 7

1. Paul Copperman, *The Literacy Hoax: The Decline of Reading, Writing, and Learning in the Public Schools and What We Can Do About It* (New York: Morrow, 1980), p. 166.
2. California Department of Education, "Student Achievement in California Schools, 1979–80 Annual Report," P.O. Box 271, Sacramento, Calif., 96802.
3. Meg Schwarz, "Broadcasting Books to Young Audiences," *RE:ACT,* Spring/Summer 1980, p. 19. Mr. Rushnell's remarks were made at a symposium cosponsored by Action for Children's Television (ACT) and the Library of Congress Center for the Book. *RE:ACT* is a non-profit journal published by Action for Children's Television.
4. Neil Postman, *Teaching as a Conserving Activity* (New York: Delacorte, 1980), pp. 77–78.
5. Jackie S. Busch, "TV's Effects on Reading: A Case Study," *Phi Delta Kappan,* June 1978, pp. 668–71.
6. Wilbur Schramm, Jack Lyle, and Edwin B. Parker, *Television in the Lives of Our Children* (Stanford, Calif.: Stanford, 1961).
7. Frank Mankiewicz and Joel Swerdlow, *Remote Control: Television and the Manipulation of American Life* (New York: Times Books, 1978), pp. 6, 15–72.
8. Neil Postman, *Teaching as a Conserving Activity,* p. 208.
9. Frank Mankiewicz and Joel Swerdlow, *Remote Control,* p. 6.
10. Bob Keeshan's remarks were made during an interview September 24, 1979, with John Merrow for *Options in Education,* a co-production of National Public Radio and the Institute for Educational Leadership of the George Washington University. A cassette recording or transcript of this interview is available by writing to *Options in Education,* 2025 M Street, N.W., Washington, D.C., 20036.
11. John Leo, "How the Hostages Came Through," *Time,* February 9, 1981, p. 52; Gregg W. Downey, "Keough Ponders the Lessons of Captivity," *Executive Educator,* May 1981, pp. 24–29.
12. Further evidence can be found in Alexander Dolgun's autobiographical

account of his role as a "storyteller" for 129 Soviet prisoners in a labor camp cell measuring 16' wide by 40' long. See Alexander Dolgun, with Patrick Watson, *Alexander Dolgun's Story: An American in the Gulag* (New York: Knopf, 1975), pp. 138–49.

13. Kornei Chukovsky, "The Battle of the Fairy Tale: Three Stages," in *From Two to Five* (Berkeley, Calif.: University of California, 1963), pp. 122–130.

14. Sylvia Ashton-Warner, *Spearpoint: "Teacher" in America* (New York: Vintage, 1974), pp. 85–88.

15. Rhoderick J. Elen, "Listening: Neglected and Forgotten in the Classroom," *Elementary English*, February 1972, pp. 230–32.

16. Paul Kresh, "Short Stories Can Make Lively Disks," *The New York Times*, December 13, 1981, pp. 28–29. The author offers an extensive listing of records and cassettes in this article and is currently preparing a book on the subject. See also "To the Dickens and Other Authors by Way of Cassette," *The New York Times*, June 13, 1982, p. 4H.

17. Marie Carbo, "Teaching Reading with Talking Books," *Reading Teacher*, December 1978, pp. 267–73.

CHAPTER 8

1. Robert A. McCracken, "Instituting Sustained Silent Reading," *Journal of Reading*, May 1971, pp. 521–24, 582–83.

2. Mark C. Sadoski, "An Attitude Survey for Sustained Silent Reading Programs," *Journal of Reading*, May 1980, pp. 721–26.

3. Richard Allington, "If They Don't Read Much, How They Gonna Get Good?" *Journal of Reading*, October 1977, pp. 57–61.

4. Michael H. Kean, Anita H. Summers, Mark J. Raivetz, and Irvin J. Farber, "What Works in Reading? Summary and Results of a Joint School District/Federal Reserve Bank Empirical Study in Philadelphia," The School District of Philadelphia: ERIC Report ED176216, May 1979, p. 8 of document résumé.

5. Martha Efta, "Reading in Silence," *Teaching Exceptional Children*, Fall 1978, pp. 12–14.

6. Robert A. McCracken and Marlene J. McCracken, "Modeling Is the Key to Sustained Silent Reading," *Reading Teacher*, January 1978, pp. 406–8. See also: Linda B. Gambrell, "Getting Started with Sustained Silent Reading and Keeping It Going," *Reading Teacher*, December 1978, pp. 328–31.

CHAPTER 9

1. Jacques Barzun, *Teacher in America* (Garden City, N.Y.: Doubleday, 1954), pp. 60–62, 136.

Bibliography

Ashton-Warner, Sylvia. *Spearpoint: "Teacher" in America.* New York: Vintage, 1974.

Barr, Donald. *Who Pushed Humpty Dumpty? Dilemmas in American Education Today.* New York: Atheneum, 1971.

Barzun, Jacques. *Teacher in America.* Garden City, New York: Doubleday, 1954.

Bernard, Harold W. *Child Development and Learning.* Boston: Allyn and Bacon, 1973.

Bettelheim, Bruno. *The Uses of Enchantment: The Meaning and Importance of Fairy Tales.* New York: Knopf, 1976.

Bloom, Benjamin. *Stability and the Change in Human Characteristics.* New York: Wiley, 1964.

Butler, Dorothy. *Babies Need Books.* New York: Atheneum, 1980.

——— . *Cushla and Her Books.* Boston: The Horn Book, 1980.

Cass-Beggs, Barbara. *Your Baby Needs Music.* New York: St. Martin's, 1980.

Cazden, Courtney B. *Child Language and Education.* New York: Holt, Rinehart and Winston, 1972.

Chukovsky, Kornei. *From Two to Five.* Translated by Miriam Morton. Berkeley, Calif.: University of California Press, 1963.

Clark, Margaret M. *Young Fluent Readers.* London: Heinemann, 1976.

Copperman, Paul. *The Literacy Hoax: The Decline of Reading, Writing, and*

Learning in the Public Schools and What We Can Do About It. New York: Morrow, 1980.

Cullum, Albert. *Aesop in the Afternoon.* New York: Citation Press, 1972.

Cullinan, Bernice E., with Karrer, Mary K., and Pillar, Arlene M. *Literature and the Child.* New York: Harcourt Brace Jovanovich, 1981.

Del Rey, Lester. *Early Del Rey.* New York: Doubleday, 1975.

Dodson, Fitzhugh. *How to Father.* Los Angeles: Nash, 1974.

———. *How to Parent.* Los Angeles: Nash, 1970.

Dolgun, Alexander, with Watson, Patrick. *Alexander Dolgun's Story: An American in the Gulag.* New York: Knopf, 1975.

Durkin, Dolores. *Children Who Read Early.* New York: Teachers College, 1966.

Egoff, Sheila; Stubbs, G. T.; and Ashley, L. F., eds. *Only Connect: Readings on Children's Literature.* Toronto: Oxford, 1969.

Fader, Daniel N., and McNeil, Elton B. *Hooked on Books: Program and Proof.* New York: Berkley, 1968.

Fadiman, Clifton, and Howard, James. *Empty Pages: A Search for Writing Competence in School and Society.* Belmont, Calif.: Fearon Pitman and the Council for Basic Education, 1979.

Fisher, Margery. *Who's Who in Children's Literature.* New York: Holt, Rinehart and Winston, 1975.

Gibson, Janice T., and Blumberg, Phyllis. *Growing Up: Readings on the Study of Children.* Reading, Mass.: Addison-Wesley, 1978.

Greene, Graham. *The Lost Childhood and Other Essays.* New York: Viking, 1951.

Haviland, Virginia. *Children and Literature: Views and Reviews.* New York: Lothrop, Lee & Shepard, 1973.

Hayden, Torey L. *One Child.* New York: Putnam's, 1980.

Hearne, Betsy. *Choosing Books for Children: A Commonsense Guide.* New York: Delacorte, 1981.

Herndon, James. *How to Survive in Your Native Land.* New York: Simon & Schuster, 1971.

Hopkins, Lee Bennett. *Books Are by People.* New York: Citation, 1969.

———. *Let Them Be Themselves.* 2nd ed. New York: Citation, 1974.

———. *More Books by More People.* New York: Citation, 1974.

Huck, Charlotte S. *Children's Literature in the Elementary School.* 3rd ed. New York: Holt, Rinehart and Winston, 1976.

Kingman, Lee, ed. *Newbery and Caldecott Medal Books 1966–1975.* Boston: The Horn Book, 1975.

Larrick, Nancy. *A Parents Guide to Children's Reading.* 4th ed. New York: Bantam, 1975.

Mankiewicz, Frank, and Swerdlow, Joel. *Remote Control: Television and the Manipulation of American Life.* New York: Times Books, 1978.

Mussen, Paul Henry; Conger, John Janeway; and Kagan, Jerome. *Child Development and Personality.* 4th ed. New York: Harper and Row, 1974.

Passow, Harry A., ed. *Education in Depressed Areas.* New York: Teachers College, 1963.

Postman, Neil. *Teaching as a Conserving Activity*. New York: Delacorte, 1980.

Prescott, Orville. *A Father Reads to His Children: An Anthology of Prose and Poetry*. New York: Dutton, 1965.

Reasoner, Charles. *Bringing Children and Books Together: A Teacher's Guide to Early Childhood Literature*. New York: Dell, 1979.

———. *Releasing Children to Literature*. New York: Dell, 1976.

———. *When Children Read*. New York: Dell, 1975.

———. *Where the Readers Are*. New York: Dell, 1972.

Rudman, Masha. *Children's Literature: An Issues Approach*. Lexington, Mass.: Heath, 1976.

Rutstein, Nat. *"Go Watch TV!"* New York: Sheed and Ward, 1974.

Schramm, Wilbur; Lyle, Jack; and Parker, Edwin B. *Television in the Lives of Our Children*. Stanford, Calif.: Stanford, 1961.

Simon, Sidney B.; Howe, Leland W.; and Kerschenbaum, Howard. *Values Clarification: A Handbook of Practical Strategies for Teachers and Students,* rev. ed. New York: A & W, 1978.

Steinbeck, John. *The Acts of King Arthur and His Noble Knights*. New York: Farrar, Straus and Giroux, 1976.

Sutherland, Zena, and Arbuthnot, May Hill. *Children and Books*. 5th ed. Glenview, Ill.: Scott, Foresman, 1977.

Winn, Marie. *The Plug-in Drug*. New York: Viking, 1977.

Wintle, Justin, and Fisher, Emma. *The Pied Pipers: Interviews With the Influential Creators of Children's Literature*. New York: Paddington, 1974.

Author-Illustrator Index to Treasury

Italics are for illustrator only; * after page number gives location of a group of books by an author or illustrator.